£14.95

182113

KW-223-888

Sport and the European Union

This project has been funded with support from the European Commission.

This publication reflects the views only of the authors, and the Commission cannot be held responsible for any use which may be made of the information contained therein.

Walter Tokarski / Karen Petry / Michael Groll / Jürgen Mittag
With the Collaboration of Matthias Gütt and Oliver Koopmann

A Perfect Match?

Sport and the European Union

Meyer & Meyer Sport

Translation: Linda Fagan-Hos, Ireland
Cover design: Meyer & Meyer Sport, Germany
Cover photo: istockphoto.com

New and revised edition of the title "Two Players – One Goal?"

British Library Cataloguing in Publication Data
A catalogue record for this book is available from the British Library

A Perfect Match?
Sport and the European Union
Walter Tokarski / Karen Petry / Michael Groll / Jürgen Mittag
– Maidenhead: Meyer und Meyer, (UK) Ltd., 2009
ISBN 978-1-84126-271-0

© 2009 by Meyer & Meyer Sport (UK) Ltd.
Aachen, Adelaide, Auckland, Budapest, Cape Town, Graz, Indianapolis,
Maidenhead, Olten (CH), Singapore, Toronto
Member of the World
Sports Publishers' Association
www.w-s-p-a.org
Printed and bound by: FINIDR, s. r. o., Český Těšín
ISBN 978-1-84126-271-0
E-Mail: info@m-m-sports.com
www.m-m-sports.com

Content

1 Preface

A perfect match? is the fully revised version of the book "Two players - one goal? The European Union and Sport" that was published back in 2004 by Tokarski, Steinbach, Petry and Jesse. Vast parts of the content of the first edition have been updated as part of this revision and aspects of sports theory in particular have been added.

This book pursues the following goals:
First of all, part one will provide those involved in sport and those interested in European sports policy with the background information on how Europe has developed and will outline the most relevant approaches to this multifaceted phenomenon. Furthermore, the European integration process is outlined from the historical perspective and the most important stages from establishment to the present day are summed up.

The second part of the book deals initially with theoretical concepts all of which explain the European integration process. It is discussed what concepts and theoretical constructs are playing a role at present in terms of general political science. It is then explained how these concepts and theoretical constructs relate to sports policy and the relevant approaches of European sports policy are outlined.

In the third major part of the book, the impact the European Union's activities have had on sport are highlighted. These can be divided into direct and indirect aspects of sports policy. Individual sub-chapters deal with topics that have become relevant and sometimes explosive for sport in recent years, for instance, the European Union's anti-doping policy, the health policy educational aspects as well as the legal framework including the most relevant acts of law and court decisions.

The fourth and last part of the book deals with organisational and structural issues. The characteristics of aspects of the sports systems in place in the individual member countries are outlined and the sport participation is described. The overall presentation has been confined to organised sport. School sport and the field of commercial and non-organised leisure sport have only been dealt with as marginal issues.

The authors wish to thank the European Commission for their assistance in creating this book as part of the Jean Monnet Programme.

2 Europe - Five approaches to a multifaceted phenomenon

What is Europe? What is special about Europe? What does it mean to be European? These questions are not easy to answer, because in order to do so, one would need to take a look at a broad range of aspects in European history. The Europe of today is the staging post of a lengthy history that is marked by many elements. What is considered to be Europe today has its own history, development and process. Life today, everyday life today has evolved, is changing into something different. Without knowing what has gone before, we cannot possibly understand what is there today, are unlikely to recognise where the process is leading to in the future (Elias, 1983: 30ff.).

The history of Europe is the history of different ages: of antiquity, the medieval times, modern times and contemporary history; it is the history of the "old world" - the Occident - though its borders are hard to define precisely; the history of peoples and nations; the history of cultures and religions; of intellectual trends and ideologies; of technical innovations and of migration; it is the history of the nobility and the bourgeoisie; of revolutions and reforms, the history of wars and peace treaties, the development of modern states and - in the recent past - the creation of the European Union (Bollmann, March & Petersen, 2004).

To be a European, therefore, not only means living in a certain part of the world, it means a great deal more: to be a European means living under certain social and economic conditions, having a certain cultural background and having certain humanitarian ideas, all of which involve taking historical processes into consideration. In European cultural science, such terms as "Europe paradigm" (Vitanyi, 1985) or "European identity" (Schulze, 1995) have been developed for this purpose: they indicate a certain way of life that is not confined to Europe, they are indicative of basic orientations and forms of awareness that determine the way in which a person thinks and acts.

Discussions about the elements that define the continent of Europe, its uniqueness, its role and aspects of European identity are controversely debated and could fill an entire library. This explains why only five distinguishing features will be outlined in the following.

2.1 First approach: Europe as a term

It is a matter of controversy to the present day where the term "Europe" originated from. No approach is in itself completely logical so that different approaches have been repeatedly used. The term Europe can be derived in etymological terms, inter alia, from the Semitic "ereb" which can be translated as "dark" or "evening" and which is attributed to the fact that the Phoenicians who sailed the Mediterranean - the most important trading people who between ca. 1400 and 750 B.C. - positioned Greece in the area of the setting sun (Sattler, 1971). If one uses the Greek root, Europe is composed of two words broad (eur-) and eye (op-, opt-) which related to the legend of Europe. The reference to Greek mythology has become very common in European history since it is considered as the eponym of the continent. Herodotus said on this continent in the 5th century B.C.: "However, no-one knows anything about Europe ... In the past, it had no special name at all, and nor did the others ..." (Weitz, 1997: 22).

Although there is no legend of the founding of Europe, such as those that exist in relation to ancient Athens, the Roman Empire or the Aztec Empire, the following legend is constantly referred to in relation to the origins of Europe:

Europa was the only daughter of King Agenor and his wife Telephassa of Tyre in Phoenicia, which lay in Asia Minor. One day, when Europa was walking along the seashore with her maidens, Zeus, the father of the Gods approached them without being recognised, in the guise of a bull, hidden in King Agenor's herd of cattle. Zeus had fallen in love with Europa because of her beauty. And when Zeus bowed down before her in the guise of a bull and offered to take her on his back, the unsuspecting Europa climbed on. No sooner had she had climbed onto the bull's back than he strode into the water, disappearing in the waves, and swam with her on his back from Asia Minor to Crete. Europa did not return to Asia Minor but remained on Crete; even her brothers, who had been sent out by King Agenor, were unable to take her back. On Crete - according to the Greek legend - she had three children and became the founder of the Minoan dynasty, which also became legendary.

In order to ease Europa's homesickness, Aphrodite promised that mankind would remember her name (Frensch, 1996: 77). The loss of her virginity was rewarded with a lasting memorial: a whole continent was named after Europa, Aphrodite had kept her word. So much for myths. Legend has it that Europa came from Asia Minor and was abducted by the father of the gods of another culture, that of the continental Greeks. The myth therefore symbolises the transformation of a culture which was transferred from the Near East to the unknown continent in the west: that was the birth of Hellenistic Europe (Weitz, 1997: 22), which thereafter became the centre of the Western world at that time (approx. 1000 B.C.). It is also regarded as the birthplace of sport, so that Greece can in a double sense be described as the force behind modern, contemporary developments (Meier, 1993).

2.2 Second approach: Europe as a geographic space

Since the seventh century B.C., Europe gained momentum not just as a mythological term but also as a geographical term. Europe can be identified as a continent on early maps. The historian and geograph Hekataios von Milet (approx. 560-485 B.C.) divided the globe into two separate halves in his world map of 510 B.C. He called the northern semicircle Europe and the southern semicircle Asia. The geographical term "Europe" gradually became accepted as the designation for the northern semicircle before the exact dimensions of the continent were known. Even though the term Europe will be used most frequently in the geographical sense in the following, people in the ancient world only had a vague idea of the size of the continent. At the time, they had little or no idea of its external coasts and borders (Schmale, 2000).

It was only gradually over the following centuries that people became aware of the geographical dimensions of Europe, with the Mediterranean defining the South, the Atlantic defining the West and the Norwegian Sea defining Europe's natural boundaries. By contrast, however, the eastern boundary of Europe remained controversial for a long time - and indeed remains so to the present day in many respects as Europe represents a peninsula of Asia in geographical terms. Whereas in southern-east Europe, a border can be drawn from the eastern Mediterranean across the Dardanelles through the Sea of Marmara and Bosporus right across to the Black Sea, it is much more difficult to draw the boundaries for the land area. The boundary of the Ural Mountains that is widely accepted today has only been considered to be the eastern border of Europe since the early 18th century. It is also heavily disputed whether Turkey has to be considered primarily as an European state (Davies, 1996).

2.3 Third approach: Europe as a defence community

When, around 500 B.C., the Greek geographers set about making a distinction between the continents of Europe and Asia, this differentiation served political purposes: it was the justification for the Persian wars, that is to say, the struggle with the Persians, who came from Asia Minor and were trying to subjugate the Greek states. The result is well-known: the Greeks won the war and prevented the Persians from marching into Europe; Europe was saved. Many historians designate this historic moment as the hour when Europe was born, as this is when first signs of awareness of European unity emerged when the Greek overcame the threat posed by the Persians. There were at least some signs that people began to realise that the region of Europe as it was known at the time differed from the customs and political organisational forms of Asia (Chabod, 1963).

Nonetheless, the term "Europe" was rarely mentioned in sources as a political term during the following centuries. For the most part, it is only used when reference is made to battlefields and to defence against the enemy, for instance, around 732 when Abd-ar-Rahman, a governor of the Caliph in Al Andalus, having won several successful battles advanced upon the Franconian national monument of the Abbey of St. Martin in Tours, and when the "Europenses" under the leadership of Charles Martel stopped the Saracens.

The external threat posed by the Ottomans and the fall of Constantinople in 1453 was another milestone in common European history. Enea Silvio de' Piccolomini (1405-1464) - who later became Pope Pius II - lamented to the people "we were attacked and defeated in Europe, i.e. in our homeland, in our own house, in our ancestral homes" (quotation by Fuhrmann, 1981: 16). When the threat posed by the Turks was staved off by the Ottomans in the Siege of Vienna in 1529, Europe was once again presented as the model of a Europe under threat. The closeness among the Europeans only lasted briefly. After successfully warding off (military) threats, new clashes broke out relentlessly between the countries of Europe which were fragmented in pursuit of their own interests. In conclusion, it can be assumed that up to the early modern period, people did not see themselves as Europeans who took jointly action (Hay, 1968: 117-125).

In the 18th and 19th century the tension between the different European nations mounted: the sovereign nation states refused to accept a higher, political instance. However, as social tension grew and legitimation crises increased, the conflicts and extremes in Europe became more pronounced. Against this backdrop, the number of peace and federation plans for Europe increased towards the end of the 19th century (Delanty, 1995). A growing number of writers and intellectuals, but also economists and lawyers sought to gain support for the concept of Europe prompted by sustained conflicts between nation states. Even though no steps were taken towards political integration until the 20th century - within the meaning of transferring competencies from (nation states) to transnational organisations with a view to achieving political unification as we understand it today, there were numerous plans for unifying the continent of Europe. Before the idea of European unification was able to take concrete shape in a political project and actually became an explicit political goal, it attracted huge interest above all among intellectuals and philosophers (Pegg, 1983).

The relentless military battles of the First World War comprising trench warfare, battles of attrition, destruction and war casualties of a hitherto unknown scale were responsible in no small measure for the 1920s becoming a decade of lively debates about Europe (Stirk, 2001). However, all attempts to foster European integration failed during the global economic crisis that following the Wall Street crash in New York in 1929. Instead of looking for common solutions, each country sought its own way out of the crisis in the course of national radicalisation. As nationalist and anti-democratic forces took power in numerous countries on the continent, ideas on European unity disappeared completely from public debate. The Second World War reduced the idea of European unity to the absurd and usurped it under the umbrella of the supremacy demands of individual countries. However, at the same time, the Second World War revived the idea of Europe in the framework of the resistance movements.

With the end of the Second World War, which leaves large parts of Europe in ruins, a rethink begins, with the aim of launching a new European unification process, which has, for the time being, culminated in the establishment of the European Union.

2.4 Fourth approach: Europe as a cultural and intellectual area

A further hallmark of the developments in this area is European man's desire for knowledge and culture: Various stages in the history of the European world reflect this development: While it was the Greeks who dominated Mediterranean European history since the 800 century

B.C. to begin with, there were the Romans, the Celts and Germanic tribes and many more who subsequently took on that role. With the passage of time, strong cultural influences from the region of Asia Minor, but also the claim to power of peoples of non-Indo-European origin, including the Huns, the Arabs, the Saracens, the Mongols and the Turks, repeatedly left their mark on Europe (Joas & Wiegandt, 2005).

Many of the major inventions in Europe can be attributed to the large groups of the Greeks, the Romans as well as the Germans and Slavs. The Greek cosmos and the Roman res publica are regarded as the nuclei of the European way of thinking and acting. Greece places at the centre of its world an interest in human experience, in the spiritual and emotional processes occurring within a person's mind and an interest in exploring the relationship between nature and mankind. This created knowledge of the spiritual values that lead to freedom and independence. The Roman Empire with its belligerent, expansionist tendencies represents a striving for power. At the same time, by asserting elements such as Latin as its language or Roman law, it contributed significantly towards the cultural development of Europe.

After the fall of the Roman Empire and the confusion of migration, the Empire of Charlemagne became the most important civilisational milestone in European history. This shifted the centre of Europe from the Mediterranean to the Northern Alps, providing major impetus in the areas of education, poetry and architecture. Yet the East of the continent also shaped Europe in no small measure. With the Byzantine Empire otherwise known as the Eastern Roman Empire having resisted the storm of migration and Islamic invasion for many years, an entire European world existed around the centre of Constantinople - which is Istanbul today. Although it differed from the Western Europe in many respects, it was also an important pillar of the common heritage.

The advance of the Arabs meant that Christianity was enclosed in Europe but that new ideas influenced the continent. In the following centuries, commerce, art, culture and science flourished, and a colourful, diverse European region with growing cities developed. The Humanist and Christian Renaissance encompassed the whole of Europe towards the end of medieval times, man became the measure of all things and the principle of individualism came into vogue. In the 17th century, science developed at a rapid pace and in the 18th century, rationalism and enlightenment began their triumphal march through Europe from Paris.

The 18th century led to a dissolution of feudal-corporatist traditions on the continent and to categories like Christianity and the Occident losing importance. At the same time, sovereign nation states emerged that were characterised by dominant ethnic nation states and numerous minorities.

National trends emerged; even though they are all interlinked, each shows certain dominant characteristics: Anglo-Saxon philosophy is empiricist, French philosophy rationalist and German philosophy idealistic. The multiplicity of states in Europe, their egocentrism and their nationalism are increasing, but so, too, is the number of republics.

2.5 Fifth approach: Europe as an economic sphere

A fifth approach to Europe is reflected in the scientific-technical inventions and the industrial revolution in the late 18th and early 19th centuries based on them. Many European countries have been deeply shaped by these developments and the evidence of a dynamic growth in the capitalist methods of production. Hence, capitalism and its counterparts also play a major role in European history. Since the industrial revolution, capitalism has been functioning as a social system and as a collective form of life more or less "automatically" on the basis of compelling its members to adapt to the "necessities of life". The interest in gainful employment that had distanced itself from the religious origins of Protestantism and the resulting effects on society were main points of criticism used by Marxism.

Socialism and communism have established themselves on this very basis - in a host of variations - with socialist and communist parties bringing their influence to bear on the world of politics in European countries. Since the end of the cold war and the collapse of the communist Eastern Bloc, the opposites of capitalism and socialism no longer exist. Capitalism has been reinforced from this historical process; Marxism and socialism lead an isolated existence in just a few parts of the world - and both are showing a growing tendency to adapt to capitalism.

In addition to the emergence of economic conflicts and their impact on socioeconomic and cultural conditions, their "pacification" is also characteristic of Europe. In this context, key importance is attached to the emergence above all of social states and welfare states which provided services in the field of unemployment benefits, social welfare, dismissal protection and pensions. Even though there are major differences between the individual social states and there was little evidence of features that are characteristic of the welfare state particularly in Eastern Europe following the system transformation of the early 1990s, the idea of developing social security systems and equal access to facilities of the welfare state began to play an important role in Europe.

2.6 Interim conclusions: towards a European identity?

Yet what is it specifically that defines Europe and is there any such thing as a European identity? And to what extent is the European Union a point of reference for this? The aspects of the linguistic, geographical, political, cultural and economic dimension of the term "Europe" mentioned in this document highlight the fact that there is a long-standing tradition to the designation "Europe". Yet they also show that the idea of Europe geared towards a political unity of the continent is a comparatively young phenomenon. This fact also has consequences for the question of a European identity.

Contrary to an individual's subjective, personal identity, a collective identity describes the specific, cognitive and emotional way in which individuals relate to an identification object. From the perspective of political science, it refers to the political community of citizens (demos) that develops from the logic of inclusion and exclusion - e.g. based on the criteria of the collective perception of the past, present and future. This collective identity manifests itself as empathy between the members of the community and creates the basis for solidarity and loyalty. A European identity is based on certain values that are also mentioned in the Treaties establishing the European Union: they include "respect for human dignity, freedom, democracy, equality, the rule of law and the protection of human rights." Yet a European identity can also be based on certain symbols. Flag, the anthem, the motto and the Europe Day are the official European symbols. In everyday life, in addition to the flag, the Euro above all is probably of the greatest practical and symbolic relevance. The European Union does not have any official pan-European ceremony during Europe Day. In more general terms, however, the celebrations marking D-Day or the liberation of Auschwitz could be classified as joint commemorative ceremonies.

The prerequisite for the deliberate development of an identity are first and foremost the basic ideas and values shared by the relevant political elite and a concrete vision of the political future of the pertinent community. It can be ascertained for Europe that these two requirements are met to a limited extent. This manifests itself, for instance, in the different visions of Europe politicians and in the development process of the Constitutional Treaty which has suffered so many setbacks. Academics are considering creating a European master narrative in order to create a European identity, although this is still in its infancy. The European Union for its part has barely considered the option of legitimising European integration so far by bringing about a common perception of history - above all because there is a lack of exemplary historical or "cultural figures" that have pan-European integrative clout extending beyond national boundaries. On the other hand, even if it turns out that a distinct European culture and civilisation - which is difficult, if not impossible, to define - is nothing more than an invention, the lively debate on the actual core content of a European identity can be interpreted as a sign that a European identity is gradually developing.

Today, Europe is the world's largest economic bloc, and the political union of 27 European countries is a unique phenomenon which is without parallel. Freedom of movement and trade, prosperity and security are important characteristics of the new Europe, and yet, a feeling of uneasiness remains. The Europe of today is more like a chaotic building site with an economic orientation and a compulsion to standardise things than a reliable, supranational entity with cultural diversity. It is precisely the economy version of the Euro-human that is to say, the one-sided economic bias of the European identity that gives rise to this feeling of unease. The fixation on the Euro as a common currency, as the only little scrap of lovely Europe left after the battles in Brussels, has brought to a standstill the attempts that have been made in the meantime to focus on diversity, culture and a citizens' Europe. This has been a bitter setback for the "European principle" and European identity, but Europe is probably unable to act any differently. The pressure of economic globalisation is simply too great. The capacity of politicians to act is falling by the wayside, and this, in turn, greatly increases the risk of social fragmentation (Hauchler, 1995: 11ff.) - a risk that the creation of a new, united Europe was really supposed to counteract. So the vision exists and is gradually instilling itself in people's minds, but the reality is still very far removed from it.

The aspirations attached to these elements, to the European citizen, to European identity were formulated a long time ago and are very ambitious: harmonisation being the magic word. That does not mean bringing everything into line, but rather joint co-ordination, yet preserving regional diversity. What is required is a new awareness and a new way of thinking, a new universalistic interpretation of history, behaviour based on reason, openness and mutual understanding. European identity can only be a poly-identity, that is to say, it is not something uniform and indivisible, but rather multi-level and multi-tiered in its essential characteristics because local, regional, national, religious and ideological elements combine to form a varied kaleidoscope.

The radical changes that have occurred over the past few years have once again altered this situation. The peoples of Europe sense that they are dependent on one another - nonetheless, they seek their own identity by setting themselves apart from their neighbours. People are in two minds as to whether they should give precedence to cultural affection for one another or to cultural concern in relation to one another. The European Union abandoned the opposites "Diversity vs. Unity" in favour of the motto "United in diversity" in an act of dialectic ambivalence, even though the motto that has been used since the turn of the century has not been incorporated into any treaties up to now. This motto expresses the intention to preserve the cultural diversity of Europe and to refrain from glossing over existing extremes but to highlight them as shared basic values. This dialectic of affection and dissociation, of care and segregation is the true distinguishing feature of the history of Europe. Europe is in the throes of a mélange between fragmentation, stabilisation, diversification and concentration. Europe was, is and will hence always be a building site.

3   The road towards the European Union

Anyone who considers the history of modern European integration after the Second World War will find the terms "deepening and widening" a useful guideline. These two key categories refer both to the
geographical widening of Europe resulting from the growing number
of Member States and deepening of Europe owing to the expansion of
legal competencies at European level (Blockmans & Prechal, 2008).

Concepts on European unity date back many years in history. In addition to individuals, movements and organisations have always sought
to gain support for the idea of a united Europe. Plans for a united
Europe that would guarantee internal peace and prosperity as well as
collective external security were presented especially in the aftermath
of two devastating world wars. It was hoped that the project on European unity would lead to a civilisation of conflicts, a democratisation
of national and political structures and modernisation of economic and
social conditions of European countries and societies. These plans
were accentuated by the resistance movements and exile governments
during the Second World War (Lipgens, 1986). The creation of permanent structures of European cooperation was considered to be an
important prerequisite for the future peace framework of the continent.

3.1 The 1940s

In the global political climate after the end of the Second World War -
and with the growing antithesis among the former war allies, there
seemed to be little or no room for ideas on European integration, at
least for the time being. The idea of Europe did not regain momentum
until Winston Churchill delivered a speech at the University of Zürich
on 19 September 1946 in which he outlined his vision of the "United
States of Europe". Churchill considered overcoming the differences
between France and Germany to be an important step towards European integration. The idea was that yesterday's opponents could become the community of tomorrow, that despite the different mentali-
ties, traditions and interests that exist, it might indeed be possible to
create a community.

In subsequent years, a large number of people in Europe sought to
gain support for European integration. With regard to the political objectives raised, federalism and unionism constituted two mainstreams

that incorporate the different ideal type concepts in post-war Europe. While the federalists pursued the concept of a federal state of Europe with an elected government, its own Parliament and Court of Justice, the Unionists were opposed to the individual nation states losing sovereignty, but were in favour of intensifying economic and political co-operation between European countries (Loth, 1996).

However, impetus for European unity also came from outside Europe. As evidence of the cold war grew, it was above all the USA that advocated intensifying (West) European cooperation. Within the framework of the European Recovery Program (ERP) - that soon became known as nothing but the "Marshall Plan" - the USA insisted that the countries of Europe enhance the coordination of their economic cooperation and agree on the distribution of funds. This fostered economic cooperation in Western Europe.

The future structure of the Council of Europe was discussed at a specific congress attended by around 750 delegates from 16 countries, including many leading politicians, economists, academics and artists in The Hague, Netherlands in May 1948. It not only generated public support for the idea of European integration, it also created the starting point for the establishment of the Council of Europe. The Council of Europe was founded on 5 May 1949. The Treaty of London or the Statute of the Council of Europe was signed in London on that day by ten states. This means the Council of Europe was the first international organisation to work towards European integration. Its structures and decision-making competencies corresponded, by and large, to the Unionist demands of the British Government. As a result, even to the present day, the Council of Europe only has limited powers - inter alia, in the fields of human rights, education and culture. Nonetheless, it barely affects national sovereignty.

3.2 The 1950s

As the Council of Europe proved to be viable only to a limited extent in terms of its expansion potential in the direction of achieving greater political and economic cooperation, considerations on finding alternatives for closer cooperation with a limited number of countries abounded. In this context, paramount importance is attributed to the declaration by the French Foreign Minister Robert Schuman in Paris on 9 May 1950 in which he presented the plan for a European Coal

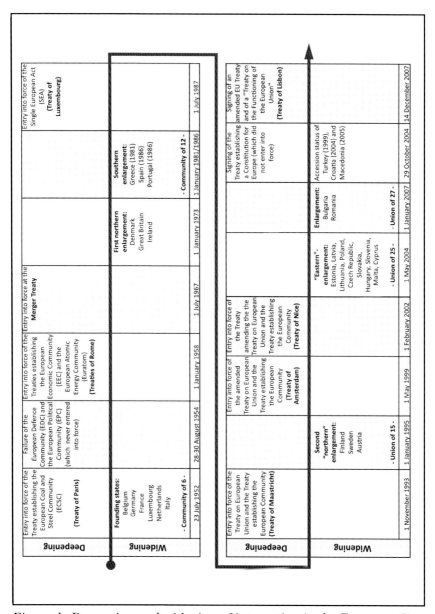

Figure 1: Deepening and widening of integration in the European Union

and Steel Community - based on considerations of Jean Monnet
(Wilkens, 2004). Robert Schuman literally said:

> (…) To that end, the French Government proposes that immediate
> be concentrated on one limited but decisive point. The French
> Government proposes that the entire Franco-German production
> of coal and steelbe placed under a joint High Authority, within an
> organisation open to the participation of other European nations.
> (...) By pooling basic production and by instituting a new higher
> authority, whose decisions will bind France, Germany and other
> Member Countries, this proposal will lead to the realisation of the
> first concrete foundation of a European federation indispensable
> to the preservation of peace.

Less than a year after Schuman's initiative, six countries signed a
treaty on 18 April 1951 to run their heavy industries - coal and steel -
under a common management (Belgium, France, Germany, Italy,
Luxembourg and the Netherlands). The European Coal and Steel
Community that entered into force on 23 July 1952 and was to expire
after 50 years created a whole new basis for European unification.
There was one basic feature that distinguished the ECSC from the
Council of Europe and all the other international organisations established in the post-war period, namely the possibility to take binding
decisions that were actionable and subject to sanctions which gave the
European Coal and Steel Community a structural feature that lent the
crucial, qualitative innovation to the European integration process and
represented the lever for its dynamic further development.

Even during the negotiations for the ECSC, the various players advocated that additional policy-making areas be added to the union which
was limited to certain sectors. However, it soon became apparent that
the idea of a further-reaching political community had reached its limits. After the French initiative for a European Defence Community
floundered in 1954, the integration endeavours experienced a serious
setback. This first major crisis for European unification was only
overcome when the six founding members of the ECSC agreed to intensify sectoral and economic cooperation. The European Economic
Community and the European Atomic Energy Community entered
into force with the Treaties of Rome in 1958. The two new agreements lent a new dynamism to the process of integration (Knipping,
2004). The cooperation agreed in these two agreements focused on
economic cooperation and pursued the goal of establishing a customs
union. The Treaties of Rome, which together with the ECSC Treaty

have created the basis for EC/EU legislation up to this very day, were oriented towards removing any barriers that stood in the way of the basic freedoms that apply within the European framework, such as the free movement of goods, services, persons and capital (European Economic Community, 1957: Article 3a, c).

3.3 The 1960s

In the first few years of the EEC, the European bodies pressed ahead with the specifications set forth in the treaties in respect of a customs union, agricultural policy and trade policy. By contrast, initiatives that focused exclusively on politics floundered in the early 1960s, including de Gaulle's strategy on European policy that was aimed at expanding the Fouchet plans to form a new "Union of States". It was also the French President Charles de Gaulle who helped to precipitate the most serious constitutional crisis the Community had hitherto experienced in 1965 when he withdrew his representatives from the EC. By adopting the "empty chair" policy, he wanted to prevent votes by a qualified majority in the Council of Ministers in important policy-making areas if and when French interests were under threat. The conflict was not solved until the Luxembourg compromise was reached in January 1966. In the practice of the EC, majority voting became a rare exception over two decades (Brunn, 2002).

In terms of treaty revision, no progress towards European integration worth mentioning was made in the 1960s. The individual communities (ECSC, EEC and Euratom) continued to be legally independent bodies. The so-called "Merger Treaty", however, led to the creation of a uniform, institutional structure. The three communities which had their own bodies up to that point, have been run by joint bodies since the Merger Treaty came into force in 1967. Against this backdrop, people began referring to the European Community towards the end of the 1960s.

3.4 The 1970s

After de Gaulle's plans to strengthen France failed in the national and international events of the year 1968 and after the turnaround in Germany's Ostpolitik implemented by the Brandt/Scheel Government, the development towards European integration entered a new phase. Some of the attempts at integration that tend to be underrated are the

political negotiating packages that identified new and enlarged problem areas as tasks that needed to be tackled by the EEC at the summit
conferences of The Hague in 1969 and Paris in 1972, defining the
Economic and Monetary Union and political union as central models.
Ideas for a "European Union" which was intended to transform all relations between the Member States were also discussed in concrete
detail for the very first time (Mittag, 2008).

In the 1970s, the governments laid the foundations for the key developments of the 1980s and 1990s, without amending primary law. The
establishment of the European Monetary System that had an exchange
rate mechanism was of lasting importance for deepening the Community. While the members of the European Community had, until then,
focused exclusively on economic co-operation, they began to make
joint efforts in the field of foreign policy (on a voluntary basis) in the
1970s with the development of the European Political Co-operation
(EPC) network.

The institutional architecture was modified and deepened by two key
reforms in the 1970s, although the Treaties were not amended. With
the creation of the European Council (1974), the heads of state and
government established an institution that enabled them to play a major role in European affairs. European citizens became more involved
in the European integration process with the introduction of direct
elections to the European Parliament in 1979 which the supporters of
a federal Europe hoped would legitimate other integration initiatives
of this body, thereby reducing the lack of democracy in the EC.

The history of European integration was ultimately marked sustaina-
bly by the first accession round: with northward expansion (1973)
when the United Kingdom, Ireland and Denmark joined the EEC, important political and economic foundations of the EU system changed
and a wider and more controversial spectrum of basic perceptions of
this new political construction emerged (Elvert, 2006).

3.5 The 1980s

Using economic projects to achieve political goals was also characteristic of the next upswing in European integration history. After a
phase of "eurosclerosis" in the early 1980s, the new President of the
EC Commission, Jacques Delors, began to strategically implement
plans for the Single European Market in order to intensify political
agreement, working towards a common security policy via a currency

union. Several previous attempts to amend the Treaties of Rome aimed at legally incorporating new policy-making areas and institutional reforms had failed. It was only after the most urgent budget and agricultural problems had been overcome at the summit meeting of the European Council in Fontainebleau in 1984 that a time window emerged for amending the Treaties, combining economic goals - particularly in relation to the Single European Market -with institutional reforms (Dinan, 2004).

The first major revision of - and supplement to - the basic treaties took place in 1987, when the Single European Act (SEA) was adopted. It reformed, inter alia, the institutional framework of the Communities, integrating into the treaties the European Political Co-operation (EPC) which, until then, had been run as an informal body: in addition, it extended the Community's competencies specifying that the Single European Market was to be established by 1 January 1993. The attribute 'single' used in the reform is perceived as a reference to the treaty links that had been established between economic and political integration with the aim of establishing a European Union.

In parallel to drawing up the Single European Act, Spain and Portugal joined the EEC. In addition to Greece, that joined the EEC in 1981, this brought the southwards expansion to a conclusion as early as 1986, when the EC comprised twelve Member States.

3.6 The 1990s

The eastward expansion of the EC following the revolutionary upheaval that took place in Europe in 1989/90 and the importance of the Single European Market increased the need to press ahead with the project of economic and monetary union in the early 1990s and also to reform the decision-making structures and systems within the Community. The 1990s were characterised by the establishment and further development of the European Union with the conclusion of the Treaties of Maastricht, Amsterdam and Nice and the addition of the EFTA countries Austria, Finland and Sweden which joined the EU in 1995.

These projects were driven by the Franco-German proposals put forward by the team of Francois Mitterrand and Helmut Kohl, building on previous partnerships such as the partnership between Giscard d'Estaing and Helmut Schmidt. Once again they were guided by the traditional motives of the respective national policy on Europe which had been reinforced by German reunification to take common integration steps.

The goal to establish the European Union was accomplished, at least in formal terms, when the Treaty Establishing the European Union (EU Treaty), also referred to as the 'Treaty of Maastricht', was adopted on 7 February 1992 and came into force on 1 November 1993. Three pillars laid the foundations for the new framework: The first pillar comprises the (revised and extended) EC Treaty including the provisions governing a common economic and monetary union (EMU). The Community received for instance new competencies in the area of culture and education in addition to several other areas. The second pillar which is based on the new EU Treaty refers to the common foreign and security policy (CFSP). The third pillar that is also laid down in the EU Treaty establishes the co-operation in justice and home affairs aspired to.

On 1 January 1995, another expansion of the EU territory took place when Austria, Finland and Sweden joined the EU, while many countries of Central and Eastern Europe applied for membership. At the same time as the European Union was undergoing institutional reform, efforts were undertaken from the mid-1990s onwards to press ahead with the accession process and initial adjustment strategies were developed. However, the enlargement process was marked by much greater difficulties than the previous enlargement involving the accession of countries in Central Eastern European and South Eastern Europe as well as Cyprus and Malta. Given that their economies are lagging way behind the further developed (West) European countries, other problems encountered involved respect for human rights and the reorganisation of administration.

The Treaty of Amsterdam replaced and supplemented the Treaty of Maastricht. Its very structure indicates that it does not represent another constitutional quantum leap towards a new, clearly structured constitution. Rather, it firms up the impression that the Treaty of Amsterdam too has taken up and strengthened the long-standing trend of development towards integration. The heads of government have once again expanded the overall scope of policy-making areas to be dealt with by the EU bodies. The numerous amendments that were made to the Treaty of Amsterdam, refer, inter alia, to aspects regarding the freedom of movement, internal security, employment and social policy, environmental and health policy, consumer protection, common foreign and security policy and the institutional organisation of the

Union. Sport was also incorporated into the regulations of the European Union for the very first time in the form of a declaration in the minutes of the Treaty of Amsterdam. With a comprehensive and detailed, descriptive chapter on the "Gradual development of an area of freedom, security and justice", the founding fathers defined a new objective that was intended to have similar programme-related affects as the visions of the 'Single European Market' in the Single European Act and the 'Monetary Union' in the Treaty of Maastricht.

However, the most important institutional adjustments of the EU failed and were deferred in the Treaty of Amsterdam. Institutional themes that set the direction such as the future size and composition of the Commission and the weighting of votes in the Council of Ministers hence became central themes at the Intergovernmental Conference held in Nice in 2000. The reform debate in Nice focused on reweighting the votes for voting in the Council. The majority of the twelve applicant states with the exception of Poland that had a population of just under 40 million, were smaller and medium-sized countries which meant there was a risk of asymmetry between the countries with a large population and those with a small population in the weighting of votes in the Council. The solution formula found in Nice following tough negotiations - spreading the votes on a wider basis - was generally rated as a technical formula compromise. In accordance with the agreement to compensate countries that have a large population by giving them more votes if they waived their entitlement to a commissioner, the larger countries obtained a substantial increase in votes. With the Treaty of Nice, the heads of state and government reformed the Union once again-particularly in terms of EU enlargement, with twelve additional countries from Central, Eastern and Southern Europe to accede at a later date.

Again sport was discussed at the conference of the European Council in Nice and sport was dealt with for the first time in a top-level political EU arena. In the conclusions of the Council Presidency published at the end of the summit in Nice, it was recommended that greater importance be attached to the social and cultural dimension of sport in the individual Member States and Community policies and that sport and its social role be promoted. In addition the autonomy of sport was highlighted. The "Declaration on the specific characteristics of sport and its social function in Europe, of which account should be taken in implementing common policies" (Declaration of Nice, 2000) is more comprehensive than the Declaration of Amsterdam. The Declaration of Nice was not incorporated into the Treaty and was merely adopted by the Council as a joint declaration which means that once again sport failed to be furnished with a legally binding character.

3.7 The 21st century

The Treaty of Nice continued to be seen as a half-hearted institutional reform that did little more than create unsatisfactory negotiating compromises. This triggered a broad discussion about the future of the European Union - though it had been established that the Community was capable of expansion. With the initiation of the European Convention following the summit of Laeken (2001), the EU developed concrete steps to further develop and deepen its constitution. The fact that the heads of state and government of the European Union used a convention to do so shows that the former method of amending the treaties had reached its limits.

In the discussions following Nice, a fresh declaration was adopted committing the EU to greater democracy, transparency and efficiency, and setting out the process by which a constitution could be reached using a "convention" as a model: this method had been tried out for the first time when the Charter on Fundamental Rights had been drawn up and was assessed as a better alternative than the model of an intergovernmental conference. Seventeen months of negotiations resulted in an initial Draft Treaty Establishing a Constitution for Europe that threatened to flounder initially but that was developed into a viable compromise under Ireland's EU Council Presidency and was signed ceremoniously in October 2004. The Treaty Establishing a Constitution for Europe was intended to combine the existing Treaty Establishing the European Community and the Treaty Establishing the European Union, to create a uniform contractual architecture and to make the European Union a legal entity. By creating new offices and transferring other competencies, European policy became more personalised and reference was made intentionally to the public.

In the Draft Treaty establishing a Constitution for Europe, sport was explicitly mentioned in two articles that call to mind regulations for the cultural sector. The two articles are in the First and Third Section of the Draft Treaty and are hence areas, in which the Union may take "supporting, coordinating or complementary action" (cf. Reding, 2003; Unger, 2006; Euractiv, 2007). Futhermore, the EU is not assigned any direct competencies for sport (Unger, 2006).

Towards the end of the 1990s, it became evident that another ten to twelve countries would be joining the EU. These were (from North to South) Estonia, Latvia, Lithuania, Poland, Hungary, the Czech Republic, Slovakia and Slovenia, plus the two Mediterranean islands of Malta and Cyprus as well as Romania and Bulgaria. Comprehensive negotiations led to the accession of Estonia, Latvia, Lithuania, Malta, Poland, Slovenia, Slovakia, the Czech Republic, Hungary and Cyprus on 1 May 2004 following parliamentary approval by an absolute majority and a unanimous decision by the Council. Since the two Eastern European countries Bulgaria and Romania joined the EU on 1 January 2007, the population in the 27 Member States of the EU has risen to around 497 million. With the enlargements of 2004 and 2007, Central, Eastern and Southern Europe have become more united than ever before. At the same time, it has been and is to the present day a matter of taking this new heterogeneity within the EU into account. It became a matter of supporting historical transitions from dictatorships to democracy, from planned economies to a market economy and from the bloc structure to national independence and of taking the new power structure in Europe into account (Gehler, 2005). Today, with its population of 497 million in 27 Member States (Eurostat, 2008), the European Union represents the largest economic and political community in the world. Further accession negotiations have been underway with Croatia, the former Yugoslavian Republic of Macedonia and Turkey.

The national ratification process began when the Treaty Establishing a Constitution for Europe was approved by the European Council. However, the ratification of the new Treaty failed unexpectedly when it was defeated by a clear majority in the referendums held in France and the Netherlands in the summer of 2005. After a self-imposed "pause for reflection", the European Union endeavoured in 2007 to incorporate important contents of the Treaty Establishing a Constitution for Europe into a modified version of the existing treaties. At the turbulent summit held in Brussels in June 2007, the heads of state and government agreed on a statutory framework that incorporated the most important results of the Treaty Establishing a Constitution for Europe und adopted a final form at the summit in Lisbon.

Yet this variant of the constitutional reform ran into obstacles as in the only referendum held - the other countries ratified the Treaty exclusively by parliamentary votes - the people of Ireland rejected Reform Treaty that is now referred to as the Treaty of Lisbon. Against this backdrop, it is not foreseeable whether and when the next Reform Treaty will be implemented.

3.8 Interim conclusions: lessons from history

The political system of the EC/EU at the beginning of the 21st century is not the systematic implementation of a carefully drawn overall architectural plan for Europe that is accepted by all parties. Rather, a final political solution (finalité politique') with greatly diverging ideas has been developed on a step-by-step basis (Mittag, 2008: 9-20).

It was specifically at the beginning of the European integration process that considerations were popular that the economic communities of the ECSC, EEC and EURATOM would result almost "organically" in a political union in the foreseeable future in the form of the "United States of Europe". An intrinsic logic was assumed as the crucial driver of this process. This intrinsic logic founded on functionalism is frequently referred to as the "spill-over-process", meaning the spill-over of integration from one area to another. Nonetheless, the development of European integration since the 1950s has shown that the integration process depends on more than one intrinsic logic that is perceived as mandatory. In actual fact, there are numerous different driving forces that are responsible for the integration process reaching a stalemate. These include, inter alia, the positions assumed by the Member States, general economic and social conditions, the international, political environment and also the activities of individuals. Nonetheless, the spill-over concept continues to be a meaningful tool for understanding what drives the integration process, although it is less manifest than had been anticipated at the beginning of the integration process.

The categories of deepening and widening of integration sum up the different driving forces. Looking back at the past six decades of European integration, there is evidence of countries reciprocally setting the course for deepening and widening of European integration. The Member States have reviewed institutions and systems time and again, supplementing and amending them in primary law based on the experience gained in a growing Union. The process of expanding the European construction cannot be regarded as completed at this point in time despite the slowing down of the dynamic trend of the 1990s. While differentiation is currently being advocated above all regarding the deepening of European integration, although not all countries are likely to agree to a further transfer of competencies to European level, we are also witnessing hesitance in the area of deepening of European integration. For fear of placing excessive demands on the accession candidates and of overstretching the Union, the current accession negotiations with Turkey (which has had accession status since 1999), with Croatia (2004) and with Macedonia (2005) have been markedly extended or deferred for the foreseeable future.

4   European integration, political science and sports: theoretical concepts and typologies[1]

Though the European integration process has attracted considerable attention in public discourses since the early 1950s it remained for many decades in the shadow of academic interest. There had been only a limited number of scientific researchers, restricted both in number and disciplines pursuing the new and developing European constructing. Political scientists - followed by legal and economic experts - were among those who first discovered this new research item while other academic disciplines such as history or sociology refrained from engaging in more detailed work on European integration for many years. Following an early initial phase in Europe, the academic debate about European integration was dominated above all by international - or to be more precise - Anglosaxon players. A large number of theoretical papers on European integration were written by US authors while the European Community was frequently passed off as a sub-category of international organisations which considered it to be one of numerous phenomena of an area of transnational interactionism until the late 1980s. "Europe" only advanced to become an area of research and teaching for numerous academic groups in the 1980s and above all since the debate was launched on the Single European Market, the Economic and Monetary Union and the Treaty of Maastricht in the 1990s. Based on these general observations, this chapter inevitably presents a very rough overview of current patterns of sport related research on European integration.

This chapter focuses primarily on the innovations of political science as the discipline that has contributed most comprehensively to the analysis of European Union politics. Political science looks for generally applicable regularities in the area of social and political reality using actual case scenarios that enable correlations to be described, causal relations to be explained and forecasts to be made. When theories, models and concepts are dealt with in this context, they are not really perceived as "hard" copies of reality, but rather as "soft" systems of generalist statements that facilitate the inclusion of theories

---

[1] Chapter 4, 5 and chapter 6 are based partly on the status document "Political Aspects of Sport in the European Union" that was published in 2008 by Michael Groll, Matthias Gütt and Jürgen Mittag with the collaboration of Oliver Koopmann and Timo Schädler within the framework of the project funded by the European Commission. The document can be downloaded at www.sport-in-europe.eu.

and typologies in a systematic and deliberate reflection of underlying preconceptions, initial assumptions and prejudice using linguistically constituted facts that are considered to be real (Meyers, 1997). Furthermore, the explicit reference to theories and typologies also provides deeper insight into the "world views" of political players. This is of paramount importance as all explanations are determined by theory and typologies within the meaning of preconceptions and world views.

For many decades, theories on European integration were derived primarily from the field of international relations. In the 1970s, there was a trend towards regulative approaches based on the interdependence theories and the regime theory. The hallmark of the last two decades was growing orientation to categories of comparative political system research. Governance and Europeanisation theories were also developed within this framework as the continuation of previous theory constructs, creating quite a stir.

Generally speaking, theories take four functions into account. They help to decipher the elements that are deemed relevant from an unmanageable abundance of available information (selection function). The very fact that a distinction is made between what is relevant and what is not shows that theories are linked to certain values. These values then help people to classify the information that has been filtered out and to structure guidelines of reality (classification function). A third function involves the explanation of ideas thus created and the establishment of causal relationships between empirical observations (interpretative function). After all, it is the awareness of the causal relationships of a constructed reality that fuels the hopes of scientists that it will be possible to predict future development trends (prediction function) on a rational basis.

Considerations on methodical approaches are closely associated with the theory approaches presented in this chapter. Contrary to the humanities that are oriented more to hermeneutic aspects, social science is based on experience and observations that arrive at generalisations in the form of laws by forming hypotheses and by evaluating empirical material - similar to the natural sciences, with these laws being combined into systematic theories. As such, empirical-analytical methods dominate in political science. These methods use a wide range of research tools, above all participatory observation, survey research and document analysis. The statistical method that determines frequencies and correlations between different variables is also of importance. Comparative approaches attempt to avoid the relative superficiality and lack of informative value of mere statistical correlations, by discussing and highlighting the systematic inclusion of comparing causal relationships.

4.1 Early integration theory debate: derivations from international relations

The probably best-known approach to discussing European integration in an exemplary and theoretical way that integrates all disciplines is reflected in the debate on integration theory. In this area, political science above all has developed a set of theoretical tools that has been elaborated on more and more in recent years to which questions and policy-making areas have always applied but which has not yet been projected onto sport (Welz & Engel, 1993; Giering, 1997; Rosamond, 2000; Wiener & Dietz, 2004; Bieling & Lerch, 2005).

Federalism, intergovernmentalism and neo-functionalism

The first wave of debates about integration theory dates back roughly to the late 1950s when the first systematic papers were published on the development of European integration. Three approaches emerged that greatly influenced the further perspective on the international system in general and the debate on integration theory in particular. They acted very much as a guideline and were closely linked to political values and objectives.

Federalism as an organising principle is aimed at combining uniformity and diversity within the meaning of Alexander Hamilton and other philosophers' explanation of the history of ideas. In the context of the European integration theory, federalism defends the establishment of general institutional conditions for a European federal state that has extensive legislative and executive powers. Whereas the federalists advocated that national sovereignty be renounced along these lines, pressing for the quantum leap (*saut qualitatif*) to be made towards a European federal state (Rougemont, Spinelli), the so-called Unionists rejected the European federal state, leaning towards the theories of the realist school as well as the loss of sovereignty by individual nation states associated with it, while simultaneously advocating that European countries intensify economic and political cooperation. In accordance with the philosophical traditions ranging from Thucydides through to Machiavelli and Hobbes right up to Meinecke's idea of the Raison d'Etat, the tendency was to distance oneself from the idea of a world ruled by peace as envisaged in Woodrow Wilson's "League of Nations". The realist or intergovernmental concept was a confederation that was based, by and large, on bilateral treaties and agreements rather than on a joint constitution and the transfer of sovereignty. Instead, the intention was for Europe to grow gradually more closely together through a network of cross-national agreements in the tradition of the concept of the balance of powers. Leading representatives of realism in the 1960s (Hoffmann, 1966) began to differentiate the European concept of realism in the direction of the intergovernmental perspective in view of the progress achieved in development towards a supranational community. They explained "The European Rescue of the Nation State" (Milward, 1992) specifically with the cooperation between European countries that goes hand in hand with it.

The so-called functionalists proposed an alternative approach by giving preference to cooperation that was limited to a few technical and economic policy-making areas over comprehensive political integration. Functionalism assumes that certain tasks and problems can only be solved by a team of experts that act at supranational level. Out of all the political theorists, it was David Mitrany above all who emphasised that modern industrial societies can only grow together if individual functional areas (such as transport or energy) integrate first. He said a network of international, function-specific organisations would gradually emerge whose services would gain growing recognition among the population. These transnational organisations promote prosperity and boost cooperation (ramification).

The theories mentioned here represent a key basis for any theory-related analysis of sport, especially when taking the underlying principles of European policy and institutional mission statements into account (Schneider, 1977: 13ff.). Mission statements are characterized by a - varying - melange of access to reality, analysis, evaluation, implicit or explicit terms of reference of political goals and propagation of political action with a view to implementing relevant programmes. They are simultaneously perception and interpretation patterns of the respective situation. For sport-related analysis this means examining what guiding principles have been pursued by which actors in the individual time periods regarding the further shaping of European sports policy and the extent to which these guiding principles have or have not been implemented.

Transactional and transnational approaches

The three theories that shaped the early years of the debate on the integration theory were frequently raised, intensified and modified in subsequent years, in fact only began to relate to European integration in the first place. It was the political scientist Ernst B. Haas in particular who projected functionalism onto European integration and evolved it into a specific variant of neo-functionalism. However, whereas functionalism highlights economic constraints almost exclusively, neo-functionalism focuses more on the political dimension.

In the context of these debates, the transnational dimension of European policies gradually became the focus of attention. The transnational sports policy (Groll, 2005) follows the same tradition as the theory of transnational policies according to Kaiser (1969), who described the growing power of social players. Transnational societies which are the prerequisite for transnational policies exist when there is social interaction between societies of nation states that have different systems. Groll (2005) proves - long after the theories of Kaiser dating back to the early 1970s - that there is such a thing as transnational societies of sport and that the interaction between them does have an impact on the political agenda of nation states and intergovernmental organisations. The model of transnational sports policy focuses on describing the dimensions of transnational sports policy as well as the tasks and goals of the players involved. This demonstrates that sports policy is not just about shaping sport, but is also about the instrumentalisation of sport. Politics, the economy, the media and sport and their relevant sub-categories are identified as relevant categories of players of the transnational society of sport. The sport-related intentional (instrumental) and non-sport-related intentional (instrumental) goals are highlighted. The processing of this issue highlights the fact that sport plays an important political role and that it is therefore necessary to look at sport from a sports policy perspective.

In the early 1970s, a second wave of discussions about the integration theory began. While the neofunctionalist approach was stagnating and its most important protagonist Ernst B. Haas, actually announced the "obsolescence of regional integration theory" (Haas, 1975), following the failure of projects such as the European Economic and Monetary Union and the increase in conflicting interests following the admission of new Member States, this school of thought began to adopt a more differentiated approach under changed auspices. Papers with a more global focus began to attract attention, above all the papers on the interdependence theory by Nye and Keohane, but also their evolution within the meaning of the regime theory by Keohane, in which integration was declared a subcategory of interdependence. The importance of the interdependence theory lies above all in the reference it makes to the networking of actors in international relations and in the simultaneous emphasis of the increase in the number of political players owing to the emergence of ever new international regimes. Regimes are not identical to international organisations, yet regimes emerge in an environment of international relations that are by and large institutionalised. According to this view, international regimes serve as an arena for all types of reciprocal political relations and are capable of providing regime-promoting services.

In view of the fact that a European sports policy is indeed emerging, it has to be examined in this context to what extent sport too is a regime. As such, special importance should be attached above all to UEFA and European wide sport (con-) federations as a quasi European regime which plays a key role in shaping sport relationships but also to actors such as the international sports federations and the International Olympic Committee (Rittberger & Boekle, 1997).

4.2 Current discussions: orientation towards political systems

The integration theory
The treaty reform of the 1990s contributed towards a renewed wave of reforms in the integration theory debate. In terms of an adjustment process - triggered by political developments at European level - the change in theory presented itself as a response to changing reality. Existing theoretical concepts were modified and evolved, for instance, the intergovernemental theory towards liberal intergovernementalism (Moravscik, 1998). A liberal component is based on the approach because Moravcsik integrates the decision-making process within societies into his analysis. However, at international level, he continues to abide strictly by the intergovernemental postulate of the sovereign nation state. In Moravcsik's view, integration arises from a rational cost-benefit analysis by nation states that felt compelled to liberalise their markets because of growing interdependency.

In addition to the incremental evolution of individual theories, the basic view of European integration is also changing. In the 1990s, there was evidence of a growing turn in the number of persons espousing theoretical integration that was characterised by a departure from approaches of international relations towards a more state-oriented approach of comparative and systems research. The "neo"-institutionalist school provided important impetus in this context. It focuses more on institutions and organisational structures, including the associated values and standards (March & Olsen, 1989).

This view was endorsed by Sven Güldenpfennig (2003), who appealed first and foremost for a systems theoretical approach to be adopted in the comments he made on the political aspects of sport. Güldenpfennig ascertains that sport as a social system has both a need for politics (sport as a cultural system) and a capability for politics (sport as an institutional system), meaning that it can be both the object and subject of politics. In general, however, this is affected by verbal over-politicisation combined with actual under-politicisation and a lack of institutionalisation within sport science. As general prerequisites for analysing sports policy, he postulates a systemic classification of sport and politics, the pre-definition of politics and a pre-definition of sport. As far as classifying the term "politics" is concerned, Güldenpfennig proposes using a definition of politics with a medium reach that includes the political system, institutional (political) action and the player-theoretical (political) action, as opposed to a minimum definition on politics based on a system of government and a maximum definition in which politics is equivalent to society.

Network and governance approaches
In addition to systems theory considerations, a growing number of approaches based on policy network analysis has been referring to the theoretical interpretation of European integration since the 1990s. For a long time, the area of sport was more or less ignored. New ground was not broken until Benner and Reinicke (1999) came onto the scene, claiming the growing insight into intragovernmental interaction processes and the suboptimal political results of classical international organisations created the foundations for the emergence of new types of cooperation such as global political networks. Based on assumptions of the network theory and the concept of cooperative international institutions, there is also evidence of global political networks developing in the area of sport for instance, in the endeavours undertaken by the European Union, nation states, IOC and other sports federations and economic players in relation to the establishment of the World Anti Doping Agency (Croci &Forster 2004). Groll only alluded superficially to the existence of political networks in sport (2005), but he

recommended that they become a key topic in more extensive papers because this is the only way the complex nature of transnational sports policy processes can be taken into account.

Since the end of the 1990s, there has been growing mention of "governance". In this context, it is argued that not only states are the focus of analytical interest as units or collective players but rather individual players. This player-focused approach is chosen in order to extend beyond abstract assumptions in relation to "national interests" and preferences of states: due to the growing influence collective and corporative players are having on the policy-making and policy-implementing process, the more widespread the assumption that modern nation states are being integrated into ever more dense intrasocietal and transnational negotiating relations. While attention was drawn to the problem of enforcing internationally binding rules of the game by way of an institutional regime, competencies for issuing rules and decision-making processes were shifted more and more to the level of negotiations which limits the state's capability for unilateral, hierarchical control. According to this version, the sub-system of politics can no longer take generally binding decisions autonomously, but rather is dependent on other players - for instance from industry. As a result of this, a new type of governing known as "governance" emerged that was characterised by a change from hierarchical, state-centred governing right up to non-hierarchical coordination of state and non-state players, incorporating all levels within the framework of so-called policy networking. Governing "beyond the state" was hence raised to become the central sign (Rosenau & Czempiel, 1992).

The concept of governance was soon applied to the European Union. In this context, the term multi-level-governance (or multi-level system) swiftly developed into a key approach of theory-based EU research. This term not only means that there is a system of vertical distribution of competencies in the EU, but also that this structure of a vertical political network is giving rise to new action patterns of the competent players. Gary Marks was among the first persons to use the approach for the EU in his analyses of European structural and regional policy by highlighting the way in which players are integrated into the overall political decision-making process. In its "White Paper on governance in the European Union", the Commission seized this integration and discussed it as being relevant for political action, the way in which decisions are taken. In the White Paper, the objective of governance in the European Union is considered "to open the political decision-making process and to involve more people and organisations in the shaping and implementation of EU policies" (White Paper of the European Commission, 2001: 4). The concept ‚governance' is also defined for the European Union as "the rules processes and attitudes that characterise the way in which powers are exercised at European level" (White Paper of the European Commission, 2001: 10).

There are two associated topics in relation to the relevance of the term "governance" for the field of sport (cf. Ronge, 2006): on the one hand the political science and sociological aspect of the term "governance" which originates from the economic context need to be developed. On the other hand, the social sector of sport needs to be examined in order to establish to what extent its interpretation as a non-profit- and non-governmental sector can be brought into alignment with the political science category "government" that is derived from the term governance. Sport as a social sector that fulfils a non-profit-making, civil societal function sets itself apart from other social sectors and is by nature neither governmental nor commercial-economic. In conceptual terms, sport belongs to the so-called third sector (along with government and the market economy) in society and can claim both non-governmental and private non-profit models. Becker and Lehmkuhl said the most striking features of sport are "single-federation structures, hierarchy and integration of the individual athletes" (Becker & Lehmkuhl, 2003). From the perspective of state "sports policy", sport represents an independent, self-administered, non-governmental social sector in which policies only intervene selectively in order to promote common welfare. This "non-governmental", politically autonomous sport sector is, in principle, deemed non-profit-making which means that sport clubs are exempt from the likes of corporation tax, income tax and turnover tax. In terms of legal form, sport clubs are "non-profit-making", i.e. they do not pursue any economic purposes. The applicability of the governance concept to sport will have to take the weak regulation (control) of the sport sector as a whole that goes hand in hand with the potency of sports federations into account.

Europeanisation of the transnational sport sector

In addition to governance approaches, Europeanisation concepts have above all been pursued within political science very recently. Up to now, the debate on Europeanisation has not led to an independent line of theory, rather a wide range of analytical concepts have been developed within the framework of increased research activities. The dazzling term "Europeanisation" which is being used to excess in the public and scientific debate subsumes above all the impact European integration is having on the individual nation states but it also includes the strategies the individual Member States have adopted to respond to the challenges posed by European integration. The term "Europeanisation" can, however, relate to regional perceptions of European policy and the adaption patterns. More and more legal instruments that are being adopted at European level also affect competencies for sport - as documented, for instance, by the Bosman ruling that relates to the Single European Market. At the same time, more and more decisions have been taken in the field of sport regarding the requirements the European Union is expected to meet.

One key issue in the debate on Europeanisation relates to the convergence and divergence theory: do the same challenges facing the EU system have 'top down' effects that change the political systems of the Member States in the direction of similar structures or even identical models? (Risse et al., 2001: 15ff.; Wessels, Maurer & Mittag, 2002). One approach that is used intensively compares European terms of reference with national structures ("Goodness of fit" or "misfit") and subsequently analyses the "mediative factors" in the Member States in order to explain national changes (Risse et al., 2001: 6ff.; Börzel, 2001: 143).

The term Europeanisation is also used in different contexts. From the sociocultural perspective, Europeanisation is discussed in terms of the development of a European identity. From the political perspective, the term is used to describe different processes and developments within the framework of the European Union (Olsen, 2002). Borneman and Fowler (1997) identify "Europeanisation" as a process which all Member States have had to undergo. Europeanisation is perceived as a "set of incremental processes through which European political, social and economic dynamics become part of the logic of national discourse, identities, political structures and public policies" (Borneman & Fowler, 1997: 489). The majority of papers on Europeanisation have been dominated by a "top-down" perspective that deals with the influence European integration is having on national policy-making. There is less evidence of opposite approaches from the "bottom-up" perspective that deal with the influence national policies are having at European level. Brand and Niemann (2007) claim in view of European sport politics that Europeanisation is not a one-way street, regardless of whether it is a "top-down" or "bottom-up" approach, saying it should be seen as a process that works in both directions. This approach highlights the interdependence between the national and European level.

Up to now the subject matter of studies have been above all policy-making areas and institutions of the Member States. It represents a central approach to transferring the debate on Europeanisation to sport (Mittag, 2007). Back in 1997, Borneman and Fowler identified five areas in which the processes of Europeanisation can be studied effectively namely language, money, tourism, sex and sport. Sport, for instance, makes its own contribution to developing a European identity, because the Europeanisation of sport is thought to promote European awareness to a certain extent. Whereas Head (2004) attempts to illustrate Europeanisation through football using episodes of Klinsmann and Eriksson in England, the social/transnational approach of Europeanisation adopted by Brand and Niemann (2007) has more to offer. In their analysis, selected Europeanisation processes in the area of football are examined on the basis of six criteria (source, dynamics, players, response, strength of the response and level of change). In doing so, it becomes clear that social areas and transnational players are important aspects of the Europeanisation process. In terms of content, there is hence a link with transnational sports policy (Groll, 2005).

Neo-corporatism and sport

Whereas the integration theory approaches are based on international relations or on political systems, corporatism and pluralism-related approaches - just like the governance approach - focus mainly on social players, specifically federations. Corporatism and pluralism are key terms in the subject area of the representation of interests by federations (Kevenhörster, 2008: 295). While pluralism emphasises the participatory and competitive aspects of representation of interests and highlights first and foremost the demands players make on the political system, corporatism focuses on the political steering processes and regulatory aspects of the state. According to the classical works of Ernst Fraenkel, pluralism is characterised by the fact that reform involves permanent change. These reforms can be attributed to conflicts of interest in industrial mass societies that need to be fought openly in order to avoid the disintegration of society. As such, the state plays an arbitrary role.

Contrary to this more conflict-oriented perspective, the term "corporatism" means the amalgamation of persons from the same class and professional groups. When corporations are heavily involved in the political decision-making process of the state, reference is made to a corporative state. Authoritarian corporatism (also known as state corporatism) was assigned in the 20th century to fascist in Italy under Mussolini and to Portugal's dictatorship under Salazar, but also to the military dictatorships of Latin America. These cases involve compulsory memberships of federations in state structures (cf. Matuschek, 1998). The term neo-corporatism (also widely known as liberal corporatism) refers to the basically voluntary incorporation of organised interests into policys and their participation in the formulation and implementation of political decisions. The scope of what is covered by the term neo-corporatism has broadened in the course of corporatism research. Whereas the term was initially used to designate "tripartite" cooperation between the state, corporate organisations and trade unions, various types of political cooperation between organised interests or with government bodies are nowadays subsumed under the term "neo-corporatism" (Voelzkow, 2003). These organised interests, mostly in the form of federations, exist in many areas. Von Alemann (1987) makes a distinction between four kinds of federations: federations in the economic and labour sector, federations in the social sector, federations in the leisure and recreational sector and federations in the religious, scientific and cultural sector. The division is a text book case, many federations nowadays have cross-divisional work areas. The umbrella and top-level federations in the European sport system are, for instance, active in all four areas.

The interplay between the political decision-makers and the local sport organisations is the prerequisite for organising the areas of sport and leisure. The question that needs to be asked is to what extent politicians determine the scope for action and whether and how sport organisations and the members of the population that engage in sports exert pressure on politicians. In principle, the relationship between the state and sport is seen as being based on the spirit of partnership or corporate models. Meier (1995) highlighted this fact back in 1988 when he established that there was greater interdependence between sport and the state in the Federal Republic of Germany than, for instance, between the state and trade unions in the economic sector.

Whereas Meier emphasised the concept and structures of neo-corporatism in sport, Heinemann published a paper in 1996 that also dealt with the relationship between sport and the state. Although Heinemann resumed the term "neo-corporatism" in his work, the principle of autonomy was the main feature of his article. He said "independence and autonomy of sport are the fundamental basic principles of the Federal Republic of Germany's sports policy" (cf. Heinemann, 1996: 178). This principle, also known as the principle of subsidiarity, differs hugely from the principle of neo-corporatism. Whereas the principle of neo-corporatism is based on state control, the principle of subsidiarity is based on independence and autonomy. In most recent times, Schimank (2002) published a paper on the debate on corporatism in sport which has not yet been conducted intensively. He sees corporatism as one of four organisational dynamics that are capable of jeopardising the internally-oriented ethos of clubs. "Corporatism involves the risk of overloading clubs with politically justified matters, that project so awkwardly into the sport meaning horizon of muscular effort, competition and the determination to win that this meaning no longer has sufficient effect to keep the actual athletes interested" (Schimank, 2002: 10).

These organisational-sociological considerations need to be pursued at the level of sport political science. This is where it would be wise to include neocorporatist findings into the theories of political networks. Kevenhörster (2008: 297f.) considers the transfer of decisions to a large number of political networks to be a general problem of corporatistic decision-making structures: "This diversification of political decision-making favoured by a high need for consensus and coordination hampers central political control, makes a clear allocation of political decision to certain institutions difficult, if not impossible, and thus prevents the allocation of political responsibility for results negotiated by way of corporatism and implemented by political-administrative means." This pessimistic outlook does not have to be shared in the sport sector as the principle of subsidiarity conflicts with central political control. Nonetheless it is importance to reach a position for sport in which the neocorporatist influence is brought to bear at national level on the one hand, enabling it to play an important role at European and international level in the global political networks of sport on the other.

4.3 EU-related sports typologies

The EU's direct and indirect sports policy
In contrast to theories, the pretension of typologies and models is less far-reaching than the theoretical approach. Relevant classification attempts are aimed primarily at classifying observations objectively and at comparing and analysing the similarities or differences of two or

more facts with the help of a number of variables. The major goal is to develop relevant basic characteristics from a large number of case scenarios that help to structure the diversity of the empirical world meaningfully into groups.

The distinction made between a direct and indirect sports policy by Tokarski and Steinbach (2001) is probably the best-known sport-related typology that relates directly to European integration and sport. Indirect sports policy refers to the impact common EU policies have on sport, whereas direct sports policy refers to the sports policy is adopted by European institutions.

Attention can be drawn to a direct sports policy in the narrower sense where the representatives of the Community, namely the Commission as the executive body, intentionally implemented relevant measures with a view to achieving an impact on sport and achieving any such effect with the help of sports for the benefit of the Union (Tokarski & Steinbach, 2001: 689).

The authors divide the direct sports policy into two phases: the Adonnino Report (1984/85) that designates sport as an area of com-munication between people and the Larive Report that defines the main lines of a coordinated sports policy can be allocated to the phase of coexistence (1985 to 1997). Other important milestones in this phase were the establishment of the European Sports Forum in 1991 and the Commission Report of 1991 "The European Union and Sport", whose main statement was that the Community bodies should deal with sport in the European Union from the perspective of sport as an important economic factor and from the perspective of sport as a suitable PR tool.

The distinction Kornbeck (2006) makes into vertical and horizontal sports policy corresponds, by and large, to the typological distinction made by Tokarski and Steinbach (2001) into "indirect" and "direct" sports policy, as the author himself emphasises (Kornbeck, 2006: 86; Groll, Gütt & Mittag, 2008: 8).

Phase models of the EU's sports politics
A second typological approach that focuses more on the process-related dimension concentrates on the emergence of phases of a Euro-pean sports policy. The question what temperoral and content-related regulations have pressed ahead with the "Europeanisation" of sport in the past few decades is important for the phase model in structural

terms. As the EU - and its forerunners - do not have any "real" competencies in sport, the question when sports policy began certainly needs
to be clarified. According to Tokarski and Steinbach (2001: 69ff.), the
phase of direct sports policy can be divided into a phase of coexistence (1985 to 1997) and a phase of cooperation (from 1998):

1. The phase of coexistence (1985-1997)
2. The phase of cooperation (from 1998)

This basic categorisation has been modified in the last years by a
number of authors who have distinguished between several historical
phases. Groll, Gütt and Mittag (2008) and Mittag (2009), for instance,
took a more differentiated view of the phases proposed by Tokarski
and Steinbach (2001) and changed the classifications in relation to the
timeframes and designations. According to younger approaches,
European sports policy can be divided into a total of at least four
phases:

The phase of disregard (1966-1984)
The phase of coexistence (1984 to 1995)
The phase of cooperation (1995 to 2003)
The phase of pre-constitutionalisation (from 2003)

1.   The initial phase of European sports policy is characterised, by
and large, by a complete disregard for the correlation between sport
and European integration. Although sport was mentioned in the
documents of the Council of Europe in the 1960s and in documents of
the European Parliament, this did not result in any closer integration
or interaction processes, at least for the time being (Sports Division,
Council of Europe, 1998). Even though a growing number of European sport competitions were established and European umbrella organisations have been set up above all since the 1950s, sporting activities during this period were confined to individual (umbrella) associations which were important players from the European perspective until the 1980s. The very fact alone that the European Parliament, the
Council of Europe and the European Court of Justice had to deal with
lawsuits by athletes as early as the 1960s indicates that a harmonisation process was underway.

2.   That the European Community began to deal intensively with sport in the 1980s - despite the lack of a statutory basis -can be attributed first and foremost to the general political conditions prevailing in the 1980s. In a bid to strengthen a European identity, the heads of state and government began to reflect on sport. One year after proclaiming the concept of a "Citizens' Europe" by the European Council in Fontainebleau in 1984, a committee drew up a list of factors that promote the Community spirit - including sport. In the course of this development and from then on, individual projects with a sport dimension were funded within the framework of other Community programmes. Both the European Parliament and the European Commission subsequently presented reports suggesting that sport be integrated more effectively into Community policy.

3.   A ruling handed down by the European Court of Justice was the ultimate driver for the development of sport-related structures at European level. The principles of the internal market which had been implemented, by and large, by 1993 developed a considerable impact on numerous policy-making areas - including sport. This manifested itself above all in the so-called *Bosman* ruling. This ruling handed down by the European Court of Justice on 15 December 1995 set a process in motion that changed sport and the organisational structure of sport. While the institutions at European level were now able to influence sport more so than ever before, sport clubs and associations realised that sport would no longer remain limited solely to the area of autonomous self-organisation. Whereas the EU institutions responded to this with numerous reports, initiatives and reform proposals under primary law, sport clubs and sports federations began to adapt their structures in view of the growing challenges facing the European Union.

4.   A Joint Declaration on Sport was attached to the Treaty of Amsterdam (1999) which highlighted "the societal importance of sport". The social dimension of sport was also pointed out in the context of the Treaty of Nice which entered into force in 2002. It too highlighted the autonomy of sport but failed to give the European Union any competency for adopting a sports policy. However, incorporating sport into the European treaties had meanwhile become a topic of serious discussion was reflected when provision was made to incorporate sport into primary law in the Treaty Establishing a Constitution for Europe and when more and more institutions began to comment on the role of sport in the European Union. This phase continues to the

present day - also against the backdrop of the Treaty establishing a Constitution for Europe which has not yet been ratified.

4.4 Interim conclusions: theoretical approaches between fashion and plurality

The theories and typologies presented are characterised by frequent upheaval and marked diversity. Whereas, for instance, some theoretical approaches (e.g. neo-functionalism) were and continue to be important throughout the entire period of integration history, other approaches are meanwhile considered to be outdated. Governance or Europeanisation concepts currently attract the strongest interest and can be regarded as fashionable from an academic perspective. To some extent, this can be explained by both concepts referring to a kaleidoscope of different social sciences and political science approaches. As scientific concepts, Governance and Europeanisaton define complex social correlations more effectively than older theories from international relations. The conclusion can be drawn that certain forms of collective coordination of action and adaptation of structures can be defined more accurately with the Governance and the Europeanisation concept than has been the case up to now.

According to Wessels, no particular integration theory can be deemed the "dominant school" at present (Wessels, 2006: 428). Even though individual researcher networks keep trying to position their key works and "beacons", this approach seems to be having more of a repressive effect as "the opportunity to gain reciprocal information is being wasted". Consequently, there are growing demands for connecting lines to be established between the individual approaches and to identify above all the correlations in a productive addendum. Against this backdrop, the area of sport also needs to "combine and delimit theoretical approaches in a meaningful way in order to tackle phenomena that are relevant for integration, if necessary, at different analytical levels (...) thereby making optimum use of the existing explanatory potential" (Wessels, 2006: 438).

Political scientists who developed considerable detail and manifold research results in their studies on the then European (Economic) Community even decades ago, may be considered overly abstract and in individual cases obsolete or refuted. Nonetheless, the approaches can enable sport scientists to shed light on a systematisation of conditions of policy and sport - in a productive combination with empirical studies that have already been carried out. This could lead to generating a further-reaching wealth of knowledge for the classification or falsification of individual results and for systematic descriptions and summaries.

5   Sport politics and polities at the European level

The relationship between European policy-making and sport is gaining momentum due to the growing convergence between sport and other social areas of activity, the unflagging importance of political players for the organisation of sport and the tangible evidence that sport is becoming ever more important at European level. However, the issue still involves so many uncertainties that it is difficult to tackle it systematically. Up to now, it has not been possible to reach a consensus on how the bandwidth of terms can be delimited (sport and politics, the political aspect of sport, sport in politics, sports policy), nor has there been any systematic debate on a European sports policy.

In order to cover the multi-dimensional nature of policy-related issues adequately, political science distinguishes between the three dimensions "polity", "policy" and "politics". "Polity" outlines permanent forms that are difficult to change and are expressed, for instance, in a constitution, but also in standards and rules. The term "politics" refers to the process-related dimensions and above all the interaction between the players involved in the political process whereas the term "policies" refers to the content-related dimension, the way in which solutions to problems are found and how policies are shaped.

Today's European Union has been shaped by a mix of treaties that have been amended throughout the history of integration over the past 50 odd years, some of them several times. The establishment of the European Coal and Steel Community (ECSC) in 1952 was followed in 1958 by the establishment of the European Atomic Energy Community (EURATOM) and the European Economic Community (EEC) within the framework of the Treaties of Rome. This framework has been modified and expanded by the Merger Treaty of 1967, the Single European Act (SEA) in 1987 and the succeeding Maastricht, Amsterdam and Nice treaty revisions. The question that needs to be asked is what rules, standards and instruments in sport and what institutions today are involved in shaping European sport and in what way? These issues are to be pursued in the following chapter.

5.1 Constitutional incorporation of sport

At present, the Treaties Establishing the European Community and the European Union and their forerunners do not contain any articles that incorporate sport into primary law (cf. Parrish, 2003; Kornbeck, 2006; Mittag, 2007). Notwithstanding this, reference is made to sport in constitutionally relevant documents - under primary law. An overall perspective of the role of sport was developed, for instance, within the framework of the conclusions adopted for the first time by the Presidency in Nice in 2000, in which sport was no longer outlined as a side issue but as an independent policy area. In this context, the European Council emphasised the autonomy of sport organisations and their right to self-organisation by creating suitable federation structures.

In the recent past, the prospect of creating constitutional coverage of sport has gained further momentum. This is expressed most clearly in the recent debate on reform: when the Treaty of Lisbon enters into force - after it has been fully ratified - sport will be incorporated into European primary law for the very first time in the history of sport. The fact that sport has not been taken into account at European level so far can be explained on the one hand by the fact that a large number of Member States have repeatedly referred to the autonomy of sport and have been rather sceptical about transferring this field of policy - and even parts of it - to European level. Furthermore, there have also been major conflict areas between the self-organisation claim of sport and already established European primary and secondary law. In the following, a chronological overview will be given of the way in which sport is taken into consideration in the documents of the European Community and European Union.

Adonnino Report

Sport was mentioned explicitly at European level for the first time in the so-called Adonnino Report. At the summit of Fontainebleau (in June 1984), the European Council set up the Adonnino Committee for a People's Europe. This ad-hoc committee - named after its chairperson Pietro Adonnino - was installed to discuss ideas that were capable of strengthening "the identity of the Community vis-à-vis European citizens and the world". In the Committee report(s), a large number of Community-promoting factors were listed, including, inter alia, uniform European passports and driving licenses, increased recognition of diplomas and proof of professional qualifications, consular assistance at all missions of Member States and even the expansion of town twinnings. Furthermore, it also says in the report that sport "has always been an important area of communication between peoples. It is an important part of life for a large number of citizens in the Community" (Bulletin of the EC, 7/1985).

The report was approved by the European Council in the summer of 1985 after which the view above all of the European Commission gradually spread that sport is an important tool for consolidating a European identity (see Groll, Gütt & Mittag, 2008: 18). As it has meanwhile been acknowledged that sport "acts as a catalyst" (Jesse, 1995: 23) for the European integration process that has helped to make the abstract construct Europe more tangible and to create a European identity, a few international sporting events such as the European Sailing Regatta have received EU funding since 1985.

However this policy fuelled incomprehension among national sport associations which criticised that the Commission only promoted popular sporting events that did not need any such promotion whereas the less funded ''sport for all' was not taken into account. The attempts made by the Commission at the time highlight the fact that sport and politics were merely coexisting in parallel worlds. This is also documented by the first sport promotion grants. The first sport promotion measure was incoherent and unsystematic so that it was not possible to draw any conclusions for future projects (cf. Tokarski et al., 2004; Jesse, 1995). At the time, the European Commission was not yet able to develop, let alone implement, a converging sports policy. This also manifested itself in subsequent years when other European institutions also began to focus more on sport.

Larive Report
At the end of 1988, the "Larive Report" of the European Parliament was published in which the author, Jessica Larive, called for a coherent and coordinated sports policy to be adopted that had hitherto been unsuccessful. She focused on four items in particular and made demands associated with them: 1. An international strategy to cope with the social aspects of sport; 2. Establishing what impact the free Single European Market is having on sport; 3. Promoting the Community dimension of sport and 4. Developing an action programme for sport.

The main focus of the report was to assess the sports policy pursued by the European Community. That policy was criticised in the report for being "one-sided and simplistic" (EU Office of German Sports, 2007). Even this document with the unequivocal and critical demands "did not change the fact that until the early 1990s, the direct sports policy of the Community was limited to an unsystematic approach which failed to rate the value of sport adequately" (Tokarski & Steinbach, 2004: 70). This is where the term "coexistence" can also be used unequivocally. The problematic relationship between the interests of sport and European policies is acknowledged and criticised by the European Parliament, but it has failed yet again in terms of practical implementation. During this phase, fears also abounded in the Member States that the Community's competencies would expand in the sports sector. Concerns that the Community would step up its activities in the sport sector cause major friction between the players (Groll, Gütt & Mittag, 2008: 19).

Pack Report

After a sustained period of stagnation in relation to sports policy in the early 1990s, the "Pack Report" of the European Parliament published in 1997 (named after the author Doris Pack) once again called upon the European Union - and the European Commission in particular - to realign its direct sports policy actions. The Parliament holds the view that the European Union should acknowledge "the important cultural, economic and social phenomenon of sport" in its foundation treaties and through the measures it implements. The author also criticises the Commission's failure of not mention sport in the White Paper on Education and Training.

In the wake of the Larive Report, the Pack Report represented a renewed attempt to handle the balancing act between sport and politics at European level using sociocultural means. The Pack Report highlights the multi-faceted nature of sport and criticises the fact that the European Court of Justice limited sport to the economic level alone. At the time, the European Parliament called for substantial progress to be made in the direction of an established EU sports policy by a) incorporating sport into the Treaty Establishing the European Community, and b) by drawing up a Green Paper including an action plan. Although these appeals only met with a limited response, there were signs of further enhanced, coordinated and more uniform cooperation between the EU institutions. The "Television without Frontiers" Directive issued by the European Parliament is a typical example of this. It was implemented in 1997 immediately after the Pack Report was published (Groll, Gütt & Mittag, 2008: 19).

Joint Declaration on Sport
(Protocol note in the Treaty of Amsterdam)

Sport was explicitly mentioned within the framework of EC/EU Treaties for the very first time in 1997 in the context of the Treaty of Amsterdam which stated the following in a "Joint Declaration on Sport":
"The Conference emphasises the social significance of sport, in particular its role in forging identity and bringing people together. The
Conference therefore calls on the bodies of the European Union to lis-
ten to sports associations when important questions affecting sport are
at issue. In this connection, special consideration should be given to
the particular characteristics of amateur sport" (Declaration on the Final Act of the Treaty of Amsterdam, Declaration no. 29). The fact that
the issue of sport was referred to as an issue for the first time in the
form of a "Joint Declaration" attached to the Treaty as a Protocol can
be attributed to the discussion prompted by the Bosman ruling on the
one hand, but also to the intensive lobbying by NGOs on the other.

With the Declaration, the societal importance of sport was, in principle, acknowledged (Tokarski et al., 2004: 68). However, the protocol
note did not give the Community any direct mandate to actively promote sport (Tokarski & Steinbach, 2001: 76), so that the Commission
was not authorised to take on funding commitments, for instance, for
the "Eurathlon" promotion programme. To sum things up, it can be
established that this Declaration did not develop any legal importance,
but it did develop political importance which was reflected inter alia
in the agenda of several European Council summits (Vienna, December 1998; Helsinki, December 1999; informal meeting of EU Sports
Ministers in Paderborn, June 1999). Against this backdrop, discussions abounded at European level and within the EU Member States
whether an article on sport should be incorporated into the treaties and
whether a legally binding declaration should be issued (Groll, Gütt &
Mittag, 2008: 20).

Helsinki Report

Even before the Treaty of Amsterdam entered into force, the European
Council, meeting in Vienna on 11 and 12 December 1998, invited the
Commission to submit a report to the Helsinki European Council with
a view to safeguarding current sports structures and maintaining the
social function of sport within the Community framework. On the basis of the Declaration on Sport attached to the Treaty of Amsterdam
which was a milestone in taking sport into account at Community

level, the European Commission presented its global vision of sport with the report it presented at the European Council summit in Helsinki in December 1999. In this report, the Commission emphasises four key aspects:

- The excessive commercialisation of sport
- The protection of underage players
- The fight against doping
- The economic dimension of sport

For several years, the European approach to sport has been affected by several phenomena, namely the rise in the popularity of sport, the internationalisation of sport and the unprecedented development of the economic dimension of sport. These phenomena provide certain advantages for sport and society. Accordingly, the number of jobs created directly or indirectly by the sport industry has risen by 60% in the past ten years. However, the Helsinki Report also warned of the negative results of these developments back in 1999, one being the need to produce results under pressure from sponsors that may be considered to be one of the causes of the expansion of doping. Other consequences are the increase in the number of lucrative sporting events, which may end up promoting the commercial approach, to the detriment of sporting principles and the social function of sport and the hazardous future facing young people who are being led into top-level competitive sport at an increasingly early age, often with no other vocational training, with the resulting risks for their physical and mental health and their subsequent switch to other employment, and last but not least the breaking apart of sport typical structures. The Commission highlights the social importance of sport and says that physical and sporting activities need to find their place in the education system of each Member State. For instance, the approximately 700,000 sport clubs in the Member States leverage the values of sport, e.g. equality, fairness and solidarity. Furthermore, sport is acknowledged as having an educational role, both in education and training programmes, and as it is an ideal platform for social democracy, existing Community programmes should make us of sport to combat exclusion, inequalities, racism and xenophobia. Summing things up, it stated "sport must be able to assimilate the new commercial framework in which it must develop, without at the same time losing its identity and autonomy, which underpin the functions it performs in the social, cultural, health and educational areas" (Helsinki Report, 1998: 6).

The Commission called upon the Member States in the Helsinki Report to orient their national competencies in sport to Community statutory provisions (specifically the law on competition and the principles governing the Single European Market). In terms of the economic activity that it generates, the sporting sector is subject to the rules of the EC Treaty, like the other sectors of the economy. The application of the Treaty's competition rules to the sporting sector must take account of the specific characteristics of sport. Any such exemptions are, for instance, organisational rules of sport organisations and events and sport rules such as "rules of the game". Rules on sponsoring agreements, transmission rights and transfer rules are not always subject to the competition rules.

With the Helsinki Report, the European Union recognises the eminent role played by sport in European society and attaches paramount importance to maintaining its functions of promoting social integration and education and making a contribution to public health and to the general interest function performed by the federation.

Yet the Commission also calls to mind that the Treaty does not contain any direct Community competencies for sport and that there is a need for a new partnership between the European institutions, the Member States and sports organisations, all moving in the same direction, in order to encourage the promotion of sport in European society, while respecting sporting values, the autonomy of sporting organisations and the Treaty, especially the principle of subsidiarity.

Nice Declaration
This discussion was continued at the conference of the European Council in Nice 2000 and sport was dealt with for the first time in a top-level political EU arena. In the conclusions of the Council Presidency published at the end of the summit in Nice, it was recommended that greater importance be attached to the social and cultural dimension of sport in the individual Member States and Community policies and that sport and its social role be promoted. In addition the autonomy of sport was highlighted. The "Declaration on the specific characteristics of sport and its social function in Europe, of which account should be taken in implementing common policies" (Declaration of Nice, 2000) is more comprehensive than the Declaration of Amsterdam. The Declaration of Nice (2000) was not incorporated into

the Treaty and was merely adopted by the Council as a joint declaration which means that once again sport failed to be furnished with a legally binding character. The Treaty of Nice entered into force in 2002 without incorporating a binding article for sport under primary law so that, for instance, the European Year of Education through Sport (2004) was implemented with a budget that was complemented by other initiatives by the Commission and Member States and by actions involving educational components financed by other parties (Groll, Gütt & Mittag, 2008: 21).

So it holds true both in respect of the Treaty of Amsterdam and the Treaty of Nice that the term "sport" is not mentioned which means the EU was not assigned any powers to act in the area of sport. This omission in terms of sports policy was of paramount importance as, in principle, the EC does not have any power to adopt laws but requires an explicit statutory basis within the Community treaties for each legal instrument (enumerative conferral).

Draft Treaty establishing a Constitution for Europe and Treaty of Lisbon

In December 2001, the European Council (which brings together the heads of state or government of the European Union and the president of the Commission) established a "European Convention on the Future of Europe" comprising representatives of governments, the European Commission, the European Parliament and of the national Parliaments as a result of the "Declaration of Laeken on the future of the European Union". Its purpose was to produce a draft constitution for the European Union. The draft Treaty establishing a Constitution for Europe presented by the European Convention in 2003 was to merge the existing EC and EU Treaties, create a uniform contractual architecture and to attribute a legal personality to the European Union. The area of "sport" is mentioned in this Treaty both in the Chapter on "Constitutional requirements" and on "Internal Policies and Action" of the Union, even though no article is devoted exclusively to sport. The Union may take supporting, coordinating or complementary action in the areas of protection and improvement of human health, culture, education, vocational training, youth and sport. The Union is to develop the European dimension of sport with a view to opening sport competitions at international level, promoting cooperation between sport organisations and protecting the physical and moral integrity of sportsmen and sportswomen, especially young sportsmen and sportswomen. To this end, the Union, "shall contribute to the promotion of European sporting issues, while taking account of the specific nature of sport, its structures based on voluntary activity and its social and educational function." (Article III - 281).

The aim to take the special concerns of sport into greater account at EU level means it is logical to draw a comparison with the contractual incorporation in the area of culture (Groll, Gütt & Mittag, 2008: 21). The Union having explicit competency for sport based on the model of the regulations for culture, vocational education or healthcare could be considered. The German Sport Federation (DOSB) gave preference to this model at the time by. A programme at the top of the Article on the regulation of culture creates the basis and the framework for the EU's promotion activity. The principle of subsidiarity would remain binding for promotion measures and precluding any harmonisation of provisions of the Member States, funding would be subject to a unanimous decision by the European Council. This would grant the wish of sport organisations involved in 'sport for all' to promote sport in EU Treaties.

In the Draft Treaty establishing a Constitution for Europe which was signed in Rome on 29 October 2004, sport was explicitly mentioned in two articles that call to mind regulations for the cultural sector. The two articles are in the First and Third Section of the Draft Treaty establishing a Constitution for Europe, and are hence areas in which the Union may take "supporting, coordinating or complementary action" (cf. Euractiv, 2007; Unger, 2006). Article III-182/282 is incorporated under the Section "Education, vocational training, youth and sport". In Article I-17, sport is mentioned alongside culture as an area in which the Union may take supporting, coordinating or complementary action (Euractiv, 2007). The harmonisation of statutory and administrative provisions of the Member States on sport is ruled out in the Draft Treaty establishing a Constitution for Europe (cf. BMI online, 2007). Furthermore, the EU is not assigned any direct competencies for sport (Unger, 2006). By classifying sport under the EU measures as "taking supporting, coordinating or complementary action", sport has by no means been assigned a separate Article that is dedicated specifically to sport - originally there was mention of a "sport article" that is dedicated specifically to sport - which means it is hence at the lowest level of the potential exertion of influence by the EU (cf. Unger, 2006)

If the Treaty establishing a Constitution for Europe were to enter into force, this would be the first time sport would have been enshrined in a uniform EU Treaty. As scheduled, the Constitution was to enter into force on 1 November 2006, following the necessary ratification by the competent national parliaments or referendums held in all of the - then 25 - Member States. However, the failure of the referendums on the Treaty establishing a Constitution for Europe in France and in the Netherlands led to the failure of the Treaty establishing a Constitution for Europe. In 2007, the initiative for a Treaty establishing a Constitution for Europe was resumed. The European Council agreed, after an extended debate within the framework of its summit held in Brussels in June 2007, that instead of introducing a new text for the constitution, it would be best to amend the existing EU Treaties to incorporate the bulk of the content of the unsuccessful Treaty establishing a Constitution for Europe into the existing EU Treaties. The amended treaties which are commonly referred to as the Treaty of Lisbon, unlike the previous Draft Treaty establishing a Constitution for Europe has been ratified in all Member States without a referendum wtth the exception of Ireland. The Treaty was signed by the heads of government of all Member States on 13 December 2007.

The relevant sport article in the Treaty of Lisbon has been incorporated verbatim into the Draft Treaty establishing a Constitution for Europe. The Article that is relevant for sport (Article III-282) states: "The Union shall contribute to the promotion of European sporting issues, while taking into account the specific nature of sport, its structures based on voluntary activity and its social and educational function". It also emphasises that "Union action shall be aimed at developing the European dimension in sport, by promoting fairness and openness in sporting competitions and cooperation between bodies responsible for sport, and by protecting the physical and moral integrity of sportsmen and sportswomen, especially young sportsmen and sportswomen" (European Commission, 2007).

With the envisaged incorporation of sport into European primary law, sport will obtain its long aspired to legal status and will be able to bring its influence to bear on the development of European law-making - based fully on the model of regulations in the area of culture. According to its wording, the Article will ensure sport is assigned its own, "vertically" constituted working area" (Kornbeck, 2006: 91). However, the EU's new sport competency has not led to any harmonisation or shift in competencies (Kornbeck, 2006). Any undercutting of the regional and national competency areas in sport is hence prevented. Fears of national sport organisations that the EU was jeopard-

ising the autonomy or self-administration of sport with a "sport article" therefore appear to be unfounded.

It remains to be seen with some anticipation whether the Treaty of
Lisbon will actually enter into force, this will be the first time in the
history of sport that it will be incorporated into primary EU law. This
would enable 'sport for all' to obtain the long aspired to financial support of the EU and would offer professional top-level sport a further
step in the direction of the desired legal security which it could invoke
in the courts. Future EU campaigns in the area of sport such as the
"Pierre de Coubertin" action plan, would have their legislative authorisation and hence the possibility of obtaining financial support
from EU funds.

The following criteria sum up the future incorporation of sport under
European primary law (Groll, Gütt & Mittag, 2008: 22):

- Sport would obtain legal certainty in EU treaties
- No desire to harmonise statutory provisions by the EU
- Limitation of the EU taking supporting, coordinating or
  complementary action
- Emphasising the specificity of sport
- The autonomy of sport is not mentioned
- The principle of subsidiarity is not mentioned

Arnaut Report (Independent European Sport Review)
As the negotiations on the amendment to the Treaty dragged on for
much longer than originally foreseen, the bodies of the European Union once again made reference to the future role of sport in documents. The Arnaut Report (Independent European Sport Review) was
the first one in 2006 (a semi-official document that originated from
the British Presidency in the second half of 2005). The British Sport
Minister Cabon used a number of major corruption scandals in Germany, Belgium and Italy as a reason to examine the situation of professional football in Europe. This plan was supported by the Sport
Ministers of Germany, France, Spain and Italy. This study was expanded and intensified by several consultations (UEFA, FIFA and the
Sport Ministers of the EU Member States) and was finally summed up
on 165 pages by the MEP and former Portuguese Sport Minister José
Louís Arnaut as an independent report in May 2006. Originally, it focused on football only, the document is also to be generally binding in
relation to governance standards in European Sport und in relation to

the protection of the European Sport Model. Because of its semi-official origin, the Arnaut Report does not have binding effect, but some parts of it were incorporated into the European Commission's White Paper on Sport. In the report, the legal situation of sport at EU level is discussed and found to be deficient. The report contains demands for greater intervention possibilities created by relevant legal authorisations to act, there is even talk of setting up a European Sport Agency as a supreme political body (cf. Euractiv, 2006; Kreuzer, 2008). It is precisely here that one sees the influence of UEFA which became the sole contact in the EU for football when it was set up, at the same time relinquishing the major problems of racism, fraud in sports betting and money laundering to the EU (cf. Kreuzer, 2008). Eichberg (2008) too claimed that the Arnaut Report was by no means "independent", but merely represented the interests of UEFA and sports federations in general. Despite this ulterior motive, the Arnaut Report does tackle a few key issues.

Belet Report

As the debate about the Treaty establishing a Constitution for Europe rages on, the European Parliament is also addressing the issue of sport, focusing on football in particular. It is noteworthy that a report by the European Parliament, that deals exclusively with a single sport discipline has so far been the only one of its kind. The crucial document published by the European Parliament in this context is the "Report on the Future of Professional Football in Europe". It was published in February 2007 and can be attributed by and large to the author, the Belgian MEP, Ivo Belet. In the run-up to the report, experts of UEFA, FIFA and individual clubs were interviewed about the subject in a public hearing.

Just like the Arnaut Report, this Report also considers the fact that sport does not have any statutory powers and that it is mentioned in the Declaration of Nice, Community law is having a growing impact on sport owing to the growing commercialisation and professionalisation of sport in general and football in particular. The Belet Report expressly describes the "European Football Model" and calls for clarity in legal matters concerning professional football. It is criticised that football in Europe faces challenges, "Football in Europe is facing multiple challenges, that cannot be tackled by the football governing bodies alone. Because of the influence of European law on the game, it is important that there is a constructive dialogue between European institutions and sport governing bodies." (European Parliament, 2006: 2).

Last but not least, the tenor of the parliamentary report was similar to the report published in the context of the European Council: the prime goal is self-monitoring - amending the general statutory conditions is also being considered. The Belet Report contains statements on the social, cultural and educational role of football (as well as on the protection of talented young athletes, fairness, racism, criminality and doping), the law on competition, the Single European Market and governance principles, with sport clubs being included in the interpretations. This has resulted in the following seven key demands:

- A regulatory framework that recognises the specificity of sports
- An action plan for European sport in general and football in particular
- Social dialogue between the Member States
- Leading football federations to enhance the transparency and legitimacy (e.g. FIFA)
- Modulated cost control system for European football
- Central marketing of television rights and the distribution of TV revenue
- The establishment of an independent monitoring body (such as a European Sports Agency)

White Paper on Sport

Generally speaking, White Papers are documents containing officially drafted proposals for Community action in certain policy-making areas. The most thorough document on sport at European level at present is hence the "White Paper on Sport" that was published by the European Commission in 2007. It contains a number of measures relating to sport that are being implemented or supported by the Commission. Ján Figel (2007), European Commissioner in charge of Education, Training, Culture and Youth, including Sport, said when commenting on the White Paper on Sport: "This White Paper is the Commission's contribution to the European debate on the importance of sport in our daily lives. It enhances the visibility of sport in EU policy-making, raises awareness of the needs and specificities of the sport sector, and identifies appropriate further action at EU level." (Groll, Gütt & Mittag, 2008: 24).

Over the two years in which it was in the making which involved two major consultative conferences, several bilateral talks and one online consultation, the Commission stressed that the White Paper on "Sport" was not starting from scratch. At the first consultative con-ference "The EU & Sport: Matching Expectations" held in Brussels on 14 and 15 June 2005, bodies representing sport that had been invited to attend discussed issues in working groups such as "The Societal Function of Sport", "Volunteering in Sport" and "The Fight against Doping", with the European Commission confining itself to "listening mode" (Euro-pean Commission, 2005). At the second confer-ence also held in Brussels on 29 and 30 June 2006 under the heading "The Role of Sport in Europe", topics such as "The Societal Role of Sport", "The Economic Impact of Sport" and "The Organisation of Sport" were discussed in the same way. It outlined the functions sport performs in the social, cultural, health and educational areas, as well as the possi-bilities of governance in sport, transparent directives on the economic impact of sport, the demand was also made that a definition of sport be found that reflects the multi-faceted nature and status of sport in society were proclaimed (European Commission, 2006). In order to fully meet the consultation requirement within EU sports policy and to ensure a bottom-up approach was adopted that could be implemented in technical and practical terms, an online consultation was organised between 7 February and 3 April 2007. Of the 777 responses received, just under 60% came from sport organisations. The largest number of responses was received from France (18.9%) and Belgium (17.5%). The results received presented the EU Commission with the following hierarchical dilemmas:

- Lack of legal security regarding the applicability of EU law in the area of sport
- Governance issues (players' agencies, protection of underage athletes, doping, racism)
- Sport finance and commercialisation tendencies
- Lack of data as the basis for policy-making
- Problems such as adiposity and lack of exercise
- Sport in education and training policy

This resulted in the following seven key areas being defined that were broken down into 1) the socie-tal role of sport (healthcare, anti-doping policy, education policy, active citizenship, social integration, the

fight against racism and violence), 2) the economic role of sport (major events, economic statistics and financing of sport) and 3) the organisation of sport (governance, specificity of sport, freedom of
movement and nationality, transfers, player's agents and rules of
competition and processed as such (Groll, Gütt & Mittag, 2008: 24;
European Commission, 2007: 12):

- Facilitate a strategic orientation of the role sport plays in Europe
- Enhance the visibility of sport in EU policy-making
- Encourage discussion about problems that are relevant for sport
- Raise public awareness of the needs and specific features of the
  sport sector above all in the social, economic and organisational
  area
- Illustrate the applicability of EU law in the sport sector
- Develop measures for the financial support of sport-related
  projects
- Enhance political cooperation in sport at EU level

If a White Paper is well-received by the Council of the European Union, this may lead to the development of a relevant action programme.
Accordingly, the above-mentioned measures create the basis of the
"Pierre de Coubertin" action plan containing 53 sport-related campaigns that will guide the Commission in its sport-related activities
during the coming years.

5.2 European institutions and sports

This chapter outlines the most important political institutions at the
European level and their relevance for sport in greater detail. Of the
institutions that have body status, the European Parliament, the European Commission and the Council of the European Union will be outlined in depth whereas the other two bodies - the European Court of
Auditors and the European Court of Justice (ECJ) - will not be regarded in detail. The European Court of Auditors is responsible for
carrying out the audit of EU finances, the European Court of Justice is
responsible for the jurisdiction of the Union. Political decisions are
negotiated at the instigation of the European Commission between the
European Parliament and the Council of the European Union.

A large number of other players play a role within these bodies. These include, among others, the Council of Europe that has created a new platform which is aimed at integrating sports organisations into the political processes. Also involdved are NGOs as well as special interest and lobbying groups in Brussels, such as the European Network of Sport and Employment, the EOC EU Office of German Sports in Brussels, the G14 and FIFPro. Besides this the national leagues, UEFA and other umbrella organisations play a certain role: UEFA itself claims to be a completely unpolitical player but is increasingly becoming a crucial cog in the wheel of European football.

European Commission

The European Commission can be characterised as the "executive" of the European Community. In some ways, it has similar functions to a government. It is a supranational body that represents not the interests of a certain member state but the interests of the European Union in its entirety. Operating in the manner of a cabinet government with 27 individual commissioners, it is divided into various Directorates-General (DG´s) that have a considerable degree of autonomy vis-à-vis the individual commissioners. There are 36 Directorates-General that cover specific policy-making areas or services. They employ approx. 24,000 staff. Sport is allocated to the Directorate-General for Education and Culture of which at the moment Ján Figel (Slovak Republic) is currently the Commissioner. On 1 January 1997, the so-called "Sports Unit" was set up as part of this Directorate-General.

Directorate-General for Education and Culture

The Directorate-General for Education and Culture is responsible for sport. The Directorate-General for Education and Culture's mission has three main goals:

- Building a Europe of knowledge
- Developing the European cultural area
- Involving citizens in European integration

Each Directorate-General is subdivided into various Directorates that are in turn responsible for individual units that handle specific tasks. At least two Directorates within the Directorate-General are involved with sport. Directorate D deals with the areas of education, training and youth. Directorate C is responsible for culture, audiovisual media and sports (CAMS).

Sport Unit

The Sport Unit of Directorate C that is responsible for Culture, Audiovisual Media and Sport (CAMS) deals with sport-related issues within the Commission. Because other Directorates-General also deal with sport-related issues, the Sport Unit regularly attends meetings in other policy-making areas that are of interest for sport. The Sport Unit set up an informal working group comprising representatives of other policy-making areas. The informal working group on sport was also involved in the preparation and drawing up of the White Paper on Sport. At the Sport Ministers' Conference held in Portugal in 2007, the Sport Ministers indicated that this working group should continue its work. The Sport Unit coordinates the European Sports Forum, the Consultative Conferences and other measures implemented within the framework of the Structured Dialogue.

European Parliament

The European Parliament is based on the ECSC assembly of 1952. Since 1979, the Members of the European Parliament have been elected directly by EU citizens. Each Member State has a number of seats in Parliament that corresponds to the size of their country. The EU Parliament controls the Commission insofar as the latter has to submit to a vote of approval by the MEPs before taking office and can even be compelled to resign in its entirety if a motion of no confidence is adopted (by a 2/3 majority - in January 1999, a vote of no confidence at the EU Parliament failed by a very narrow margin, prompting the Commission to yield to the pressure exerted by Parliament and to resign en masse for the very first time in the history of the EU in March 1999). Furthermore, the Parliament has to approve the EU budget before it is adopted.

The European Parliament basically performs three functions: It has legislative, budgeting and control powers. The work of the European Parliament is organised by Standing Committees that are responsible for certain policy-making areas. Sport is an issue of the Standing Committee "Culture, Youth, Education, Media and Sport", the so-called Sports Intergroup. This is a working group that is independent of parliamentary groups and discusses topical sport-related issues and meets every three months. At the level of the European Parliament, the Sports Intergroup Meeting is a communication and cooperation interface between the members of the European Parliament and the sport organisations (cf. Spindler, 2005). If it needs to deal with specific problems that arise, the Parliament can also set up sub-committees and temporary committees.

Council (of the European Union)
The Council (of the European Union), referred to in the Treaties, is composed of twenty-seven national ministers (one per Member State) and should be distinguished from the European Council which is an assembly of EU heads of state or government and the President of the European Commission. Although the council is a uniform body, it acts in different formations as it deals with different policy-making areas. Although there is no official Council formation for sport, the EU Sport Ministers gather frequently at informal meetings, for instance, during Germany's EU Council Presidency under the chairmanship of German Minister Schäuble on 12 and 13 March 2007 in Stuttgart. The meetings are informal insofar as no decisions are adopted at the two-day meetings, recommendations are merely issued. However, these meetings at which topical issues are discussed are becoming increasingly the rule. The meeting in Stuttgart was overshadowed by recent challenges, such as hooliganism in football stadiums but also doping. Sport economical aspects and aspects of integration through sport were discussed too.

Council of Europe
The Council of Europe, a pan-European organisation with 47 Member States, was founded on 5 May 1949 in order to develop joint and democratic principles. It is totally separate from the European Union. The Council of Europe deserves to be mentioned not least because of its importance in terms of the history of sport. The "sport for all" movement began in 1975 with the Charter of the Council of Europe. Of the total of four Directorates-General, DG IV Education, Culture, Youth and Sport and the Environment deals with sport-related issues. Within this Directorate General, the Directorate for Youth and Sport deals with the issues referred to in the title. The European Cultural Convention creates the framework for the Council of Europe's sport-related activities. Up to then, the Committee for the Development of Sport (CDDS) had been responsible for the implementation and coordination of activities in the area of sport within the framework of the

draft budget 2006, however the Secretary General of the Council of Europe proposed finding a new structure for cooperation in the field of sport.

Until the end of 2005, the Sport Department of the Council of Europe consisted of the Committee for the Development of Sport (CDDS) and the two Council of Europe Conventions on Sport (Anti-Doping-Convention and Convention against Spectator Violence), that give substance to the work performed by the Standing Committees (T-DO as the Committee for the Anti-Doping-Convention and T-RV as the Committee for the Convention against Spectator Violence). The CDDS has also been responsible for all matters relating to cooperation and coordination in the field of sports. The CDDS was entrusted with organising ministerial conferences which took place every two years and had all the signatories of the European Cultural Convention as participants.

The year 2006 was a transitional year in which a group of experts (ad-hoc Committee for the "Accord sur le sport") (CAHAS) was commissioned to conduct a study on the future of sport in the Council of Europe ("Feasibility study on the proposed Enlarged Partial Agreement on Sport"). The results of this study were presented at the 17th informal meeting of the European Sport Ministers that was held in Moscow on 20 and 21 October 2006. The Sport Ministers recommended that an "Enlarged Partial Agreement on Sport" (EPAS) be concluded with a view to regulating future cooperation in the Council of Europe.

EPAS is to take over tasks of the CDDS and is also to ensure that the two European conventions, namely the Anti-Doping Convention and the Convention against Spectator Violence develop a framework for a pan-European platform of intergovernmental sports co-operation. The new structure has the following contents:

- The Governing Board of EPAS meets twice a year (the costs are borne by the Member States for their selected experts)
- The Bureau of the Governing Board of EPAS meets twice a year (here too the costs are borne by the Member States)
- The sports federations are integrated into the decision-making process for EPAS programmes and campaigns by representatives on the Consultative Committee. They have the right to advise the Governing Board of EPAS

- EPAS aims to establish international standards and to define political guidelines. As the European Sports Charter or the Code of Sports Ethics, the new standards are not legally binding but are to be mandatory to a certain extent
- Every two years, EPAS will be commissioned by the Ministerial Committee to prepare Ministerial Conferences for all the Member States of the Council of Europe
- EPAS is responsible for examining joint programmes with other international organisations such as the EU, UNO or others

5.3 The structural model of sports in the European Union

The organisation of sport in Europe can be viewed from two different perspectives. The first perspective refers to the organisational structures of sport in the individual Member States of the EU. Many of these organisational structures are pyramid-like, which also explains the generalisation of the pyramid model of sport and of the European Sport Model as a pyramid. As such, sport clubs form the base of the pyramid, which are members of their respective regional associations that are all combined at national level in the national umbrella sport organisations. In each country, there is, for instance, only one umbrella football association. Each European federation only accepts one umbrella organisation per country as a member. Another feature of the pyramid structure is the interactions of the different levels in sport competitions. In theory, a club from the lowest division can move up to the highest division and qualify for a European competition, or alternatively may be relegated again. This system of promotion and relegation is a "feature of European Sport" (European Commission, 1998). This traditional, open sport system in Europe differs from the North American closed professional sport model where relegation is not possible. However, this dividing line cannot be drawn unequivocally anymore as some European leagues are meanwhile based on the American model, such as the German Ice Hockey league (Deutsche Eishockey Liga, DEL) (Groll, Gütt & Mittag, 2008).

By contrast, the second perspective from which the organisation of sport in Europe can be viewed refers to the network structures that represent the organisations of sports and the political institutions at European level. These structures are illustrated by the following diagram in which the political institutions are illustrated in white and the sport organisations have a grey background. The structural model of sport in the European Union is illustrated according to GO´s (governmental organisations) and NGO´s (non-governmental organisations).

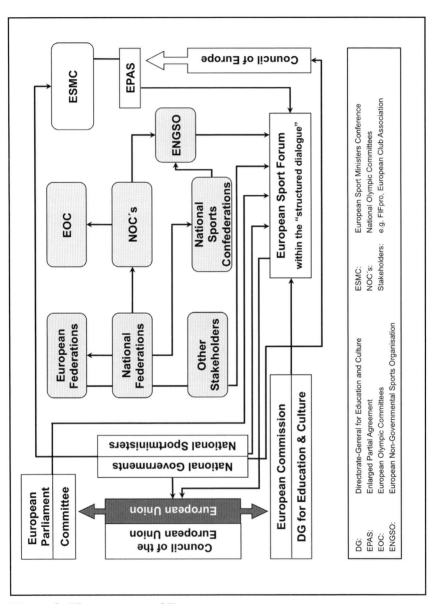

Figure 2: The structure of European sport

Governmental organisations

The governmental organisations include the bodies of the European Union and the institutions of the Council of Europe. Within the Council of Europe, the Steering Committee for the Development of Sport (Comité directeur pour le développement du sport) (CDDS) has been dealing intensively with sport-related matters for 30 years and organises the Conference of European Sport Ministers (ESK) every two years. In 2005, the Sport Ministers decided that the only solution for sustained pan-European sport cooperation was to transform the CDDS into an "Enlarged Partial Agreement" (EPA) in order to be able to focus on continual, more intense cooperation. Due to savings measures, the CDDS was removed from the budget of the Council of Europe. The work of the CDDS has been continued since 2007 through an EPA which interested countries from all over the world can accede to. The pioneering role the Council of Europe plays in sport-related initiatives has hence been brought to a final conclusion as this body can only be assigned symbolic character (Groll, Gütt & Mittag, 2008: 28).

Within the EU, the Sport Unit which belongs to the Directorate-General "Education, Culture and Youth" is responsible for sport within the European Commission. The Sport Unit has acted as the first service point for sport-related matters at European level since it has been established in 1997. It is responsible for cooperation between national and international sport organisations and associations (European Commission online, 2007). In order to enhance the flow of information between the Commission and the sport organisations of the Member States, so-called EU Consultative Conferences are held which are presented in detail in the White Paper on Sport.

The European Parliament itself has a Committee for Culture, Youth, Education, Audiovisual Media and Sport. The European Council, by contrast, only deals with sport-related issues at so-called "informal meetings" that have no binding effect.

Non-governmental organisations

National federations comprising around 700,000 sport clubs (European Commission, 2004: Special Eurobarometer 62.0) create the basis for the European sport system. In nearly all EU countries, sport is represented by an umbrella organisation in which the national federations are represented (National Sports Confederation). A typical example of this is the German Olympic Sports Confederation which was founded on 20 May 2006 by a merger of the Deutscher Sportbund (DSB)

(German Sports Association), and the Nationales Olympisches Komitee für Deutschland (NOK) (National Olympic Committee for
Germany). The National Olympic Committees are either representatives of the Olympic Sport Movement in their country or are also
commissioned, as in some EU Member States, to act as umbrella organisations. Accordingly, the umbrella organisation of NOC´s at
European level is the EOC (European Olympic Committee). At European level, the national sports federations are in turn organised in
European federations, as, for instance, UEFA (Union of European
Football Associations). European National Sports Confederations and
National Olympic Committees, if they are the national umbrella organisations for sports, form a separate association, the "European
Non-Governmental Sports Organisation" (ENGSO) which is a non-
profit-making or distributing organisation with public responsibilities.
The members represent sport in the widest sense and expressly respect
the diversity of the manifestations of sport, the various target groups
and the diverse social and cultural dimensions of sport (ENGSO,
2007).

The by and large autonomous structure of the European sport system
gives rise to the question why the Union deals with sport-related issues. There are huge differences of opinion on this subject even within
the non-governmental organisations (Groll, Gütt & Mittag, 2008).

5.4 Decision-making processes of European sports politics

Whereas the rule and institutional structure of European sports policy
is marked above all by the bodies of the European Union and its position papers which have a certain degree of constitutional importance,
the political will formation and decision-making processes are marked
more by the formal and informal political negotiation and law-making
processes. In the following chapter, special focus will be placed on
both the institutionalised forms of information exchange and on the
emerging ad hoc constellations. Special attention will be paid to non-
governmental players, including NGO´s as well as interest and lobbying groups in Brussels, such as the European Network for Sport and
Employment in the third sector, the EOC EU Office of German Sports
in Brussels or even the European Club Association - the successor to
the G 14 - and FIFPro. This includes above all the national leagues
and UEFA.

European Sports Conference (ESC)

The European Sports Conference is a consultative conference organised every two years since 1991 that is majorly important for the development of European sports policy. The European Sports Conference was set up in 1971 - the first ESC was held in Vienna in 1973 - and is a tool of the national umbrella organisations of sport (cf. König, 1997). Similar to the Council of Europe, the ESC acts at pan-European level. The ESC was hugely important above all in the 1970s and 1980s as it represented quasi the only possibility of exchange between the countries of the Eastern bloc that were under Communist rule and the other countries of Western Europe on sport-related issues. The ESC does not have an independent, central Secretariat; the Executive Committee has five members.

To the present day, the ESC is an important institution as - according to the member of the Executive Board Felix Netopilek - a unique forum and the only platform that brings all governmental and non-governmental organisations from all European countries together at all levels and on the basis of equality so that they can discuss shared interests and sport-related problems openly and without restrictions (Netopilek, 2003).

The last European Sport Conferences which representatives of governmental and non-governmental organisation attended as well as the Sport Unit of the Council of Europe were held in Greece in 2005 and in Romania in 2007. The 17th. European Sports Conference took place in Athens in 2005 was held under the auspices of "The Evolution of Sport in Europe". The main topics addressed at the ESC were European structures, financial aspects, ethical values and ideals as well as education, sport in art and future trends. One new achievement of the ESC in Athens was the inclusion of the European working group "Women and Sport" in the agenda.

Structured dialogue

The structured dialogue within the framework of the EU also has a pan-European dimension as it is oriented above all to integrating the countries of Central and Eastern Europe. The structured dialogue launched in 1993 was part of the EU strategy to align the countries of Central and Eastern Europe to the EU. The structured dialogue consisted of regular meetings of heads of state and government, a number of ministerial conferences and theme-specific concerted actions with the bodies of the European Union. The structured dialogue is used today for a number of subject areas, inter alia, for a new rather informal youth policy tool which the European institutions wants to use to reach out to the young people of Europe.

One new feature is the fact that the "structured dialogue" tool has been transferred to the area of sport. The basic principles governing the structured dialogue were defined in the White Paper on Sport. In an accompanying document to the White Paper, "The EU and Sport: Background and Context", the structured dialogue is also referred to as it is in the "Action Plan Pierre de Coubertin" that contains 53 proposals and is also part of the White Paper on Sport, action point no. 49 of the "structured dialogue" is mentioned as a follow-up to the White Paper on Sport. In November 2007, the discussion paper on the "Structured Dialogue with Sport Stakeholders" was published. The contents of the discussion paper are:

- Context for a sport dialogue at EU level
- Proposals put forward in the White Paper
- Launch of a structured dialogue
- European Sport Forum
- Thematic discussions with sports stakeholders
- Use of existing cooperation and dialogue structures
- Practical requirements

Social Dialogue Committee

In July 2008, the Social Dialogue Committee set up by the member of the EU Commission Vladimir Spidla (Commissioner responsible for Employment, Social Affairs and Equal Opportunities.) and Ján Figel (Commissioner responsible for Education, Training, Culture and Multilingualism) convened for the very first time. The Committee which brings together representatives of the European Professional Football Leagues, the European Department of the Fédération Internationale Des Associations de Footballeurs Professionels, usually known by the abbreviation FIFPro, a worldwide representative organisation for professional football players and the European Club Association under the auspices of UEFA highlights the fact that this new forum is dedicated fully to European professional football. The discussions were and are to focus on: agreements on minimum standards in the fields of healthcare, occupational safety and health, health insurance, education and training for young players, the rights and obligations of players, conflict solutions and image rights.

Consultation conferences
Consultation conference that were held in 2005 and 2006 at European level involving many players under the headings "EU & Sport - Matching Expectations" represent a less formalised forum within the framework of will formation and decision-making processes. The topics were: "The social function of Sport", "Volunteering in Sport", "Fight against Doping", "Economic Impact of Sport" and "Organisation of Sport".

One issue that is always controversial in the consultative processes is who is to be invited to participate. Failure to invite national, regional and local players in 2006 - which were merely represented by the EOC European Olympic Committee - sparked such strong criticism that in the spring of 2007 an online consultation was initiated also among these institutions and organisations. At the consultative conference itself, representatives of organised sport criticised that there is too much emphasis on professional football and too little on amateur sport.

European Sport Forum
The European Sports Forum was established in 1991 with a view to creating a platform that enables the European Commission, the umbrella federations and national federations, the National Olympic Committees and the Sport Ministers of the Member States to discuss sport-related issues. Together with MEPs, representatives of the Council of Europe and other observers, the European Sports Forum is generally held once a year. However, it was not held in the years between 2005 and 2007. Instead, the above-mentioned consultative conferences were held.

The revival of the European Sports Forum was announced in the White Paper on Sport. This is elaborated upon in the discussion paper on the Structured Dialogue from November 2007. It says that the Forum will be held in the autumn of each year. Ideally, the Forum should be linked with a conference of EU Sport Ministers in order to facilitate informal talks between the non-governmental sport stakeholders and the EU Sport Ministers. That happened in 2008 when the European Commission - following an initiative of the French presidency - organised the first EU Sport Forum since the adoption of the White Paper on Sport. It took place in Biarritz on 26 and 27 November 2008 and was linked with the informal meeting of EU Sport Ministers. The European Sports Forum is to focus on the following issues:

- Progress report by the Commission on the implementation of the White Paper and of Coubertin Action Plan
- General debates on the specificity of sport
- Report by the EU Presidency on political cooperation in sport at EU level
- Progress report by the Commission on preparations on the implementation of the future provisions on sport in the Lisbon treaty
- Report on the thematic discussions and other measures within the framework of the Structured Dialogue
- Progress report on the Social Dialogue in Sport
- Discussions on the financing of sport
- Discussions about other topical issues

Thematic discussions

The so-called "thematic discussions" with selected participants offer another dimension. In the White Paper on Sport so-called thematic discussions involving different players from the world of sport are re-ferred to in addition to the European Sports Forum. The discussion paper on the "Structured Dialogue" provides more information on the identification of stakeholders and on the type and dates of these dis-cussions. All in all, seven interest groups are mentioned: 1) European top-level sports federations in the field of professional sport; 2) Euro-pean sports federations in the field of 'sport for all'; 3) Smaller or less professionalised European sports federations; 4) National sports fed-erations; 5) European federations that represent employer and em-ployee interests; 6) International umbrella organisations and 7) Other European associations that may not represent sport but are involved in the field of sport. Thematic discussions are to be flexible by nature and be organised on an ad-hoc basis. There are plans to organise writ-ten surveys, seminars, questionnaires and meetings of experts.

Eurobarometer surveys

In addition to the institutionalised forms of exchange of information between selected stakeholders of sport and the European Commission, collecting statistics and data material is part of the basis for will for-mation and decision-making processes. The information provided by the Statistical Office that is, however, based by and large on the proc-essing of national statistics, also includes information about attitudes and preferences of European Union.

This is the prime purpose of Eurobarometer surveys. According to an initial survey commissioned by the European Community in 1970 and a further pilot study conducted in 1973, the so-called Euro-barometer 1974 was installed as a biannual survey (that is carried out in spring and autumn) among the Member States of the European Community. The surveys produce reports of public opinion on certain issues relating to the European Community and the European Union across the Member States and hence help to shape information policy and public relations work accordingly. With the opinion polls the goal is also to bring the citizens of the Community closer, by enabling them to learn more about their European neighbours. Eurobarometer surveys are also carried out at the same time. They comprise the same questions in all 27 Member States and candidate countries.

Due to the continuity of the surveys, it is possible to identify and comprehend trends over extended periods. There are a number of different Eurobarometer surveys. The 'standard' survey is carried out twice a year in order to identify long-term trends and tendencies. From the very outset, these surveys dealt with two major areas: modules and the self-characterisation of European societies. The European identity and perception of European Communities were the subject matter of the survey in the latter area.

The "Special Eurobarometers" are ad-hoc (face to face surveys). The third type of survey is "Flash" involving ad-hoc telephone surveys on the latest events and trends, frequently with special target groups such as companies, physicians, young people etc. The surveys implemented on the issue of sport and physical activity comprised the following studies:

Special Eurobarometer number 183-6, Wave 58.2, Title: "Physical Activity" (2002):
The contents of the first Special Eurobarometer on the issue of Physical Activity are not specifically tailored to sport. In three chapters it is outlined how prevalent physical activity is among the European population from a number of aspects (age, gender, Member States) and the perception of environmental opportunities for physical activity, in a number of different contexts. The fourth chapter contains basic information about the methods used and physical activity in general.

Eurobarometer Spéciale number 197, Wave 60.0, Title: "Les Citoyen de l'Union Européenne et le Sport" (2003, only available in French):
The first special Eurobarometer on Sport was only published in French. The content of this Eurobarometer covers participation in sport (frequency, motives, level of organisation), the effects of engaging in sporting activity, the social dimension of sports (e.g. integration, education, media) and more general aspects of the subject area "European Union und Sport" (inter alia individual Member States' possibilities of cooperation also in relation to anti-doping measures or dedicating an article to sport in the Treaty establishing the European Community).

Special Eurobarometer number 213, Wave 62.0, Title: "The citizens of the European Union and Sport" (2004):
The third Special Eurobarometer was basically a continuation of the second Eurobarometer. The contents of this Eurobarometer are identical to the contents of the French Eurobarometer and also deal with participation in sport (frequency, motives, level of organisation) or the social dimension of sport.

Informal representation of interests in the area of sport
Contrary to the formal types of decision-making processes that are aimed in particular at incorporating institutionalised governmental and non-governmental players, the area of informal decision-making refers above all back to lobbying activities which non-governmental players engage in. The term "lobbying" originates from the Anglophone designation "lobby" (a hall or large anteroom) of Parliament, where interested groups from the population tried to convince MPs of their viewpoints. Since the beginning of the 19th century, this type of representation of interests refers to a "group of persons that seek to influence the legislative process" (Pfeiffer, 1995; Nonen & Clamen, 1991). Lobbyism is a method of deliberately bringing one's influence to bear on decision-making processes and players within the political environment. Players representing these interests are called lobbyists.

The lobbyists' activities are always rated with a certain degree of ambivalence as they tend to pursue their own specific interests. By contrast, reference is made to the role lobbying associations play as agents and transmission belts of knowledge. Whereas government players tend to lack the proximity and expertise in specific subject areas, interest groups or NGOs that frequently deal with certain subject areas only tend to be superior government institutions because of their expertise. This means the state has to rely on the willingness of interest groups and NGOs to share their knowledge and to exchange information, in this sense knowledge is power in the long term. Although the government can prevent decisions from being taken, it will have to take the arguments of critics on board in the long term. According to research conducted by political scientists there are "no realistic and basic alternatives" to the existing pluralistic representation of interests against this backdrop in which modern, capitalist democracies "are not a realist and basic alternative", as lobbyism represents one key possibility of incorporating interests and knowledge into legislative processes (Lehner, 1983: 114).

The analysis of the representation of political interests is reflected both in the various integration-related theories (neo-functionalism, multi-level governance research), and in a set of strategies relating to associations and interest groups (neopluralism, neo-corporatism). However there continues to be a lack of detailed theory formation in the field of EU-based lobby research that can also be attributed to the lack of quantifiable empirical data on political lobbying processes at European level (Michalowitz, 2007: 49),

At EU level, endeavours are currently being undertaken to tighten regulation and the controllability of representation of European interests. The Constitutional Committee of the European Parliament decided in 2008 to introduce a mandatory register for EU lobbyists with a view to safeguarding transparency. This means a certain type of supranational regulatory mechanism was introduced for lobbying.

At present, it is estimated that there are approx. 15,000 lobbyists (Woll, 2006; Greenwod, 2007) in the political environment of the EU. This demonstrates that EU lobbying has become an important and integral part of European policy (Michalowitz, 2007: 200). As there is an imbalance between extensive competencies and the lack of a mandate at the European Commission (by contrast, the Council and Parliament are either elected directly or indirectly and have hence been legitimated, at least partly), the Commission is endeavouring to create a kind of legitimation of its decisions by enhancing the participation of lobbyists. According to Michalowitz (2007: 193), this participation in civil society is at the expense of formal types of participation (parties, associations etc.). Nonetheless, she acknowledges that lobbyism is the only realistic possibility of articulating interests in legislative processes that can also contribute towards democratic governance.

The players who play a key role in the political decision-making process within the framework of European sports policy are to be outlined briefly in the following.

UEFA
The "Union of the European Football Associations" (UEFA) was established as a confederation at the end of October 1954. The individual member associations preserved their sovereignty with the exception of election procedures, decision-making took the form of recommendations" (50 Years UEFA, Vol. 1: 46). UEFA decisions did not become binding for all member associations until the statutes were amended in 1961. The establishment of an institutionalised representation of interests was intended to enhance the representation of interests in the international arena and vis-à-vis FIFA to serve above all coordination purposes.

The "Union of the European Football Associations" (UEFA) which has its headquarters in Nyon (Switzerland) has been endeavouring for several years to improve the dialogue with the European Union. The fact that UEFA has opened an office in Brussels that is being managed by Jonathan Hill shows how important these relations are. In technical terms, UEFA's EU Office is connected to the Communication and PR Department. UEFA estimates that in future it will be possible to take a growing number of political decisions relating to football at European level. UEFA would like to maintain a constant dialogue with the EU on various factual issues, such as the sale of TV broadcasting rights, the freedom of movement, doping or racism.

FIFPro
The Fédération Internationale des Associations de Footballeurs Professionels, usually known by the abbreviation FIFPro, is a worldwide representative organisation for professional football players. At the moment there are 42 national players associations who are members of FIFPro. FIFPro itself designates itself the representative of all professional football players. Following the Bosman ruling of 1995, UEFA and FIFA recognised FIFPro as the representative organisation for professional football players. In 1998, the European Commission too espoused this view. The Commission's decision was attributed not least to the dissatisfaction with the players' agent system that had existed up to then. New regulations governing players' agents that also met with the approval of the European Commission (cf.

www.FIFPro.org) were issued in cooperation with FIFA. In subsequent years, FIFPro was repeatedly involved in the activities. The currently valid transfer system, for instance, was negotiated by FIFPro in cooperation with UEFA and FIFA. FIFPro continues to be one of the stakeholders of European sport that the European Commission asks to participate in consultations and discussions. The new subject areas to be tackled by FIFPro are gradually emerging. There is need for discussion about the international transfer system, for instance, and about the 6+5 rule adopted by FIFA in May 2008 which basically provides that a club team must start a match with at least six players that would be eligible for the national team of the country in which the club is domiciled.

European Club Association and G14

The European Club Association (ECA) is an organisation representing football clubs in Europe. Formed on the dissolution of the G-14 group in January 2008, it has 103 members, with at least one from each of the 53 national associations. The precise number of clubs from each member association is established every two years at the end of the UEFA season on the basis of UEFA ranking of its member associations according to the following principles. The ECA is the successor of G-14, an amalgamation of leading football clubs in Europe that was established in September 2000. Before the G14 was established, some of the subsequent member clubs met in the early 1990s for an informal exchange of opinions and to discuss positions. In the year 2002, four other top European football clubs joined the G14. The key objective of the ECA was to raise participation in TV revenue generated from national and European competitions. In addition, the G14 has also long been advocating that revenues be guaranteed by a fixed participation system in the Champions League. Karl-Heinz Rummenigge was the first Chairman of the organisation. On 15 February 2008, the decision was taken to dissolve the G-14 in order to transfer the role of being the sole, independent representative of football clubs in Europe.

Whereas the predecessor organisation G-14 had an office in Brussels, ECA is thought to have less influence on the European Commission. ECA is to represent the interests of football clubs vis-à-vis FIFA and UEFA and will hence seek to establish its headquarters near UEFA. It cannot yet be foreseen to what extent direct contact will be made with the European Commission. The goals of ECA relate to the payment of clubs for releasing players for national teams and to reduce the number of matches played by national teams in order to give players more time to recover for their club's matches.

European Professional Football Leagues

EPFL (European Professional Football Leagues) is an organisation that was originally set up in1997 under the name "Association of the European Union Premier Professional Football Leagues" (EUPPFL). Its members include the professional football leagues of 15 countries. National professional football leagues normally include the active professional football clubs in the first or top football league (sometimes also the professional leagues of the lower leagues). EPFL pursues the following objectives:

- To develop and foster cooperation between leagues
- To cooperate with UEFA for the benefit of professional football leagues across Europe, in particular via UEFA Commission for Professional Football
- To promote the interests of its member leagues
- To develop and promote relations between EPFL and non-member leagues
- To create a uniform system, maintaining the freedom of movement between member leagues

EPFL elects five representatives onto UEFA's professional football committee and is entitled to appoint representatives for the FIFA Dispute Resolution Chamber. EPFL is also represented in UEFA discussion round "UEFA, Leagues and FIFPro Panel". National leagues have to deal to a growing extent with the political and legal conditions in the European Union, above all in relation to the internationalisation of sponsoring and of capital markets. As far as the Europeanisation and globalisation of professional football is concerned, EPFL intends to be the common voice of Professional Football Leagues across Europe on all matters of common interest. It represents the interests of national leagues that consider themselves not be insufficiently represented by established football associations. With its headquarters in Brussels, EPFL also has greater opportunities for representing its interests at the European Commission, mainly in relation to TV broadcasting rights and the law on competition.

EOC EU Office

The EOC EU Office was established in 1993 at the initiative of the German Sports Confederation (DSB), the National Olympic Committee for Germany (NOC) - which has meanwhile merged to become the German Olympic Sport Confederation - and the regional sports confederations (LSB). Since then, several European sport organisations have become cooperation partners of the office: the umbrella sport organisations of the Netherlands, France, Austria, Denmark, Finland, Sweden, Norway and the United Kingdom. In 2009 the EOC EU office takes over the activities of the former "German EU Office of Sports". Its aim is to monitor, identify and analyse subjects of relevance to sport at European level and to represent the interests of the EOC and its members (national and European non governmental sports organisations) towards the European institutions. As European legislation and policy seldom reveal their impact on sport at first glance, it is indispensable that the organised sport, as the biggest citizen movement in the community, represents its interests in Brussels and establishes itself as a contact for dialogue with EU institutions. (cf. www.eu-sports-office.org).

5.5 Interim conclusions: growing differentiation

If the decision-making and will formation processes of European sports policy is considered in a synopsis, what is immediately striking is the considerable differentiation. It also applies to the sports sector that growing expansion of the policy-making areas dealt with in the EU (sectoral differentiation), was reflected in the growing catalogue of issues dealt with. However, the growing number of institutional "co-players" in the area of sports policy is also significant. There is also a growing number of representatives of interest of various origins involved in the political cycle (player differentiation). It is above all UEFA and FIFA which steered the affairs of European and international football almost autonomously for decades that had to relinquish competencies, whereas politicians and an ever growing number of stakeholders are becoming increasingly involved. Last but not least, the regulatory autonomy of umbrella organisations was called more and more into question, while the power of clubs was distributed differently. Within this framework, there are also signs of a vertical differentiation. The growing involvement of national clubs and regions means more fellow players are participating in EU policy-making.

6   Areas of European sports policy

The areas of European sports policy presented below are merely a selection. There are, of course, many other areas of sports policy (such
as social inclusion, racism and violence in sport, sport and environmental protection, sport and development policy, etc.) which, under-
standably, cannot all be included in this chapter.

6.1 EU health policy

The main responsibility for health policy and healthcare for European
citizens lies with the Member States. The European Union's health
strategy therefore focuses mainly on strengthening cooperation and
coordination, on promoting the exchange of secure information and
specialist knowledge and on supporting decision-making at the national level. To this end, the EU is developing a comprehensive health
information system which is intended to provide EU-wide access to
reliable and current information on key issues in the health area.

The first strategy paper presented by the European Commission was a
Communication on the framework for action in the area of public
health in 1993, which was to be used to develop the efforts being undertaken in the area of public health. A coherent and coordinated
health policy concept was first outlined in May 2000 with the European Community's Health Strategy. As part of this first Action Programme, over 300 projects and other actions received a total of   354
million in subsidies between 2003 and 2008. The Programme focused
mainly on the areas of health information, rapid response to health
threats and health promotion through taking health factors into account. A new Health Strategy entitled "Together for Health: A Strategic   Approach   for   the   EU   2008-2013"   was   adopted   on
23 October 2007. This new Health Strategy created an overarching
strategic framework for measures in the health sector at EU level and
points the way forward for the years to come. However, the Strategy is
not only focused on public health but is also intended to help integrate
health-related issues into other policy-making areas. The basis of the
Strategy consists of the four principles and the three strategic objectives for improving health in the EU which are outlined in a separate
White Paper. The fundamental principles of:

- A value-driven approach in a joint Health Strategy
- Recognising the links between health and economic prosperity
- Integrating health into all policies across borders and sectors
- Strengthening the EU's voice in global health

underpin the following strategic objectives in EU health policy:

- Fostering good health in an ageing Europe
- Protecting citizens from health threats
- Supporting dynamic health systems and new technologies

Both the current and the "old" Health Programme are based on Article 152 of the Treaty Establishing the European Community. The Health Programme 2008-2013 is intended to complement, support and add value to the policies of the Member States and contribute to increased solidarity and prosperity in the European Union by protecting and promoting human health and safety and by improving public health. In order to ensure cooperation between the different policy-making areas, numerous partnerships have already been established, for instance in the areas of pharmaceutical products, demographic change and ageing, health promotion via Structural Funds or health in the information society.

The Executive Agency for Health and Consumers (EAHC) (formerly Public Health Executive Agency (PHEA)) manages the implementation of the Programme in the area of public health. The EAHC's remit includes, inter alia, organising, reviewing and coordinating symposiums, public tenders and projects. It handles all the technical details and is subject to the control of the European Commission.

The budget for the Programme is   21.5 million. To ensure full participation in the Programme by organisations which promote a health agenda in line with the Programme objectives, a wide variety of financing mechanisms is available, including cofinancing of projects or of the operating costs of non-governmental organisations, specialised networks and joint financing of public bodies by the Community and one or more Member States.

6.2 EU anti-doping policy

There has been a particular focus both on the economic and social aspects of sport and on the anti-doping issue, not only by the German EU Council Presidency in 2007 but also generally within the framework of European sports policy.

In terms of the subsidiarity concept and the content of the Treaties Establishing the European Community, the European Union, as an independent body, basically does not have unlimited power to proclaim its own anti-doping policy (cf. European Commission, 2002: 22; Feiden & Blasius, 2002: 70). Hence, EU's measures focus particularly on co-ordinating and harmonising individual countries' policies and on supporting research and the gathering of information on the problem of doping (cf. Vieweg & Siekmann, 2007: 38). Therefore, in general terms, the promotion of a coordinated and joint approach within a pan-European anti-doping policy cannot be directly related only to the European Union. It takes place - as do other areas of politics - in a dense web that encompasses nation states as well as national and international non-governmental sports organisations (cf. chapter 7.2).

Despite this conflict, concrete directives on joint European Union anti-doping measures do exist. They can generally be broken down into competencies regarding action and competencies regarding harmonisation. Competencies regarding action do not include formal legal measures, such as in respect of information and prevention (Röthel, 2000: 113).

Areas where the EU can, however, intervene more or less independently in the fight against doping include, in particular, its competence regarding the legal and illegal circulation of drugs, its programmes in the areas of research, youth, education and training and cooperation between the judiciary and the police. Furthermore, Article 152 of the Treaty Establishing the European Community, which provides for support measures via the healthcare system that aim to protect and improve human health, allows the EU also to take action against doping without any harmonisation of the Member States' legal and administrative regulations in this area. (cf. Feiden & Blasius, 2002: 71; Siegert, 2008: 32). The Directorates-General of the European Commission which are hence the most heavily involved in the fight against doping are the Directorate-General for Health and Consumers and the Directorate-General for Justice, Freedom and Security.

The EU's efforts in the fight against doping began with the Resolution of the Council of the European Communities of 3 December 1990 on Community action to combat the use of drugs, including the abuse of medicinal products, particularly in sport. It was emphasised that the goal was to complement the work of the Council of Europe. On this basis, on 8 February 1992, a Code of Conduct against Doping in Sport was drawn up, which, in addition to research promotion and informa- tion tasks, contained, inter alia, anti-doping measures in areas of health policy. Following parliamentary requests, the Commission, via directives on the use of drugs, subsequently also approved a ban on taking "doping drugs" as the latter, if they were not used for purposes of diagnosing or treating recognised pathological findings, would con- travene current Council directives. Owing to the numerous doping scandals that hit the headlines in the late 1990s, the EU became equally active and adopted, ten conclusions on the fight against dop- ing at the informal Sports Ministers' meeting held in Paderborn, Ger- many, and subsequently also adopted a concrete plan on the EU's con- tribution to the fight against doping.

The White Paper on Sport also touched on the issue of doping in Chapter 2.2, where the Commission states that at "European level, the fight against doping must take into account both a law-enforcement and a health and prevention dimension" (European Commission, 2007: 5). The EU would like to play a facilitating role in relation to its Member States, the Council of Europe, WADA and UNESCO and calls on its Member States to implement the UNESCO Convention against Doping in Sport. In this context, the EU has already estab- lished an informal network that currently comprises 14 national anti- doping organisations of Member States.

Co-operation with WADA
On 10 November 1999, the World Anti-Doping Agency (WADA) was set up in Lausanne as a foundation based on Swiss law. The European Union had previously agreed with the IOC on 2 November 1999 that the statutes would be drawn up jointly. The EU, as the representative of national interests, managed to bring its influence to bear on the structure of WADA. The IOC initially provided start-up capital to the tune of CHF 5 million for WADA. The 32 seats on the Foundation Board, WADA's supreme decision-making body, are divided up equally among government and non-government representatives. The

EU received 2 of the 4 European seats reserved for government organisations.

The European Union was heavily involved in the setting up of WADA and indeed worked with national governments to restrict the IOC's influence on WADA so that WADA could operate transparently and independently. Even though some initial joint successes were achieved (for instance, introducing the Athlete's Passport or developing an e-learning website), co-operation between the EU and WADA ran into major problems once the launch phase had been completed. The EU ceased co-financing WADA for budget-related reasons that were due, among other things, to the fact that the EU was not responsible for sport. The EU Member States took over the European Union's share of WADA financing for 2002 as a transitional solution, which will safeguard European representation on WADA's Foundation Board for the time being. However, the influence the EU intends to have over the work performed by WADA will depend on how this problem can be solved. A further EU objective, namely to transform WADA from a private institution that merely has recommendation powers into a public agency has not yet been accomplished either.

With the Commission's communiqué presented by the competent Commissioner Viviane Reding on 3 December 1999, the Commission ultimately defined the principles governing the European Union's anti-doping policy: The Commission particularly considers developments associated with the growing commercialisation of sport to be one reason for the growing problem of doping in sport. The Commission identified three focal points for its strategy against doping in sport (see below), which were explained in the communiqué "Plan for the Community's Contribution to the Fight against Doping" (cf. European Commission, 1999):

Expert opinions on the ethical, legal and scientific significance of doping
An opinion by the "European Group for Ethics" (EGE) constitutes the "ethical" substructure of the EU's anti-doping policy. In this opinion, the term of doping in sport was defined:

- Ethical guidelines were set for athletes, federations, sports physicians etc.
- Target groups who are at particular risk were identified

- Guidelines for the areas of doping analysis, research and information were drawn up and
- Conditions for the independence and credibility of a World Anti-Doping Agency were defined

Mobilising the Community instruments
The EU's anti-doping policy envisages not just making greater use of and harmonising repressive measures, but also strengthening the preventative strategy as part of the objective of mobilising Community instruments. The "Plan for the Community's Contribution to the Fight against Doping" specifically includes:

- Intensifying doping research
- Developing standardised, scientific criteria and control structures has also been identified as a priority
- Integrating the LLP and YOUTH programmes into the awareness campaign and doping prevention
- Making full use of all the possibilities for police and judicial cooperation that are available as part of the programmes
- Providing more information about drugs
- Developing measures in the field of public health

In March 2002, Commissioner Viviane Reding announced two further concrete measures: on the one hand, a report on the opportunities that could be seized within the framework of the EU's existing competencies and on the other, an action plan that focuses on educational and preventative measures.

A comparison of national anti-doping legislation
Based on the heterogeneous legal situation as regards doping in the EU Member States, it is even problematic to establish what the term "doping" actually means in the first place. Definitions in national legislative texts exist alongside definitions used by the Council of Europe, the EU, federations, the IOC or WADA.

The same applies more or less to cases in which the respective anti-doping regulations that are in force are breached. Both athletes and persons as well as organisations involved in the peripheral area of sport face very different consequences if they commit a doping offence, depending on what nationality they are or what federation they belong to. This unequal treatment within the EU Member States seems to be problematic in respect of professional athletes - not to mention considerations of fairness - also in connection with various articles of the EU Treaty (e.g. Article 12, Article 82).

Detailed overviews of national legislation relating to doping in sport have already been submitted elsewhere (European Commission, 2000; Bögeholz, 1998). A compilation made by the IOC that provides a comprehensive overview of legislation, definitions of doping, banned substances and potential penalties in over 50 countries deserves special mention (International Olympic Committee, 1998) in this regard.

In the following, we will therefore merely provide a brief outline of how heterogeneous the existing legal and structural prerequisites for the fight against doping in sport currently are in the Member States: Not all Member States have independent anti-doping laws, such as those in France, Belgium or Italy. As a rule, the doping problem is covered by existing laws on sport (Spain, Portugal) and/or by other non-sport-specific laws (e.g. Drugs Law in Germany). The status of agencies responsible for the prevention of doping at national level differs in the individual Member States, depending on the type of sports system that exists there. As a public institution, the "Conseil de Prévention et de lutte contre le dopage" (Council for the Prevention of and the Fight against Doping) in France for instance, has different powers than the National Anti-Doping Agency in Germany, which is based on federation law. The level of penalties athletes who have committed doping offences can expect to face if they are caught ranges from disqualification from competitions, which is common in all countries, right through to penal consequences that may even involve imprisonment under certain circumstances (Greece, Italy). There are fewer problems regarding the standardised implementation of anti-doping measures in centrally organised sports systems (e.g. France, Greece) than in countries in which the sports system grants the individual sports federations greater autonomy and/or federalist administrative structures exist (e.g. Germany, Austria, Belgium).

6.3 The economic dimension of sports in the EU

The question of the economic dimension of sports policy centres, in particular, around the key issue of the extent to which sport, under strict free market laws, is subject to the free play of forces or the degree to which the special characteristics of sport are taken into consideration and can also find legal expression in special regulations.

The White Paper on Sport also states in broad terms that sport generally is a dynamic and fast-growing sector with an often underestimated macro-economic impact. A study presented during the Austrian Presidency in 2006 suggested that sport in a broader sense generated added value worth €407 billion in 2004, accounting for 3.7% of EU GDP, and provided employment for 15 million people or 5.4% of the labour force (European Commission, 2007: 11). This contribution of sport should be made more visible and promoted in EU policies. The European Commission (2007) states that sport can "contribute to the Lisbon objectives of growth and job creation. It can serve as a tool for local and regional development, urban regeneration or rural development. Sport has synergies with tourism and can stimulate the upgrading of infrastructure and the emergence of new partnerships for financing sport and leisure facilities." However, overall, it is difficult to calculate the quantifiability of sport's potential as an economic factor as the latter is usually relatively narrowly defined from an economic perspective. In order to remedy this shortcoming, the European Commission, inter alia, set up a Working Group on "Sport and Economics" with the aim of developing a common statistical definition of sport as well as a method for illustrating the economic impact of sport across the EU (Groll, Gütt & Mittag, 2008).

To an increasing extent, however, the economic importance of sport is connected particularly with the generation of income: sponsorships, copyright and merchandising, licensing, trademarks and also photo and media rights. As such, the enforcement of intellectual property rights also has a major role to play in the increasingly globalised, commercialised and dynamic sports business sector.

Furthermore, it is important for end users to be guaranteed the possibility of cross-border access to different sporting events within the EU. In this regard, media policy decisions taken by the Directorate-General Information Society and Media also have an influence on the economic aspects of sport. The "Directive on Audiovisual Media Services", which was revised in 2007, has given Member States the option of drawing up lists of designated (sporting) events of major national interest that must be broadcast on free television and this also involves marketing strategy considerations. In addition to other considerations, such as the problem of licensing, which is mainly handled by the Directorate-General Internal Market and Services, whose main role is to ensure the free movement of persons, goods, services and capital within the European Union, sports business policies focus mainly on the marketing of sports that are popular with the mass media.

In this regard, the Directorate-General for Competition, in particular, has to deal with an increasing number of sports-related cases. Most sports-related cases come under antitrust law, which prevents anti-competitive agreements and practices (Treaty establishing the European Community, Article 81) as well as abuse of a dominant position within the common market (Treaty establishing the European Community, Article 82). A ruling made by the European Court of Justice on 18 July 2006 in the so-called Meca-Medina case recently provided support to the Directorate-General in dealing with the aspects of competition law that relate to sport (cf. Legal Aspects of Sport). In this context, another important document on EU competition policy in sport is the working document that accompanied the White Paper on Sport, entitled "The EU and Sport: Background and Context" (SEC, 2007: 935) with its subject-specific Annex I "Sport and EU Competition Rules".

While the EU Commission and the European Court of Justice view the application of, and compliance with, competition law, also in sport, as being important and necessary, both are also keen, however, to take into account the major social and cultural role that sport plays as well as its other specifics when handing down decisions. One result of this is, for example, conditional approval of the central marketing of sports leagues, which the Commission investigated, where TV rights and revenue are not negotiated by each club individually, but, rather, a certain balance is achieved between big and small clubs in central negotiations with the media.

6.4 EU Educational policy[2]

The educational activities of the European Commission are based, inter alia, on the objective formulated by the European Council in Lisbon in 2001: The EU wants "to become the most competitive and dynamic knowledge-based economy in the world, capable of sustainable economic growth with more and better jobs and greater social cohe-

---

[2] Chapter 6.4 is based on a report that was published in 2008 by Karen Petry, Matthias Gütt and Christoph Fischer within the framework of the AEHESIS project (cf. Petry, K., Gütt, M. & Fischer, Ch., 2008).

sion" (strategic goal for 2010 set for Europe at the Lisbon European Council in March 2000).

Lifelong learning was identified as an essential element of European education policy in this so-called Lisbon strategy:

> Lifelong learning is an essential element of the European Higher Education Area. In the future Europe, built upon a knowledge-based society and economy, lifelong learning strategies are necessary to face the challenges of competitiveness and the use of new technologies and the improve social cohesion, equal opportunities and the quality of life. (Communiqué of the Meeting of European Ministers in charge of Higher Education in Prague on May 19th, 2001).

Therefore the European Commission has increased the budget for its activities in the area of education and training significantly (For the period from 2007 till 2013 the Commission adopted a budget amounting to   6.97 billion. This is about twice the sum invested in preliminary programmes). Besides this financial change the structure of the funding system has also been modified under the Lifelong Learning Programme (LLP). In order to promote student and staff mobility, the community has been running the ERASMUS mobility programme since 1987. This programme has contributed to the enormous increase in the mobility of undergraduate students over the past fifteen years. By introducing the SOCRATES programme, the European Commission expanded the ERASMUS programme in 1997 by adding further Europeanisation measures. Since then, the mobility of lecturers and the introduction of a uniform, pan-European system of credits (ECTS) have been fostered, among other things.

Relating the quintessence of European education and training dimensions to the sector of sports, the White Paper on Sport states, that through

> its role in formal and non-formal education, sport reinforces Europe's human capital. The values conveyed through sport help develop knowledge, motivation, skills and readiness for personal effort. Time spent in sport activities at school and at university produces health and education benefits which need to be enhanced. (European Commission, 2007: 5).

European Organisations acting in the Field of Sport Education

The external environment and the institutional demand within education and training have changed in terms of the European Union's policy. Now and for the near future, the "Education and Training 2010" objectives are at the heart of this policy. Referring to the Special Eurobarometer Survey on Sport (EC, 2004), sport not only transfers high social dimensions, its role within the education system also needs to be fostered (pp. 8-10). Therefore, sport has often been a sector with pioneering status within the overall development in education and training in recent years. Several European organisations acting in the field of education, employment and sport science were created, all in all to promote the exchange of know-how in the sport sector (Petry, Gütt & Fischer, 2008):

European Network of Sport Science, Education and Employment (ENSSEE)

For the European Network of Sport Science, Education and Employment the task of implementing EU policies and improving the quality and effectiveness of education and training systems in sports and physical education has been a challenge for more than a decade. Since the first few years, ENSSEE combines education and employability at the European level.

European Observatory of Sports and Employment (EOSE)

EOSE is a non-profit organisation of national, regional and local observatories specialising in the analysis of the sport labour market and in the production of dedicated methodologies and tools for the collection and processing of data in quantitative and qualitative terms.

European College of Sport Science (ECSS)

The ECSS is an independent association of individual sport scientists. It was founded in 1995 and its main aim is the promotion of sport science at the European level. It is dedicated to the generation and dissemination of scientific knowledge concerning the motivation, attitudes, values, responses, adoption, performance and health aspects of persons engaged in sport, exercise and movement.

European Association of Sports Employers (EASE)

EASE is a European non-profit-making organisation for employers operating in amateur and professional sport, recreation, fitness and the outdoors. It aims to promote social dialogue in the sport field linked to business issues and the quality of industrial relations at European level. Its aims are to negotiate at European level on behalf of employers in sport as well as to seek and to develop any means likely to ensure the harmonious development of the sport sector.

European Association for Sport Management (EASM)

EASM is an independent association of individuals involved or interested in sport management in the broadest sense. Its aims are to promote, stimulate and encourage studies and research, as well as scholarly writing and professional development in the field of sport management.

European Health and Fitness Association (EHFA)

EHFA is a not-for-profit European social dialogue organisation within the fitness sector that has its registered office in London. It brings together employers, employees and training organisations through membership and in general promotes and enhances the sector of health and fitness in Europe.

European Committee for Sport History (CESH)

CESH coordinates European projects on the history of physical education and sport to assure better European and international cooperation. In particular, it helps in the exchange of ideas, students and staff between European universities, in order to assure a high standard of teaching in sport history, to help young scholars in developing a European dimension to their work and to prepare a European doctorate in sport history.

European Sport Workforce Development Alliance (ESWDA - The Alliance)

In the light of the Education and Training policy in Europe, a consortium of selected European sport organisations involved in education, training and employment have started developing, implementing and evaluating a European Sport Workforce Development Plan with short, medium and long term goals. As a result, the strategic committee called "European Sport Workforce Development Alliance" was set up.

To sum things up, all organisations and initiatives undertaken by them constitute a European and trans-national base for building a common strategy related to education and training in sports as well as related sectors and will lead to important references for all of them.

The Bologna Process

The area of education, especially higher education, was excluded from the endeavours of the European integration process for a long time. Compared with the attempts towards harmonisation undertaken by the European Union this policy area remained principally a domain of the Member States (Witte, 2006: 1).

Not until the French minister responsible for higher education Claude Allègre came together with his colleagues from Italy, Germany and the United Kingdom in May 1998 at the Sorbonne University an initiative leading to the harmonisation of higher education in Europe was launched. Within the so-called Sorbonne Declaration, the four ministers established the basis for further developments. The fact that only one year later the ministers in charge of higher education of 29 European countries met in Bologna showed that there was a need for a voluntary integration process. At this conference all of the 29 ministers present signed the Bologna Declaration stating their intention to create a European Higher Education Area by the year 2010.

The Bologna Process is a process of voluntary convergence. It expressly acknowledges the need for convergence of European higher education systems and also calls for a further strengthening of the mobility of students in Europe. The Bologna Declaration is no longer just a political statement; it has become a binding commitment to a common action programme. The Bologna Process is both a consequence of and a contribution to the European integration process in higher education. The Bologna Declaration is having a major impact on the debate about the relationship between higher education and professional life - in particular concerning the preparation of students for the labour market. "The Bologna Declaration has reinforced the debate and increased awareness that employability is an issue all over Europe" (Haug & Tauch, 2001). The general setting in the respective countries is naturally having a major impact on the employment situation.

Yet it is understandable in a converging Europe that the number of
people wishing to study or work outside their homeland is increasing.
One of the goals of the Single European Market is to promote this
mobility. As such, two different goals are being pursued: one objective in recognising diplomas and qualifications for the purpose of enabling persons to freely practice their profession is the implementation
of a common European career area from Portugal to Estonia and from
Finland to Cyprus.

The Development of the Three-Cycle Study Structure

Before the Bologna Process, a number of country-specific approaches
to organising higher education structure existed - and unfortunately
continue to exist in some of the Bologna regions. According to Witte,
these structures can be roughly categorised between (1) countries that
have a long tradition of consecutive study programmes such as France
and the United Kingdom and (2) countries that have parallel structures
with shorter application-oriented and longer mainly theory-oriented
study programmes like Germany or the Netherlands (Witte,
2006).Within the Sorbonne Declaration the aligning of study structures was introduced as an instrument for the harmonisation of European Higher Education:

> A system, in which two main cycles, undergraduate and graduate,
> should be recognised for international comparison and equiva-
> lence, seems to emerge (Sorbonne Declaration, 1998).

The statement in this declaration was limited to the implementation of
a consecutive study structure. The Bologna Declaration took up this
idea one year later and added the aspects of duration and labour market relevance:

> Adoption of a system essentially based on two main cycles, under-
> graduate and graduate. Access to the second cycle shall require
> successful completion of first cycle studies, lasting a minimum of
> three years. The degree awarded after the first cycle shall also be
> relevant to the European labour market as an appropriate level of
> qualification (Bologna Declaration, 1999).

The common duration of the study cycles emerged in the further
course of the Bologna Process; it was three to four years for the first
cycle and one to two years for the second cycle with both degrees lasting no more than five years (Tauch & Rauhvargers, 2002). Furthermore, the number of credits dedicated to one study year was 60, so

that the first cycle comprised 180 to 240 credits and the second cycle 60 to 120.

Unlike the duration of the study cycles which was developed outside the official Bologna documents, the consecutive character of the study structure was advanced within these statements. Within the Bologna Declaration, the Master and doctoral studies formed the second cycle in a parallel manner. Beginning with the Berlin Communiqué, a three-tiered structure was implemented, where the "First cycle degrees should give access [...] to second cycle programmes. Second cycle degrees should give access to doctoral studies" (Berlin Communiqué, 2003). Following the most recent studies on the Bologna Process, 82% of higher education institutions in Europe had implemented the three-cycle study structure by the year 2007. In the preliminary study undertaken in 2003 it was only 53% (Crosier et al., 2007: 15).

Employability - the link between higher education institutions and the labour market

One of the main tasks of the Bologna Process is to improve the employability of university graduates, first and foremost of the graduates from the first cycle study programmes (see among others Bologna Declaration, 1999; Haug & Tauch, 2001; Crosier, Purser & Smidt, 2007). This aspect constitutes the largest point of contact between the labour market and the higher education institutions.

One of the first tasks is to find a common definition of what employability stands for. By nature, the approaches to the academic and the occupational area are often very different. Owing to this problem, it became widely accepted practice to involve representatives or at least to incorporate information on the labour market into the development of new study programmes. In Germany, for example, the participation of representatives of the relevant labour market is compulsory for the official accreditation of study programmes at the Bachelor and Master Level.

Besides involving representatives of the labour market, several other changes and innovations in accordance with the Bologna Reform to foster the employability of graduates include:

- The change of the educational paradigm
- The implementation of the first study cycle

- The possibility of creating vocationally-focused study programmes

The change of the educational paradigm is one of the key requirements for the implementation of the Bologna Reforms. It envisages the change from input-orientated to learning outcome-orientated teaching in higher education. The focus of teaching will shift from the mere dissemination of contents to the teaching students skills and competencies.

As the duration of the first cycle and thereby the first (academic) vocational qualification is reduced, graduates will enter the labour market sooner. This means potential employers could use this time span to foster more particular specialisations within their enterprises.

One further aspect which enhances the employability of graduates is the possibility to create vocationally-focused study programmes either in the first cycle or in the second; e.g. through the increased integration of practical higher education modules such as internships or close cooperation with enterprises. Also giving students the opportunity to leave university after completing the Bachelor's degree and to return to it after a few years to complete a Master's programme is a big step towards creating a more permeable educational and vocational system.

Based on the resolutions of the Bologna Declaration, the introduction of Bachelor and Master Degrees (BA/MA) throughout Europe is currently being discussed in sport science faculties. The Member States that already have a tiered system of study are evaluating the respective higher education systems against the backdrop of pan-European convergence of the curriculum. A number of countries have been undertaking reforms in their higher education systems over the past few years. The reforms related, inter alia, to the following:

- Architecture of learning structures (the relationship between first degree and higher degrees). Discussions involved questions such as: how long should initial degree courses last? How can initial degrees be recognised by employers?
- Flexibility and structure of qualifications. Main tools of flexibility are: credits, modules and semesters - the question is, how flexible are institutions? How can transparency be ensured within a flexible system?

- Competition in the European Higher Education Area. Higher education institutions are competing with each other for scholars, research grants, students, reputation. How can quality assurance be implemented? What role do professional organisations play in the accreditation process of degrees?

The Ministers of Education discussed this controversial issue in Bologna in 1999 and ascertained that the individual education systems of the European countries differ hugely in terms of their structure. The fascinating thing about the present developments in Higher Education is the fact that countries which have thoroughly different starting situations such as Finland and Spain or France and Estonia are implementing similar reforms:

The Bologna Process has demonstrated that problems that may seem inherent in a national system or certain subjects do actually have a European dimension and can therefore be solved most effectively in close co-operation (Haug & Tauch, 2001: 5).

Tuning Educational Structures in Europe

In the outlined course of various political resolutions regarding education and training in Europe, as mentioned above, in 1999, the Bologna Process was initiated, implicating strong change regarding higher education systems. In particular, as a direct effect of the political decision to converge the different national systems, e.g. through the implementation of the Bachelor and Master degree system by 2010, (nearly) all European higher education systems and programmes are in the throes of reform.

> For higher education institutions these reforms mean the actual starting point for another discussion: the comparability of curricula in terms of structures, programmes and actual teaching. In this reform process the required academic and professional profiles and needs of society (should) play an important role (Tuning, 2007).

Whereas up to now, many activities focused only on organisational systems within education, this initiative was based on educational structures and the content of studies. In this regard, the "main aim and objective of the project [was] to contribute significantly to the elaboration of a framework of comparable and compatible qualifications in each of the (potential) signatory countries of the Bologna process, which should be described in terms of workload, level, learning out-comes, competences and profile" (González & Wagenaar, 2003).

Bearing in mind the aims and methodology of the Tuning Project, and again the overall objectives of the Bologna Declaration and the Lisbon Process, all these elements also constitute a basis for building a com-mon strategy related to education and training in sports and all sport related sectors. The process to establish the European Higher Education Area in the sport sector by 2010 is one of the major reforms ever made to university and non-university programmes. The higher education institu-tions across Europe are deeply commited to the Bologna Process and it is necessary to support them as much as possible in their development (cf. Petry, Froberg, Madella & Tokarski, 2008).

European Year of Education through Sport 2004
The inclusion of the educational element stems from the proposal put forward by the Member of the European Parliament, Doris Pack, aimed at facilitating financial subsidies for sport. The factors of edu-cation and training have contractually binding force and, as a conse-quence, they provide a legal safeguard for sport. The actual idea of implementing a "European year of Sport" failed owing to this prob-lem. Linking sport and education is a "device" as the EU Commission does not have the contractual basis to subsidise sport. EYES strongly contributed to sport at EU level being accepted both as an important cross-sectoral issue and as an independent policy area representing the first signs of European sport's future legislative roots. The aim of EYES was to promote the establishment of interdisciplinary and inter-institutional networks between education and sports science. In Ger-many alone, 20 sports-related projects received financial support from the Commission. Nonetheless, it would certainly be appropriate to analyse the longer-term effects on enhanced cooperation between sports organisations and educational institutions that EYES was in-tended to stimulate (cf. Petry, Jesse & Kukowka, 2006).

International sporting events such as the European Football Champi-onship in Portugal and the Summer Olympics in Athens provided EYES 2004 with a platform that generated major media interest. The aim was specifically to incorporate the "social, educational and cul-tural functions" of sport into EU policy and to have the responsible Directorate-General of the European Commission perceive sport as an independent sphere of activity. Hence, the issue of sport was imple-mented indirectly, via an "education policy to which sport had been added", as a new policy area in Europe. The EYES message targeted both existing EU Member States and EFTA/EWR countries as well as potential future EU member countries. Measures were implemented as part of EYES both at national and at Community level, involving 28 states. The focus of the measures introduced at Community level was the information and promotional campaign implemented by an external company, as part of which, inter alia, a communication strategy and also a logo and slogan were produced and PR work involving different areas was performed. Two Eurobarometer surveys on sport provided the scientific back-up for EYES.

An analysis of the objectives and implementation of EYES allows the functionality of the "European Year", which has been launched at irregular intervals since 1983, to be examined by way of an example, as a political control instrument at European and national level. Overall, EYES was able to promote the instrumentalisation of sport for formal and non-formal education and also as an integration factor for values education. If the instrument of the "European Year" is viewed as a strongly target group-specific communicative measure aimed at achieving a political focus throughout Europe, it certainly appears to work as a control instrument. In selected areas, it was possible to design new methods and to develop best practice models. The greatest achievement of EYES is the permanent establishment of new cross-sectoral networks (Eureval-C3, 2005). It was not possible to reach the broad European public and the players in sports organisations and educational institutions to the desired degree. Nor was it possible to successfully achieve cooperation with other EU policy-making areas. Nevertheless, EYES was judged as being a "Community added value" (ibid.) and, with the measures that were implemented, serves to point the way forward for future EU policy in the area of sport. EYES played a major role in sport being identified as a "cross-sectoral area" of European politics and hence being accepted as an independent policy area.

6.5 Interim conclusions: different approaches

Health, Doping, Education and the Economy are areas of sports policy, where the European Union takes over responsibility in order to reform the situation europewide:

The integration of the health aspect into the Lisbon Agenda, which is considered to be the most important political instrument in the EU focused on economic growth and productivity, can be regarded as one of the greatest successes of cross-policy integration of the health dimension. Concerning doping, the EU sees its responsibilities in the area of law enforcement as mainly involving coordination, training and networking. With regard to the health-hazard aspects of doping, the Commission calls on sports organisations to develop rules of good practice to ensure that young sportsmen and sportswomen, in particular, are better informed and educated.

Sport's points of contact with business and its economic aspects are numerous and varied. The Directorate-General for Employment, Social Affairs and Equal Opportunities, for instance, which plays a key role in promoting positive interaction between economic, social and employment policies, deals, in the area of sport, with players' transfer rights. In this regard, the European Commission recognises the right of sports organisations to draw up sport-specific transfer market guidelines as long as they do not infringe upon the general legislation on competition and the labour market within the EU's internal market structure.

The objective formulated by the European Council in Lisbon in 2001, that the EU wants to become a competitive and dynamic knowledge-based economy, identified lifelong learning as the essential element of European education policy. The overall objectives of the Bologna Declaration and the Lisbon Process built a common strategy related to education and training in sports and all sport related sectors.

7 The legal framework based on EC/EU law

Thomas Dehesselles & Michael Siebold

General

The European Court of Justice has repeatedly considered the position of sport in relation to the common public interest and economic competition and has had to justify the role of sport under European law.

Sport has remained outside the remit of community responsibilities regardless of whether one is referring to sport as a leisure activity or to professional sport. Rules under sport laws in the so-called "narrower sense" are rules that relate to the right to participate in sport competitions and to organise sport competitions; for instance, promotion and relegation rules, penalties, doping etc. Sport law is the law imposed by sports federations on the basis of their autonomy that is protected by their constitution in their own area of activities, regardless of whether they are set forth in statutes, general regulations, implementing regulations, rules of arbitration or the like, provided this law has just been standardised. In addition, the relationship between the members themselves and the federation bodies can, but need not necessarily, be organised in terms of rights and obligations. This refers, for instance, to sport tribunals of sport federations, codes of ethics, catalogues of penalties etc.

Rules under sport laws in the so-called "broader sense" in this context are rules that affect those participating in sport - federations, clubs, athletes - and are indirectly associated with sporting activity. Commercial regulations come under so-called sport law in the broader sense. As so-called "sport law in the broader sense", economic regulations come under both national and European laws, unless they are based on other rules. As they frequently involve commercial issues, the general competency regulations that apply to the non-sporting, economic sectors apply to the sport sector, too. Overlapping with the rules under sport laws in the "narrower sense" means that in individual cases the legal aspects of the autonomy of sports have to be weighed up against the general rules of commercial law.

Sport-related disputes frequently involve public law that encompasses EU regulations, laws on general taxation and subsidies, but also emission protection acts and police laws, for instance, which have an impact on sporting facilities just like construction laws and the full scope of commercial civilian law, particularly civil law, trade law, antitrust law and labour law. In the final analysis, there are some elements that are relevant under criminal law particularly in the field of sport fraud, gambling/lotteries and doping. This is where there are some aspects of sport that have a special publicity effect even though they are actually subject to special law where general rules apply.

Autonomy of sports

No practical rules facilitating unequivocal classification have been found for amateur sport or for delimitation in particular. The ECJ claims that objective criteria should be used to distinguish amateur sport from professional sport. This is comprehensible insofar as it cannot be within the sovereignty of sports federations, for instance, to specify the applicability of Community law using relevant "selection" (Deliége - ECJ series, 2000: 2549 marginal number 46). After the criterion of having a fixed payment limit was rejected to the referring diversity of conditions in the European Union, but also in the various disciplines, the level of payment must be used as the benchmark. Only activity that is purely marginal and ancillary would not come under European law (Levin - ECJ series, 1982: 1085 marginal no. 13; Steymann - ECJ series 1988, 6159 marginal no. 13). However, as long as the content has neither been declared "marginal" nor "ancillary" and is not based on other comprehensible criteria, the impression remains that a reliable delimitation is virtually impossible to achieve and that the respective decision must be respected in each individual case. The ECJ has held the view which has been consistently reflected in its case law since 1974 that professional sport at least is deemed economic activity within the meaning of Article 2 of the Treaty Establishing the European Community when it says:

> In view of the Community goals, sporting activity only comes under Community law insofar as it is part of the economic system within the meaning of Article 2 of the Treaty Establishing the European Community. If any such activity can be classified as paid work or services, it is subject to the regulations of the Treaty Establishing the European Community based on the circumstances of each individual case (sic!). (Walrave - ECJ series, 1974: 1405 marginal no. 10).

This case law attracted maximum public and media attention with the ruling handed down in the Bosman case (ECJ series, 1995: 4921). Although a number of federations and governments claimed that sport and disciplines like football do not represent economic activity in the majority of cases but that they concur in structural terms with the definition of culture set forth in the Treaty Establishing the European Community, the ECJ ruled otherwise. The freedom of movement which workers are guaranteed is so fundamental that its relevance may not be limited by invoking the limited powers of the Community in the cultural sector (Bosman - ECJ series, 1995: 4921 marginal no. 7). The ECJ did not focus on the issue of the "proximity" and structural compatibility of sport and culture for formal reasons.

Whether or not sporting activity can be classified as paid work is the main criterion for invoking the freedom of movement for workers as set forth in Article 39ff. of the Treaty Establishing the European Community and the freedom to provide services within the meaning of Article 49ff. of the Treaty Establishing the European Community. In the opinion of the football associations of the Federal Republic of Germany, for instance, the threshold of payment is as little as a monthly flat-rate remuneration of   150. Against the backdrop of so-cial insurance, the argument is frequently used that the limit for mini-jobs is currently   400 a month. If one were to apply this to ordinary market conditions, this would mean that vast areas of competitions hitherto construed as "amateur sport" would come under economic regulations of the EU legislative procedure and that there would be no need to distinguish between work that is subject to directives and work on a self-employed basis (II. Internal rules - freedom of move-ment of workers/freedom to provide services).

7.1 Internal rules - sports law

Shareholders

A large number of European top-level sports leagues are meanwhile not only permitting clubs but also corporations to take part in competi-tions. Moreover, the shareholders of these corporations are no longer linked exclusively to the parent clubs but to third parties too - entre-preneurs or private individuals - who may have a minority or majority stake in the corporation. Sometimes shares in sport corporations are traded on public stock markets; the conditions are as widely diversi-fied in this area as they are in other regulatory areas of the European Community.

There is a growing trend among both strategic partners like media companies, marketing companies and manufacturers of sportswear and strategic investors to participate in sport corporations under company law; some of them acquiring multiple stakes. As soon as an individual or a company acquires a substantially larger share than a sport company participating in the same competition, there is a risk this might create the impression that competition could be distorted by that individual's or company's ability to influence the actual sporting behaviour. From the sport perspective, it is a matter of safeguarding the integrity of competition and of preventing the possibility of manipulating the results, for instance, by "transferring" players within the clubs on unjustifiable grounds, a tendency that was observed frequently in the countries of the former Eastern Bloc. Players in the sport business are well aware of the problem and it has also been addressed in a number of solution approaches (cf. Weiler, 2006).

The rules adopted by the sports federations make a distinction between a majority and minority stake and a simple or multiple stake. Having a majority stake is prohibited for the field of professional football in Germany but having a multiple stake is not. The European professional football leagues in neighbouring European countries have different rules; the majority of them assume that club competitions can be spun off into corporations which third parties can obtain multiple stakes in. The top leagues at national level - football, basketball, ice hockey, handball - have different rules on the (optional) participation of corporations in club competitions and on the extent to which it is possible to acquire a stake in sports organisations. Multiple stakes are subject to terms and conditions. Since 1999, it has been possible for corporations to become involved in football leagues, with the participation of third parties being subject to restrictions because the parent club must always hold 50% + X of the voting rights. In the case of limited partnerships, this restriction only applies to limited liability companies, the corporation can sell all its shares which, for instance, Borussia Dortmund did when it went public. One argument in favour of restricting third party shares to "50% - X" of the voting rights is that no influence can be brought to bear on sporting competitions. Anyone who finances a business has considerable potential for bringing their influence to bear on competitions. The same applies to the main sponsors and patrons of a club who support the club financially either by making donations or because of their desire to act as a patron. There is no doubt that they are capable of influencing sporting competitions. A glance at other leagues shows that there is either less evidence of anti-competitive influence in other disciplines or that it does not occur in the first place; if and when companies are (majority) stakeholders in these disciplines, this does not necessarily mean they are bringing an illegal influence to bear on professional sports. "Traditional" links are said to be equally harmless. Even if the main impression gained is that partners are willing to invest vast sums of money in German professional sports even when they do not have a stake under company law, they will certainly be looking for some kind of links with company law in the long term in order to secure their investment. Professional sport associations have vast autonomy when it comes to the organisation of their internal rules ensuing from the unrestricted freedom of association set forth in Article 9 of the Basic Law. This also includes governance of corporations in competitions. As the monopoly federations organised in Germany on the basis of the so-called "single place principle" are frequently the only "provider", the latter is obliged to observe certain boundaries. It may only adopt rules to the extent necessary to represent their sportrelated goals, although the provider is granted a certain level of assessment and discretionary scope.

As it is possible to acquire majority stakes and sometimes even multiple stakes in international clubs, the question arises whether German clubs could not invoke the European ban on discrimination. UEFA wishes to ensure that holding stakes in several teams competing in a competition is prohibited, for instance, for the Champions League which it organises (cf. CAS 98/200 and EU Commission of 25 June 2002: no. 37806). In view of the fact that international competitions are gaining momentum specifically in financial terms, German clubs are hence being deprived of a significant source of internal finance. The permissible minimum stake cannot be deemed adequate compensation. German clubs therefore tend to be at a disadvantage in financial terms too, they are becoming less competitive and may even be experiencing discrimination within the meaning of Article 81 para. 1 and Article 56 para. 1 of the Treaty establishing the European Treaty (competition, capital transactions). There are no restrictions on stakeholding in other disciplines or countries. The rules limit competition between potential partners and strategic investors in stakeholding and likewise affects the possibility sport corporations have of advertising for investors invoking Article 81 para. 1 of the Treaty establishing the European Community.

Transfer of players - switching clubs

It is no longer just insider information but basically common knowledge that European regulations and case law in the area of the protection of workers' rights have set milestones in professional sport. The relevant ruling [Bosman L.c.] is certainly one of the best-known rulings in legal history, the consequences of which are meanwhile being recognised by national courts and courts of appeal, having overcome initial resistance; it is merely the top-level sports federations and FIFA in particular that persist in issuing rules that may not stand up to legal scrutiny at European level. The applicability of the relevant rules is hence limited to the non-European professional sport sector, particularly professional football in South America and Africa.

Since 1996 (Bosman - ECJ series, 1995 I: 4921) all sports federations in the European Union and associated states know that professional athletes can only be kept under contract with their club within the framework of a permanent employment relationship and that there is no statutory basis on which a professional football player who is a citizen of one Member State may not, on the expiry of his contract with a club, be employed by a club of another Member State unless the latter club has paid to the former club a transfer, training or development fee. It literally stated:

> 1. Article 48 of the Treaty Establishing the European Community precludes the application of rules laid down by sporting associations, under which a professional football player who is a citizen of one Member State may not, on the expiry of his contract with a club, be employed by a club of another Member State unless the latter club has paid to the former club a transfer, training or development fee.

> 3. The direct effect of Article 48 of the Treaty Establishing the European Community cannot be relied upon in support of claims relating to a fee in respect of transfer, training or development which has already been paid, or is still payable under an obligation which arose before, the date of this judgment, except by those who have brought court proceedings or raised an equivalent claim under the applicable national law before that date.

The Court ruled that keeping the player under contract where a system of licensing is used is, in principle, possible and permissible under

European law. The European Court of Justice did not render the issue of athletes' participation in competitions problematic, which means that any existing "internal rules" are basically at the discretion of the sports federations. There is hence no need to consider in any great depth whether the internal conditions relating to the admission of athletes to professional competitions could be subject to restrictions imposed by European law or based on European case law.

The transfer rules of the sports federations that were the subject matter of the dispute which had abided by the rules imposed by FIFA and by the Union of European Football Associations (UEFA) found three different legal relationships to begin with. The membership of the player in the national federation and his membership in a club were not the subject matter of the dispute, as they are internal rules. The third legal relationship was the so-called "entitlement to play", which is regularly referred to colloquially as a "license", which explains the term "licensed player". Transfers and the transfer of players refers to the process in which a player terminates his legal relationship with his club or even his legal relationship with his club and his federation in order to enter into a legal relationship with a new club or federation, giving the player the entitlement to play for the new club which constitutes the necessary prerequisite for participation in official competitions.

If a player is still involved in a legal relationship with his club, he cannot change to another club without his club's consent; this reflects the current legal situation. The club releasing the player usually requests a payment to release the player, providing the basis for so-called "transfer fees". The question that is frequently debated in legal circles whether these payments are compensation by nature or are made on the basis of a mutual agreement between the clubs concerned is not to be highlighted as a problem in this context as it is not an issue that is relevant under European law. Furthermore, legal practice has accommodated this so that no disputes arise when players switch clubs within Europe.

The sport federation's transfer rule under dispute also envisaged even players whose contract had expired not being permitted to switch to a different club unless a transfer fee was paid. According to these rules, so-called "compulsory transfers" were also permissible which meant that the club releasing the player did not have to agree to the new club paying a so-called "training fee", which was calculated by multiplying the player's gross annual income by a coefficient based on the player's age. If the club refused to pay this fee, the player's new club risked facing sanctions by the federation that could even lead to the club being excluded from competitions. If the player on his part refused an offer by his previous club to extend his contract on the same terms as the previous year, the club was entitled to ban this player, i.e. the player was no longer allowed to take part in the competition. After two periods of inactivity, the player was allowed to change clubs without any fees being paid.

The European Court of Justice established that these rules disproportionately impeded the player's freedom of movement, in particular as Article 48 of the Treaty Establishing the European Community contains a fundamental right according to which the freedom of movement of citizens of EU Member States is not just protected by a direct prohibition of discrimination on grounds of nationality but that non-discriminatory obstacles to the freedom of movement of workers are impermissible too. The ECJ established that the rule is certainly capable of impeding the player's chances of changing clubs as it incurred "higher expense" for the club engaging the player even if no employment contract existed with the club that is releasing the player. In addition to the player's future salary, the club signing up the player would also have to raise the transfer fee.

While the national sport federation and UEFA argued that the transfer rules are justified by the need to maintain a financial and competitive balance between clubs and to support the search for talent and the training of young players, the ECJ refuted this allegation. In this context, it is also expounded as a problem whether transfer rules can be justified by the special status of sport even though they violate the basic right of the freedom of movement of workers when they pursue the legitimate purpose of maintaining the financial and competitive balance between clubs and of supporting the search for talent and the training of young players. It ruled that the measure was not suitable for doing so. Those rules neither preclude:

> the richest clubs from securing the services of the best players nor prevent the availability of financial resources from being a decisive factor in competitive sport, thus considerably altering the balance between clubs, (…).

> However, because it is impossible to predict the sporting future of young players with any certainty and because only a limited number of such players go on to play professionally, those fees are by nature contingent and uncertain and are in any event unrelated to

the actual cost borne by clubs of training both future professional players and those who will never play professionally. The prospect of receiving such fees cannot, therefore, be either a decisive factor in encouraging recruitment and training of young players or an adequate means of financing such activities, particularly in the case of smaller clubs (…).

Finally, the argument that the rules in question are necessary to compensate clubs for the expenses which they have had to incur in paying fees on recruiting their players cannot be accepted, since it seeks to justify the maintenance of obstacles to freedom of movement for workers simply on the ground that such obstacles were able to exist in the past" (Bosman - ECJ series, 1995 I: 4921).

Last but by no means least, the ECJ established that it was merely transfers within Europe that were affected but not relationships between the national federations of the Member States and those of third countries. This is where different rules could certainly apply. The question was not answered whether the freedom of movement of workers would also be impeded if a player signed his first so-called professional contract. This is where sports federations and indeed FIFA have meanwhile created rules that apply to "young" players who have been the focus of the European Commission and the European Court of Justice. As the national associations are oriented to FIFA rules which do not represent directly applicable law within the European Union, since they only become binding when they are incorporated into the statutes of the national associations, the following contains excerpts of the text (www.FIFA.com. - search "Regulations on the Status and Transfer of Players"):

Article 19 - Protection of underage players
1. International transfers of players are only permitted if the player is over the age of 18. The following three exceptions to this rule apply:
a) (…)
b) The transfer takes place within the territory of the European Union (EU) or European Economic Area (EEA) and the player is aged between 16 and 18. In this case, the new club must fulfil the following minimum obligations:
(…)

The Players' Status Committee shall be competent to decide on any dispute arising in relation to these matters and shall impose appropriate sanctions in the event of violations of this provision.

Training compensation

If a professional is transferred before the expiry of his contract, any club that has contributed to his education and training shall receive a proportion of the compensation paid to his former club (solidarity contribution). The provisions concerning solidarity contributions are set out in Annexe 5 of these regulations.

Solidarity mechanism

If a professional is transferred before the expiry of his contract, any club that has contributed to his education and training shall receive a proportion of the compensation paid to his former club (solidarity contribution). The provisions concerning solidarity contributions are set out in Annexe 5 of these regulations.

Solidarity contribution

If a professional moves during the course of a contract, 5% of any compensation, not including training compensation paid to his former club, shall be deducted from the total amount of this compensation and distributed by the new club as a solidarity contribution to the club(s) involved in his training and education over the years. This solidarity contribution reflects the number of years (calculated pro rata if less than one year) he was registered with the relevant club(s) between the seasons of his 12th and 23rd birthdays:

It is remarkable that no specific sums are specified but that clubs face the uncertainty of (arbitrary) specification by FIFA. Some state federations and national associations have hence drawn up their own "compensation models" (cf. for instance www.nfv.de - "Training compensation calculator"). It is rather doubtful that these rules would stand up to legal scrutiny regarding the freedom of movement of workers when the arguments outlined above are considered.

Nationality clauses

The ECJ also established whether the so-called nationality clauses that limit the number of "non-nationals" who can be fielded in competitions are compatible with European law. At the time, the so-called "3+2 rule" had actually been drawn up in collaboration with the Commission. This rule permitted each national association to limit to three the number of foreign players whom a club may field in any first division match in their national championships, plus two players who have played in the country of the relevant national association for an uninterrupted period of five years, including three years as a junior. On this issue, the Court also ruled that the violation of the freedom of movement of workers and the abolition of any discrimination based on nationality between workers of the Member States as regards employment, remuneration and conditions of work and employment was not permissible. It said it was irrelevant that the restriction only applied to players being fielded in official competitions and not to the basic employment in a club. It also said that participation in a competition was greatly reduced for the activity of a professional athlete and that a player's actual ability to be fielded was reduced. This hence represented an unjustified, unlawful restriction under European law (Bosman-ECJ series, 1995 I: 4921).

Although the ECJ acknowledged that rules or practices which exclude foreign players from playing in certain matches for non-financial reasons that are associated with the specific nature and framework of these matches are not necessarily unlawful, it ruled that any such limitations must be tied to a specific purpose. As the so-called nationality clauses are not limited to certain matches but apply to all of the respective club's official matches, participation in competitions being the essential purpose of a professional player's activity, nationality clauses are hence incompatible with the freedom of movement of workers. For restricting the right of clubs to field players to the Member State in which it is domiciled is not necessarily associated with its sporting activity. This even ensues from a parallel assessment of restricting the right of clubs to field players from other regions, towns or localities in such matches:

> Even though national championships are played between clubs from different regions, towns or localities, there is no rule restricting the right of clubs to field players from other regions, towns or localities in such matches.

Furthermore only clubs that have achieved a certain sporting result in their national association are allowed to participate in national competitions regardless of the qualification or origin of individual players. It is not necessary either to prove a certain nationality. In the final analysis, the clause maintaining a balance between sport clubs would be useless, which in turn means it would be inappropriate as the clause would enable the richest clubs to secure the services of the best national players, giving them a competitive edge over other clubs. Finally, the EU Commission which was involved in developing the so-called "3+2 rule" was wrapped over the knuckles and told that it was not entitled to issue any guarantees regarding the compatibility of certain behaviour with European law. It is certainly not allowed to approve of any behaviour that contravenes Community law (Bosman - ECJ series, 1995: 4921).

7.2 Doping

Case law has meanwhile initiated major trends, amid much media fanfare and creating furious uproar among top-level sports federations in doping cases, clarifying its position. The starting point was provided by a ruling that is likely to have a similar impact as the decision on the freedom of movement of workers (Meca-Medina - ECJ series, 2004 II: 3291).

At the level of the European Union, there have been wide-ranging political and fewer legal activities in the fight against doping (cf. chapter 6.2). It is true that the European Commission has played an active role in the World Anti-Doping Agency (WADA); it has issued a large number of policy statements and organised a large number of anti-doping conferences. Nonetheless, the European Union does not have any original competency to adopt rules and the statutory basis for action is much disputed even among legal scholars. In legal terms, Article 5 of the Treaty Establishing the European Community must be observed.

Article 5
The European Parliament, the Council, the Commission, the Court of Justice and the Court of Auditors shall exercise their powers under the conditions and for the purposes provided for, on the one hand, by the provisions of the Treaties establishing the European Communities and of the subsequent Treaties and Acts modifying and supplementing them and, on the other hand, by the other provisions of this Treaty."

This means it needs to be clarified whether the fight against doping in sport involves first and foremost health aspects, aspects of criminal activity or of fairness in sport; in any case the normative basis of pan-European regulations is different. In some countries of the European Union, doping is a criminal offence, in other countries it is merely an administrative offence and in third countries, athletes merely face sport sanctions but no official sanctions. Whereas to begin with the general view held was that the main responsibility to fight doping lay with the athletes, clubs and sports federations, there now seems to have been a shift in trend manifested by a desire for legal solutions. Considering both ethical aspects and aspects of public healthcare, the European Parliament-Committee on Culture, Youth, Education, the Media and Sport organised an initial hearing that has led to the demand for a pan-European information database, harmonisation of legislation regarding the possession and use of stimulants in sport. Following the events at the Tour de France, demands for a harmonised anti-doping strategy - not primarily legal measures - increased once again among all political and legislative bodies.

The majority of observers think substantial, transnational progress has been made in the area of police and judicial cooperation, but not in the area of cross-border-trafficking in drugs and pharmaceuticals. There is police and judicial cooperation in the prevention and prosecution of trafficking in drugs. The practical problem that exists in the field of doping that is relevant for sport is, however, that not all substances come under the definition of "drugs". On the contrary, the majority of substances originate from medical treatment and /or tends to be administered in quantities that are sanctioned as doping for athletes that would normally not be subject to any sanctions at all. Furthermore, it almost impossible to imagine medical treatment without many of the substances that are banned for athletes or are derived from the body's own substances which certainly cannot be classified as drugs. However, it is mandatory for medical products that the patient information leaflet contain both a list of all the substances contained and a warning, for instance, that use of the product may lead to a positive doping test (Directive 2001/83/EC-Article 59 para 1 c.). The right to a con trolled fight against drugs and prevention of drug addiction is to create the authorisation basis for European lawmaking in the field of anti-doping policy. There is specific mandatory labelling for products that come under the definition of the term "drugs", cigarettes, for instance. Article 6 para 4, Article 29, Article 32, Article 152 para. 4 of the Treaty Establishing the European Community are relevant for the criminal aspects of an anti-drugs policy, for instance, trafficking and trading in illegal substances or the criminal liability of persons supporting athletes:

Article 6
(…)
(4) The Union shall provide itself with the means necessary to attain its objectives and carry through its policies"

Article 29
Without prejudice to the powers of the European Community, the Union's objective shall be to provide citizens with a high level of safety within an area of freedom, security and justice by developing common action among the Member States in the fields of police and judicial cooperation in criminal matters and by preventing and combating racism and xenophobia.

That objective shall be achieved by preventing and combating crime, organised or otherwise, (...) illicit drug trafficking and illicit arms trafficking, (...) through closer cooperation between police forces, customs authorities and other competent authorities in the Member States, both directly and through the European Police Office (Europol), in accordance with the provisions of Articles 30 and 32, closer cooperation between judicial and other competent authorities of the Member States including cooperation through the European Judicial Cooperation Unit ('Eurojust'), in accordance with the provisions of Articles 31 and 32."

Article 32
The Council shall lay down the conditions and limitations under which the competent authorities referred to in Articles 30 and 31 may operate in the territory of another Member State in liaison and in agreement with the authorities of that State."

Article 152
(…)
(4) The Council, acting in accordance with the procedure referred to in Article 251 and after consulting the Economic and Social Committee and the Committee of the Regions, shall contribute to

the achievement of the objectives referred to in this article through adopting:

a) measures setting high standards of quality and safety of organs and substances of human origin, blood and blood derivatives; these measures shall not prevent any Member State from maintaining or introducing more stringent protective measures;

b) by way of derogation from Article 37, measures in the veterinary and phytosanitary fields which have as their direct objective the protection of public health;

c) incentive measures designed to protect and improve human health, excluding any harmonisation of the laws and regulations of the Member States.

The Council, acting by a qualified majority on a proposal from the Commission, may also adopt recommendations for the purposes set out in this Article."

Assuming that 152 para. 4 accords legislative power to the European Union in the area of public healthcare only in a strictly limited number of cases, any action pursuant to Article 136ff. could be more effective. Assuming that athletes who have committed doping offences are employees, the EU could have the power to intervene on the basis of the protection of workers' rights. The European Union has the right to issue minimum demands in respect of working conditions and occupational safety and health.

The ECJ has recently reiterated that it reserves the right to issue its own ruling in the narrower sporting sector - also - in cases involving doping if and when other basis rights are affected (Meca-Medina - ECJ series, 2004 II: 3291). Two professional swimmers involved in doping practices gained the backing of the European Court of Justice which reversed the ruling of a European Court of First Instance. Bans imposed owing to the use of prohibited substances are not exempt from the due judiciary and jurisdiction of the ECJ. Anyone assuming that sanctions imposed for violation of the rules of competition, such as doping, would fall within the natural and exclusive competence of the expert (sporting) regulator was proven wrong. The two-year ban from swimming imposed on the two swimmers was challenged under the European law on competition - antitrust law. Unlike the Court of First Instance, the ECJ rejected the complaint that anti-doping rules were pure "sports rules" that fall outside the scope of EU competition law that cannot be allocated exclusively to the economic, ethical area of sport, but rather examined whether the sport rules were proportionate in terms of the law on competition. This means there will hardly be any internal rules on the participation and organisation of competition under sport law that the European Court of Justice will be unwilling to examine.

7.3 External regulations - commercial law

Value-added tax - general introduction

Even (non-profit-making) sport clubs are subject to the rules of taxation of turnover insofar as they meet the other definitions of the VAT Act or of the VAT Directive (VAT Directive 2006/112/EC - still referred to as the 6th EC Directive 777/388/EC up to 31 December 2006). There is no special law that applies to sport. There is, however, a special provision which deviates from German VAT law and has therefore recently become the subject of litigation. The VAT Directive allows every taxpayer to invoke it, which will be the case, in particular, if the provision is more favourable for the taxpayer than the German VAT Act. Based on their duty to cooperate pursuant to Article 5 of the Treaty Establishing the European Community, national courts also need to grant the legal protection that ensues from the direct impact of provisions of Community law (Factortame - ECJ series 1990 I, 243). If a European legal provision has not been implemented, or has not been implemented adequately, and if it is not possible to interpret national legislation in conformity with a directive, either the national court or the European Court of Justice grants the taxpayer the relevant legal protection if he invokes the provision in the directive that is favourable for him (Soupergaz - ECJ series 1995 I, 1883). In this regard, it is primarily a matter of examining whether, taking into account the actual circumstances of the particular case and ECJ case law, the principle of the neutrality of value-added tax has been violated or, in relation to tax exemptions, whether or not services of the same type have been provided (Turn- und Sportunion Waldburg - ECJ series 2006 I, 589). The Member States have discretionary powers in terms of granting tax exemptions where the tax exemptions involved are for services that are primarily provided by public institutions but could also be handled by private corporations, such as in the area of initial and advanced vocational training, education and higher education or culture, Article 132 (1) h) and l) of the VAT Directive.

Article 132

(1) Member States shall exempt the following transactions:

h) the supply of services and of goods closely linked to the protection of children and young persons by bodies governed by public law or by other organisations recognised by the Member State concerned as being devoted to social wellbeing;

l) the supply of services, and the supply of goods closely linked thereto, to their members in their common interest in return for a subscription fixed in accordance with their rules by non-profit-making organisations with aims of a political, trade union, religious, patriotic, philosophical, philanthropic or civic nature, provided that this exemption is not likely to cause distortion of competition;

Both public corporations and private individuals are entitled to the tax exemption that is granted in this way, although the latter may have to meet certain requirements for recognition purposes. If there is no specific recognition process, the national authorities which are under the control of the national courts are required, as specified by the Federal Fiscal Court, to determine which institutions are to be recognised as being comparable (Federal Fiscal Court ruling of 21 March 2007: 687). European law specifies that institutions which are to be given equal status in this way must not systematically seek to make a profit (Kügler - ECJ series, 2002 I: 6833). Therefore, where German corporations are organised as non-profit associations pursuant to Article 21 of the German Civil Code, as is the case with sport clubs, this element applies. A club whose purpose is not to operate as a commercial business gains legal status by being entered into the register of associations held by the relevant district court. Furthermore, where a sports club is also recognised as being non-profit-making, which should be the rule; this is additional proof that it meets the requirement of not systematically seeking to make a profit. This ensues from Articles 52 para. 1 and 55 para. 1 of the German Fiscal Code (Abgabenordnung).

A corporation pursues charitable aims if its activity is designed to give altruistic assistance to the general public in a physical, intellectual or moral sense. (…).

Assistance or support is provided altruistically if, in doing so, a corporation does not pursue goals primarily serving its own financial interest - for instance, commercial or other profit-making goals. (…).

The VAT treatment of non-profit-making sport clubs is problematic, particularly against a backdrop where similar - not necessarily identical - and potentially competing service providers may not be treated differently in respect of value-added tax (JP Morgan Fleming - ECJ ruling of 28 June 2007 - RSC 363/05). Article 132 (1) m) of the VAT Directive (previously Article 13 A (1) m) of the 6th EC Directive) applies to sport clubs; reexemption from value-added tax:

> the supply of certain services closely linked to sport or physical education by non-profit-making organisations to persons taking part in sport or physical education.

By contrast, Section 4 subsection 22 b) of the VAT Act limits the exemption such that only sporting events which are held by non-profit-making organisations and the remuneration for which consists solely of attendance fees are exempted. Unlike Community law, German law narrows the facts as not every service linked to sport is at the same time a sporting event. As such, VAT law follows on from public benefit law and requires a so-called dedicated activity (Federal Fiscal Court ruling of 9 August 2007, UR 2007, p. 811). A sporting event is an organisational measure initiated by a sports club that is more than just the surrender of the use and benefit of sports equipment or facilities and is more than an actual service, such as a training session for an individual athlete or transportation to a sports competition. These differing requirements are viewed as a departure by national law from the EU rule, which it may not be possible to cure through interpretation (see earlier Federal Fiscal Court ruling; different view: Rhineland-Palatinate Fiscal Court, ruling of 9 November 2006, EFG 2007, 1995).

To sum it up, one can say that services which are not sporting events in the sense of the dedicated activity mentioned above are taxable and subject to taxation under national law but should be exempted under European legal rules. European law defines the term "sporting event" and thus retroacts on national law. The existence of services that are taxable and subject to taxation does not necessarily only result in an increase in charges through the addition of the relevant value-added tax. The right to deduct the value-added tax shown on purchase invoices - so-called deduction of prior VAT - then also exists. In connection with extensive external services provided by third parties, the right to deduct prior VAT can provide significant benefits in terms of financing to entrepreneurs who are liable to VAT, and this is illustrated by the following simplified arithmetical example:

The cost of building a gym or training ground amounts to   100,000; as the entire facility is being constructed by a building contractor, the latter adds on German value-added tax at a rate of 19%, bringing the total cost to   119,000. The sports club charges its members   5 an hour and non-members   10 an hour for the use of the sports facilities. As it is providing services that are liable to VAT, it can deduct the invoiced   19,000 immediately as prior VAT, thereby reducing its building costs to the net amount. Members are to be charged 7% VAT and non-members 19% VAT for the use of facilities, the payable VAT proportion of the charges therefore amounting to   0,33 per hour for members and   1,60 per hour for non-members. The benefits ensuing from the deduction of prior VAT from current accounts such as energy, cleaning etc. can be added. It is obvious that it would require a very lengthy period to offset the benefits arising from the deduction of prior VAT; it assumes almost 10,000 hours of roughly constant letting to members and non-members.

Membership fees

The VAT treatment of membership fees, too, has been the subject of legal disputes, also before the European Court of Justice. Fees which are the same for all and are levied on all members based on a uniform standard of assessment or which are, if necessary, scaled according to criteria that are the same for all members are not liable to VAT under national law, as so-called "genuine membership fees" (Section 4 of the VAT Guidelines, Federal Fiscal Court ruling of 4 July 1985, UR 1986, p. 62; Federal Fiscal Court ruling of 7 November 1996, UR 1997, p. 184).

By contrast, the ECJ takes the view, with regard to sport clubs' membership fees, that there is usually a direct connection between the membership fee and a service, for instance, permanently maintaining and hiring out sports facilities or providing coaching sessions. It holds the view that even the fact that the fee is classified as a fixed annual membership fee and is not allocated to any particular use in an individual case is unimportant. It further states that it cannot be a matter of whether the recipient of the service - the club member - actually makes use of it. Besides membership fees, admission fees and the personal services of a member as stipulated in the club rules also need to be taken into account in this context as they are also directly connected with the possibilities for participation or for using the sports facilities created by admission to the club (Kennemer Golf Club - ECJ series, 2002 I: 3293).

Taxpayers cannot avoid VAT liability either by taking the view, together with recipients of services, that a service is zero-rated. Rather, as a consequence of ECJ case law, it would be mandatory for tax authorities to determine the total charges paid by members of sport clubs by adding membership fees, special payments and assessing personal services and subsequently to demand a corresponding VAT payment. On the other hand, the club could claim its deduction of prior VAT, although it needs to be able to submit the relevant records. Furthermore, it should be noted that only transactions which are specifically referred to in the VAT Directive, i.e. services between which there is a closer connection, are exempted, but not measures between which there is a "broader" connection. Here, the question similarly arises, as in sports law generally, as to where the boundary between "closer" and "broader" connection lies. In the area of VAT, too, one line of argument that is certainly permissible relates to the degree of commercial relevance or whether or not the work as such is of a commercial, sporting or health prevention nature.

As the taxpayer has an option based on the above-mentioned "invocation of greater advantage" and can re-exercise it in each tax assessment period, ensuing from the rule of final taxation which is also enshrined in the VAT Act, this gives rise to different possibilities with different economic effects. Therefore, the taxpayer can either invoke the tax exemption to which he is entitled under Community law or he accepts taxation - possibly downstream - of his transactions in order to maintain his deduction of prior VAT. The deduction of prior VAT may be adjusted if capital goods with a long life are purchased and the deduction of prior VAT is claimed in full in the year of purchase but transactions liable to VAT are not generated with the capital goods over a sufficiently long period of time (Wollny - ECJ series, 2006 I: 8297). Whether and when national legislatures will introduce a relevant amendment to bring matters into line with European law, so as to create a clear and standardised legal position, and what transitional periods might apply in respect thereof, is unclear at present (Gemeente Leusden - ECJ series, 2004 I: 5337). What one can say is that there is a difference between European law and national law in this area which the taxpayer has the option of invoking or not invoking and which leads to different economic results. In terms of the harmonisation provision in the European Union, this is certainly questionable, however it is not prejudicial to the economic interests of the sport clubs concerned.

Athlete's withholding tax
Article 49
Within the framework of the provisions set out below, restrictions on freedom to provide services within the Community shall be prohibited in respect of nationals of Member States who are established in a State of the Community other than that of the person for whom the services are intended.

Article 50
Services shall be considered to be "services" within the meaning of this Treaty where they are normally provided for remuneration, insofar as they are not governed by the provisions relating to freedom of movement for goods, capital and persons.

"Services" shall in particular include:

(a) activities of an industrial character;
(b) activities of a commercial character;
(c) activities of craftsmen;
(d) activities of the professions.

Without prejudice to the provisions of the Chapter relating to the right of establishment, the person providing a service may, in order to do so, temporarily pursue his activity in the State where the service is provided, under the same conditions as are imposed by that State on its own nationals.

Section 50 a of the Income Tax Act (Einkommenssteuergesetz (EStG))

(4) For taxpayers subject to limited tax liability, income tax shall be levied by means of a tax deduction

1. in the case of income which is generated through artistic, sporting, circus artists' or similar performances delivered or sold within Germany, including income from other services connected

with these services, irrespective of who receives the income (Section 49 subsection 1 para. 2 d),

2. in the case of income generated by engaging in or selling an activity as an artist, professional sportsperson, writer, journalist or press photographer, including such activities for radio or television (Section 49 subsection 1 para. 2 to 4), unless the income originates from paid employment, which is subject to tax deduction from wages pursuant to Section 38 subsection 1 sentence 1 para. 1,

3. in the case of income emanating from payments for the use of commercial property or for transferring the exploitation of, or the right to exploit, rights, in particular copyright and industrial property rights, and commercial, technical, scientific and similar experience, knowledge and skills, e.g. plans, designs and systems (Section 49 subsection 1 para. 2, 3, 6 and 9); the same shall apply to the transfer of rights pursuant to Section 49 subsection 1 para. 2f. (…).

The full amount of income, including amounts pursuant to Section 3 para. 13 and 16, shall be subject to tax deduction. (3) Deductions, e.g. for business expenses, incomerelated expenses, special expenses and taxes, shall not be allowable. (4) The tax deduction shall amount to 20% of income, and 15% in the case of corporations subject to limited tax liability pursuant to Section 2 of the Corporation Tax Act (Körperschaftsteuergesetz). (5) (6) In the case of artistic, sporting, circus artists' or similar performances delivered within Germany, it shall amount to the following for income

- Of up to   250: 0%
- Of between   250 and   500: 10% of the total income
- Of between   500 and   1,000: 15% of the total income
- Of more than   1,000: 20% of the total income

Sentence 5 para. 4 shall not apply in the case of corporations subject to limited tax liability pursuant to Section 2 of the des Corporation Tax Act. (7)

After the German revenue department asserted, and was also backed up by case law in this respect, that the regulation complied with Community law, it was not possible to maintain this jurisprudence as a result of an ECJ ruling which was clearly to the contrary (BFH/NV

1994, 864; Gerretse - ECJ series 2003 I, 5933). Subsequently, the basis that was applied was that German tax law shall, in principle, grant a deduction of business expenses, despite the wording of the law to the contrary, if it is not already occurring as part of a deduction at source in a simplified refund procedure (BFH IstR, 2004: 244).

The latter has also been clearly countered by European case law, which states that the need for the tax deduction system to function properly justifies the requirement of a certificate of exemption, as provided for in the Double Taxation Agreement (DTA), with a view to avoiding disproportionate administrative costs and bearing in mind the potential loss of tax revenue through non-resident artists (athletes). If there are no cross-border collection options, this argument is accepted by the ECJ. In conclusion, the ECJ does not hold that intracommunity activities involving citizens of all nationalities domiciled in a different Member State are protected via the freedom to provide services and it refers to the wording of Section 49 subsection 2 in this regard. It further holds that the freedom to provide services only extends to citizens of other states if it has been approved by a qualified majority at the proposal of the Commission, although such a measure has never actually been implemented (the draft Directive of 12 February 1999 was withdrawn by the Commission in 2004). And that therefore a recipient of a cross-border service designated for the purpose of protecting Community law needs to make sure of the nationality of his opposite number (Scorpio - ECJ series, 2006 I: 9461).

The withholding tax deduction system, which is intended for athletes subject to limited tax liability, was examined in order to determine whether the deductibility of costs needs to be permissible even at the withholding stage and whether a corresponding double taxation agreement should be allowed despite the aforementioned standard tax exemption. In the interim, infringement proceedings brought by the European Commission against the Federal Republic of Germany on the grounds that its tax laws may contravene Community law are pending. (As specified by the ECJ, a withholding tax provision applied to domestic income of non-resident athletes creates discrimination because national contract partners are faced with administrative costs which they would not have incurred if they were to work with athletes subject to unlimited tax liability/Germans. In the year of litigation, it is possible that the tax intake had not yet been secured and that the deduction of withholding tax was therefore justified. However, as Council Directive 2001/44/EC of 15 June 2001 amending Directive 76/308/EEC on mutual assistance for the recovery of claims resulting from operations forming part of the system of financing the European Agricultural Guidance and Guarantee Fund, and of agricultural levies and customs duties and in respect of value-added tax and certain excise duties had in the meantime been extended to include the recovery of direct taxes. This justifying argument would no longer have applied and far less burden some means would have been available, also casting doubt on the proportionality of the rule (Directive 76/308/EC, as amended by Directive 2001/44/EC). It would, in principle, still be possible to have a deduction system for non-resident athletes (Scorpio - ECJ series, 2006 I: 9461).

The approach adopted by the ECJ, which has already been discussed elsewhere and under which the principle of proportionality, in other words the minimum required, appropriate means, must be applied in respect of legal rules, is also followed here. In case of dispute, the ECJ clearly holds that the deduction of direct costs must be allowed at source. Nor do the costs need to be documented vis-à-vis the debtor - in other words, the athlete's sponsor. Rather, it is sufficient to notify the latter of the costs so that he can declare the amount, which is then reduced, as part of the deduction system (Scorpio - ECJ series, 2006 I: 9461).

The ECJ has issued clear guidelines as to how a withholding tax system needs to be structured in line with Community law. At present, the German tax authorities do not comply with these guidelines and, consequently, the German withholding tax system, which applies solely to non-residents, contravenes Community law. The infringement proceedings which the European Commission has instituted against Germany are thus likely to end up being brought before the ECJ.

In the area of professional football, a solution to the problem has in the meantime been found at national level to the effect that, where the relevant reciprocity exists, a deduction is no longer necessary in Germany for competitors from EU and EU associated countries. Although UEFA clearly stated in the past, for instance, that finals were no longer to be played in Germany, German stadiums and arenas now again have a realistic chance if they put in bids to stage UEFA Cup Finals. It has not yet been fully clarified whether reciprocity is to be guaranteed via a Double Taxation Agreement (DTA) or in some other way. Thus, there is no longer any need to try and find out competitors' nationalities and to withhold a proportion of the money to which they are entitled. Only other sports or footballers from non-EU countries or

EU associated countries will continue to be subject to withholding of tax at source in future, with payment to be reduced accordingly. The actual opportunity, or at least the attractiveness of sporting events undoubtedly depends to a major extent on the sporting quality and also on the international nature of the participants. Hence, the taxation at source that was to be undertaken up to the decision of the Federal Ministry of Finance, i.e. the deduction of up to 20% of net income, including both actual prizes and paid travel and hotel expenses, etc., served as a deterrent in the past.

Therefore, the case law of the European Court of Justice has also pointed the way forward in the area of taxation or income assessment of athletes, which the German tax authorities or legislature had and still have to comprehend in order to find regulations that comply with European law.

Subsidies

Common public interest

The majority of German sport clubs not only meet the compulsory requirements of non-profit associations in accordance with the German Civil Code, i.e. they do not pursue economic goals but are recognised as non-profit-making organisations as they meet the formal and substantive requirements set forth in the German Fiscal Code. According to their statutes the actual way in which they are managed, clubs must promote the public at large altruistically, exclusively and directly, for instance, by promoting sport. Clubs that are recognised as being non-profit-making result in preferential treatment under the individual tax law - Corporation Tax Act (Körperschaftsteuergesetz) (KStG), Trade Tax Act (Gewerbesteuergesetz) (GewStG), the Income Tax Act (Einkommensteuergesetz) (EStG) and the Inheritance and Gift Tax Act (Erbschaft- und Schenkungsteuergesetz) (ErbStG). What is more, clubs recognised as being non-profit-making are entitled to deduct funds (donations) allocated to these corporations. This incentive is often of greater practical importance for smaller clubs in particular than the above mentioned tax exemptions.

Once a sport club has been recognised as non-profit-making in accordance with the above mentioned principles, it is entitled to accept funds from natural and legal persons - patrons, companies - tax-free which they can claim as donations that reduce their tax liability. Since 2007, tax payers have been able to claim 20% of their total income and 4 ‰ of their total revenue, wages and salaries as tax-deductible expenditure. However, one requirement that has to be formally confirmed by the sport club receiving donations is that the latter will be used in the non-profit-making area, i.e. not in the economic area. This formal requirement does not apply to small donations up to   200; a remittance slip or transfer slip is all that is needed. Since donations do not increase the recipient's tax liability but reduce the donor's tax liability, the fact that they are tax-free means that they do, at the very least, represent indirect subsidies.

Persons who provide training or coaching services as a sideline are entitled to a flat-rate, tax-free allowance of   2,400 a year as a so-called tax-free allowance for sport coaches; this also applies to coaches in sport clubs that do not operate in a so-called commercial business. This tax-free allowance affects a large number of corporations, for instance, in the fields of science, culture and sport alike, which is an argument for equal treatment under European law. There is also a special regulation for the area of sport according to which persons who provide training or coaching services as a sideline on a self-employed basis can be paid sport coach fees of up to   450 per month tax-free and duty-free; however, coaches are obliged to declare this income in their own tax returns. Persons who have a second job in a non-profit-making sport club in the non-profit-making sector qualify for a tax allowance of   500 a year. This tax-free allowance cannot be deducted from taxable income generated from another main source of income or sideline employment. Evidence of higher expenditure actually incurred can be furnished and claimed.

This favourable treatment of non-profit-making sport clubs can be relevant in terms of European rules if they represent subsidies or state aid.

Sporting facilities
Whereas subsidies in sporting facilities have been practically irrelevant in legal assessments by the courts and the European Commission in the past, they have slowly but surely become the focus of European state aid law following the major investments made in state-of-the-art sport palaces. This applies to the one-off building and, if applicable, the subsequent modernisation and day-to-day running of the sporting facility. Yet there are various types of subsidies, primarily user fees (rent or lease) and utilities such as electricity, water, waste water, maintenance etc. To what extent this should also include interest payments depends very much on the constellation selected; as a rule each

municipality finances its services via the capital market on favourable terms - as a municipal loan or other similar loans mostly so that the ongoing interest payments also represent subsidies.

When reference is made to subsidies - referred to as state aid - within the framework of European law, it needs to be checked under Community law on state aid whether the allocation of funds by the public sector represents a case of so-called state aid. This is indeed the case if a third person or third persons are favoured by the allocation of funds. The element of favouring defined in Article 87 para. 1 of the Treaty Establishing the European Community exists if there is no reasonable ratio between the public service and entrepreneurial counter-service received, namely if the third party receives an unreasonably high payment from the public sector. (cf. Koenig & Kühling, NJW 2000 and in depth Koenig, Kühling & Ritter, 2001).

Article 87
(1) Save as otherwise provided in this Treaty, any aid granted by a Member State or through State resources in any form whatsoever which distorts or threatens to distort competition by favouring certain undertakings or the production of certain goods shall, in so far as it affects trade between Member States, be incompatible with the common market.

State aid exists if the favouring of certain undertakings or the production of certain goods distorts competition; this is the case if there is no reasonable proportion between the public service and the entrepreneurial counter-service received. In order to assess the adequacy of service-counter-service relationships, the EU Commission, having abandoned its initial reluctance to use this test, has shown a growing tendency to use the so-called "market economy investor test" Alfa Romeo [ECJ series, 1991, I: 1603 (1604 f.) marginal number 19ff.]. For this test to be satisfied it must be demonstrated that a private investor, whose purpose is to profit in the long run, would have acted in the same way the state did in its capacity as a shareholder (cf. D'sa, 1998: 67ff.; Koenig, ZIP 2000: 53, 57ff.).

Since the DMT rulings (ECJ series, 1999, I: 3913 (3932 f.), marginal number 17ff.) and Cityflyer Express (series 1998, II: 757, 776) marginal number 51), this approach has also been adopted in relation to payment accommodations and loans. It is not clear to what extent the same regulations also apply to venues such as stages, theatres and operas etc., both de facto and de jure, this is not the subject matter under review. Nonetheless, it is certainly worth mentioning a comment made by the former mayor of the city of Frankfurt, Achim Vandreike, in this context. He was responsible for sport at the time and oversaw the construction of the Commerzbank Arena in Frankfurt (podium event of 29 January 2008, ISPO Conference of Sport Sponsoring, Munich). When asked whether he thought the major investment the municipality of Frankfurt had made in the Frankfurt World Cup stadium was a wasted subsidy, the municipality having every reason to assume when it agreed to make the investment that at least 50% of its investment would be wasted, he basically replied that considering the much higher annual subsidies that are allocated to urban and state theatres it should certainly be permissible, all the more so given the enormous interest and importance of the sport (football) among the population.

In the absence of an exemption, Community law on state aid applies to ongoing state funding of sporting facilities. Both the case law of the ECJ and the legal practice of the Commission on this issue have progressed but they have not always concurred, which is not surprising given the large number of diverging case scenarios. However, when one attempts to identify a uniform regulation in respect of subsidies at operator level, any favouring of the users of an infrastructure that distorts competition, particularly the main club leasing the infrastructure, is to be counteracted by ensuring sporting facilities are extended to become multifunctional and offer non-discriminatory access. This is the most likely and effective way of refuting the allegation of inappropriate favouring.

Even though it can be assumed that the majority of sporting facilities represent a user-specific infrastructure, which is likely to hold true at least of football stadiums that do not have a running track, inappropriate favouring of undertakings can be ruled out in view of the appropriateness of non-discriminatory usage fees. In this context it is often necessary to incorporate a relevant compulsory arrangement into operator agreements concluded between the public sector and the private operator. In doing so, the public sector can ensure that an enforceable obligation has been imposed on the private sector, ruling out inappropriate favouring of undertakings.

The jurisprudence and decisions quoted prove that in addition to the public sector offering direct financial benefits, the provision of energy, water, sewerage generally by public utilities without doubt represents state aid within the meaning of Community law unless they receive adequate levels of pay that are customary in the particular market. Even though public utilities are generally privately-owned companies, they tend to come closely under the jurisdiction of the municipalities, be it as majority shareholders or as a member of the Supervisory Board, fulfilling municipal tasks, meaning that the legal relationships they enter into come under the scope of application of Community law on state subsidies.

7.4 Acts of law and court decisions

Up to the mid-1970s, European bodies did not produce any publications dealing with the issue of "sport". Nonetheless, during the past 35 years, a dense network of legal regulations has emerged, derived, in particular, from the court decisions of the ECJ, which the latter did not hand down for purposes of sport, but rather based on a general interpretation and specification of EC or EU law. These legal cases, which have hitherto been examined more from a legal than from a political science perspective, play a key role as regards future policy analyses.

In the case of European sports policy, "policies" are closely linked to the constitutional dimension. The individual cases, acts of law and court decisions which have been cited here as examples have provided major impetus in terms of shaping the legal structure of European sport. Particularly as a result of having to deal with sport in the context of the Bosman ruling, EC/EU bodies began to look at sports policy more closely. They drew up a number of opinions on the area of sport, on the one hand addressing the "lack of coordination" and, on the other, highlighting the social importance of sport. These cases are briefly outlined below.

Walrave and Koch case
It all began with the Walrave and Koch case which resulted from the problematic situation of two Dutchmen who wished to work as pacemakers for the cycling teams of other Member States at world championships but who were prevented from doing so by the statutes of the International Cycling Union (UCI). The two sportsmen brought an action before the ECJ. The Court found that "the practice of sport is subject to Community law only in so far as it constitutes an economic activity within the meaning of Article 2 of the Treaty" (Walrave & Koch case, 1974). The ECJ further ruled that the prohibition on discrimina-

tion based on nationality does not affect the composition of sports teams, in particular national teams, "the formation of which is a question of purely sporting interest and as such has nothing to do with economic activity" (Walrave & Koch case, 1974). In this ruling, sport was, for the first time, perceived as an "economic activity" in the context of Community policy (Groll, Gütt & Mittag, 2008: 40).

The increasing economic importance of sport was also reflected in the changed international sporting environment. In the autumn of 1981, the 11th Congress of the IOC and the IOC Session in Baden-Baden immediately following it conferred on sports federations the right to decide independently whether they would allow professional athletes to participate in the Olympic Games, which had previously been strictly forbidden by the Amateur clause. Then, three years later, in 1984, the first Olympic Games featuring a significant number of professional athletes were held in Los Angeles. As a consequence, the economic importance of sport increased enormously. This commercialisation of sport was also a decisive factor in the development of European sports policy. Parrish cites the commercialisation of European sport as being one of the major reasons why a relationship between sport and the EU exists at all (Parrish, 2003: 9).

Donà/Mantero

In 1976, in the "Donà/Mantero" case, the European Court of Justice dealt with a complaint filed by the Italian player's agent Gaetano Donà, who challenged the restrictions on nationality that applied in Italian professional football leagues at the time. Donà had been hired by the then president of FC Rovigo to recruit new players for the club. When Donà presented the club president with Belgian players, the president refused to consider his offers or to pay the expenses that Donà had incurred, referring to statutes of the Italian Football Federation that only allowed Italian players to participate in matches in the Italian football league. Donà was of the opinion that this provision was contrary to the freedom of movement provisions in Articles 39 and 49 of the Treaty Establishing the European Community and he sued Mantero for payment of his expenses. In order to clarify the applicability of the freedom of movement provisions, the court in Rovigo initiated a preliminary ruling procedure before the European Court of Justice. The applicability of Community law to sport was again the overriding issue being submitted for decision in this case (Grodde, 2007: 110f.).

In its opinion, the ECJ confirmed its observations in the Walrave and Koch case, however it emphasised more clearly than previously that sporting activities were always part of economic life and hence Community law was applicable in this case if the activity could be characterised as gainful employment or remunerated service. Just as in the Walrave and Koch case, the competent court did not make a conclusive ruling in the Donà/Mantero case. Therefore, it was still unclear whether a professional footballer is to be classified as a worker pursuant to Article 39 EC or as a service provider pursuant to Article 49 EC.

Over time, the players involved lost sight of this purely legal dispute between the EC and the sports sector. In addition, no other noteworthy events requiring a detailed definition occurred, so that one can speak of a lengthy phase of "coexistence" between sport and EC politics. In the narrower sense, it was not until the Bosman ruling of December 1995 that the foundations for a reorientation of the content framework of sports policy were laid.

The Bosman ruling of 1995
How strongly the ECJ has influenced the legal framework of European sports policy is shown by the so-called "Bosman ruling" made by the European Court of Justice on 15 December 1995. The basis of the dispute was the right to freedom of movement laid down in Article 48 of the Treaty Establishing the European Community, which the Belgian professional footballer was also claiming for the case of a transfer to another football club. Jean-Marc Bosman took legal action against his former club before various Belgian civil courts at different levels, submitting that the club should not be permitted to demand a transfer fee as this was not compatible with European Community law and the provisions relating to the fundamental freedoms in the single market as a result of which a worker can freely choose his place of work in the European Union.

In its ruling of 15 December 1995, the European Court of Justice - which had been asked to make a preliminary ruling in the Bosman case - ruled wholly in favour of the applicant Bosman, holding that the transfer system could not be reconciled with Community law. Unexpectedly for both the general public and sports experts, in the law on transfers and the nationality clause, the judges in Luxembourg set aside two key regulations that characterised professional football (Mittag, 2007; Pfister, 1998; Fritzweiler, 1998). Once a professional footballer's contract expired, clubs were no longer allowed to demand a transfer fee if the player moved to a different club within the European Union. In addition, teams within the European Union were now able to field an unlimited number of EU foreigners. The ruling changed the "core structures of football" (Mittag, 2007: 209). Within a very short space of time, the percentage of foreigners playing in western European leagues and also players' salaries increased enormously because the money that had previously been paid as transfer fees between the clubs was now passed on directly to the professional players (cf. Mittag, 2007).

The ECJ's ruling subsequently led to considerable legal uncertainty in the sporting world with regard to the relevance of EU competition law (Parrish 2003, 12). As a consequence, the European Commission received numerous sport-related complaints (Siekmann & Soek, 2005: 26). The European Commission's Directorate-General for Competition (DG IV), for instance, received 55 complaints in relation to sport. These touched on issues such as the role of sports organisations, television rights or commercial sponsorship (Groll, Gütt & Mittag, 2008: 42).

The transfer dispute of 2001
The fact that the European Commission also exerted a strong influence on the content of European sports policy alongside the ECJ is evidenced by the dispute regarding the law on transfers. It all began with Competition Commissioner Mario Monti's attempt in August 2000 to bring the transfer system used in football fully into line with Community law in economic terms (Mittag, 2007). Monti's idea was that football players should in future be treated just like normal workers. In addition to the complete abolition of transfer fees, Monti called for the introduction of a right of notice for professional footballers, which would have given the latter the same status as other workers and the right to give three to six months' notice. For clubs, this would have meant that players could have opted out of a current contract almost at will.

After a lengthy tug-of-war between the European Commission, FIFA and UEFA - in which the G14 also continually weighed in with critical objections - an agreement was finally reached on modified transfer legislation. At a summit meeting in March 2001, at which FIFA was represented by Sepp Blatter, UEFA by its President, Lennart Johansson, and the European Commission by Commissioners Monti (Competition), Reding (Education) and Diamantopoulou (Social Affairs), agreement was reached on a solution that would, among other things, see football players having to sign a contract for a minimum of one year in future, but would limit contracts to a maximum of five years.

The Kolpak and Simutenkov cases

In May 2003, the ECJ dealt with the restrictions on foreigners in the handball players' regulations for non-EU countries. Kolpak is the "Bosman of handball", as it were. Based on the fact that an Association Agreement existed between Slovakia and the EU, the Luxembourg judge was of the view that the interest of unrestricted exercise of one's profession in the single Community market outweighed the sporting grounds cited by the federations, such as the argument of support for young athletes (cf. Schmeilzl, 2004). The prerequisites for exercising one's profession are proper residence in the EU and a legal contract of employment (Groll, Gütt & Mittag, 2008: 42).

Another ruling made by the ECJ in 2005 further specified and reinforced the importance of EC/EU law for sport. In its ruling regarding the Russian professional football player Igor Simutenkov, the ECJ found that a nationality clause which, unlike with the Bosman ruling, concerned a non-EU sportsman was unlawful. Simutenkov, who was a player at the Deportivo Tenerife club, had a Spanish work permit and residence permit. The Spanish Football Association had also issued Simutenkov with a licence for non-EU players, the regulations stating that only a limited number of players from non-Member countries could be fielded. With reference to an Association Agreement concluded between the European Union and Russia, Simutenkov submitted an application for an unrestricted licence. The ECJ confirmed Simutenkov's view, stating that nationality clauses in European professional sport were invalid if the Association Agreement concluded with the EU regulated equal treatment in respect of working conditions.

In the "Simutenkov" case, the ECJ consistently followed its precedent from 2003. Even in the Kolpak ruling (see above), the judges emphasised that the equal treatment stipulated in the Association Agreement between the EU and Slovakia also applied to other sports federations. In view of the consistent legal decisions in the "Kolpak" and "Simutenkov" rulings and the large number of Association Agreements between the European Union and third countries (e.g. the Coto-

nou Agreement with 77 ACP states), it is to be expected that existing
nationality clauses will continue gradually to disappear.

Deliège and Lehtonen case

Based on the fact that the Nice Declaration refers to the special characteristics of sport, the ECJ felt obliged to consider the special features of national sports federation law before EU law in the Deliège
and Lehtonen rulings made in 2000. In the Deliège case, national judo
federations were given the right to continue to set selection criteria for
international competitions for their athletes themselves. The Lehtonen
case deals with the time limit on transfers where the player is still to
be fielded during the current season. The ECJ declared that the sub-
missions in respect of the issues raised under competition law were
inadmissible as such interventions could be justified on non-economic
grounds. The change in the legal position, which is undoubtedly the
most effective instrument for exerting influence, highlights, in these
examples, the cooperative development process of sport and European
legislation (Groll, Gütt & Mittag, 2008: 42).

Meca-Medina and Majcen ruling

The Meca-Medina and Majcen ruling of 2004 is a further example.
The ruling is the first case where the ECJ applied Articles 81 and 82
of the Treaty Establishing the European Community to the sports sector and this is why it is to be examined in more detail. The reason for
the ruling was the action brought by two professional swimmers who
had lodged a complaint with the European Commission against the
anti-doping rules of the International Swimming Federation FINA
(Fédération International de Natation Amateur) because they unlaw-
fully infringed their economic freedoms. In their complaint, the appli-
cants challenged the compatibility of certain regulations adopted by
the IOC and implemented by FINA and certain practices relating to
doping control with the Community rules on competition and the freedom to provide services. According to the complaint, the application
of those rules led to the infringement of the athletes' economic freedoms, guaranteed inter alia by Article 49 EC and, from the point of
view of competition law, to the infringement of the rights which the
athletes could assert under Articles 81 EC and 82 EC. The EU Commission rejected the complaint on the grounds that the rules were
purely sports rules. The European Court of First Instance (ECFI) concurred with this view. Although the ECJ, to which the athletes had ap-

pealed, quashed the ECFI's ruling, it still rejected the complaint. In its reasons, the ECJ intimated that the EU rules on competition were generally applicable to the rules of sports federations and that an exception could only be made in individual cases if matters of a purely sporting nature were involved which did not affect competition. However, in the case of the swimmers who had lodged the complaint, the ECJ concluded that anti-doping rules did not constitute an unlawful restriction of competition because they served a legitimate purpose. Legal scholars consider the ruling to be as far-reaching for European sports federations as the Bosman ruling (Groll, Gütt & Mittag, 2008: 43).

The Gambelli and Placanica lottery rulings

The most important lottery rulings at European level - the Gambelli ruling of 2003 and the Placanica ruling of 2007 - also show that sport has increasingly been interfacing with business. In the "Gambelli" proceedings, the European Court of Justice had to rule on whether a monopoly that confers the sole right to organise sports betting on the state is compatible with the fundamental freedoms of the European Union in respect of the freedom of establishment and the freedom to provide services under Articles 43 EC and 49 EC. The backdrop to the proceedings was the conviction handed down to the Italian businessman Piergiorgio Gambelli for having illegally organised betting in Italy as an intermediary for the bookmaker Stanley International Betting Ltd., which is licensed in England. Gambelli was prohibited from engaging in the business practice of accepting bets in Italy and forwarding them to England on the grounds that this constituted an offence of fraud against the state. The European Court of Justice, however, held that the Italian regulation upon which the decision was based was a restriction on Europe-wide freedom of establishment and freedom to provide services. The actual novelty of this ruling had already been preceded by the "Schindler" (1994), "Läärä" and "Zenatti" (both 2000) lottery rulings, where the court had found "that the State cannot, on the one hand, invoke the maintenance of public order while, on the other, being allowed to call upon people to participate in sports betting, lotteries and other games of chance and generating significant revenue therefrom".

The gambling market in Italy was partially liberalised at the time of the proceedings in the "Placanica vs. Italy" case. In Italy, unlike in Germany, a limited number of licences (for sports betting: 1,000) had been issued for the organisation of gambling. Massimiliano Placanica, after whom this ruling is named, and other persons were charged before a national court with having collected bets without a licence and having forwarded them to a British bookmaker. However, the competent court questioned the compatibility of the licensing system enshrined in Italian law with European Community law and, against this backdrop, turned to the European Court of Justice, requesting a decision of general principle in this case. In the "Placanica" case, Articles 43 EC and 49 EC were interpreted "as precluding national legislation, such as that at issue in the main proceedings, which excludes - and, moreover, continues to exclude - from the betting and gaming sector operators in the form of companies whose shares are quoted on the regulated markets" (ECJ C-338/04 in conjunction with C-359/04 and C-360/04). Hence, the European Court of Justice held that the limitation of licences in Italy was in breach of European law. Community law places restrictions on Member States' jurisdiction in respect of national criminal penalties (imposed on the accused). In this regard, the European Court of Justice stated that "a Member State may not apply a criminal penalty for failure to complete an administrative formality where such completion has been refused or rendered impossible by the Member State concerned, in infringement of Community law".

7.5 Interim conclusions

Neither the EU Commission nor the European Court of Justice claim to have any direct case law or legislative power for the area of sport. The autonomy of sports in terms of its internal rules and participation in the narrower sense is untouched. Nonetheless, other authorisation bases are having an indirect impact on the internal relationships of sport. In addition, sport enjoys the privilege of exemption in some areas, for instance, in the selling of broadcasting rights, the transfer of "young" athletes and the nationality clauses that limit the number of "non-nationals" who can be fielded in competitions. Tolerated deviations from other European regulations exist in the areas of tax benefits and the financing of sporting facilities.

Sports federations - corporations and clubs - are subject to separate regulation by European rules in terms of their economic activities and in relation to the organisation of employment and the signing up of athletes. This is where the provisions of the law on competition and protection of the freedom of movement of capital, the freedom of establishment and the freedom of movement of workers come into the picture.

The problem associated with making a distinction between sporting activity that is "also deemed economic activity" outlined in the introduction and "non-economic" sporting activity therefore cannot be fully solved. Insofar as the specific characteristics of sport are mentioned, this argument is frequently used to justify conditions that do not comply with European law in terms of their alleged necessity, an argument that is rarely verifiable. The problem of delimitation cannot be solved at the level of rules. As the large number of conceivable cases scenarios and the different conditions in the individual countries of the European Community make any specifications appear arbitrary and possibly even unreasonable, "flexible" case law as opposed to "rigid" rules would appear to be more appropriate even if this contravenes the pursuit of legal certainty and calculability. However, strengthening the autonomy of sport and the specific regulation of additional exemptions could also create greater legal certainty. Insofar as exemptions such as the selling of television rights or the approval of subsidising sporting facilities has been created by formal legal means or have been tolerated up to now, the burden of proof continues to be on sport, which has to prove that the exemptions constitute special regulations that are justified. This is where greater focus will be placed on coherent lines of argument in future that do not contravene European law, but are compatible with it.

8 Sports organisation in Europe

In order to be able to understand every single development process at European level, it is necessary to be familiar with and to refer to the background of the individual conditions at national level and to developments in the countries involved. The distinct approach adopted by the French government regarding the doping problem and the comparatively cautious approach adopted by the German government have to be seen against the background that a direct, governmental response in Germany stands in contrast to the principle of non-governmental sporting organisations (i.e. the "autonomy of sport", which were in charge of the problem of doping for a long time), whereas in France the responsibility for this specific sports-related topic (as sport in general) comes under the government's direct remit. National sporting systems in competitive sport not only appear as partners (e.g. in the fight against doping), they actually compete with each other and with the sport systems of the non-EU-countries. Referring to this context, Digel says, "...that it is surprising how few responsible persons in various disciplines of competitive sport are familiar with the structure of their competitors, how intensively some sport associations persist in their traditional pattern of action and how infrequently federations are ready to subject the work they perform in competitive sport to scrutiny" (Digel, 2001: 244). Especially whilst drawing comparisons with other systems, one could easily resolve one's own "operating-blindness" and identify the weakness in one's own system. Moreover the organisational structures of sport are subject to ongoing change. Notably within the new EU Member States in Eastern Europe, the process of adapting sport to the framework of democracy and market economy is still very much ongoing. Efficient and suboptimal efficient systems can assume a model function and can contribute to achieving success and to avoiding mistakes. The dynamism of the various systems needs to be seen beyond the problem of limited comparability of the sport systems. This can be illustrated by taking Great Britain as an example. Sport has been ministerially organised since 1990; initially, the competence lay with the Minister of Ecology, afterwards with the Minister of Education and Science, three years later the Ministry of National Heritage was placed in charge of sport and since 1997, sport has been integrated into the competence of the Department of Culture, Media and Sport.

Detailed structures of sport-related legislation and the national sporting systems can be taken from the country profiles of the EU Member

States. To begin with, the structural and organisational characteristics that create the framework of the country profiles shall be described in brief, beginning with the general organisation of sporting activity and the development of sport clubs in combination with the societal role of sport. This breakdown follows the multi-level system in the European Union ranging from individual level, via the level of clubs and providers right up to national level and the interaction between all these levels which characterises sport in the European Union.

8.1 Organisation of sporting activity

The populations' involvement in sporting activity is associated with the political concept "Sport for All", which was developed at the European Council's level and which is being implemented in many countries today. The success of the national policies can be shown by the participation-rate, thus this section of the population that exercises or plays sport indicate that they do engage in sporting activity.

Sport possesses three basic organisational forms: self-organisation, club organisation and miscellaneous organisations (such as commercial and other provider). Another possibility is of course to divide sport into two categories as suggested by Wopp (2008), namely formal and informal organisational forms. However, we will use the three basic organisational forms in order to emphasise the differences between sport clubs and other sport providers.

While sport was mainly practised in clubs from the 1960s to the 1980s, the image has gradually changed over the last twenty years. In contrast to the absolute monopoly of sport clubs before, privately-organised sport has increased enormously and commercial providers have even become more attractive to people interested in sport. Regarding developments at European level, commercial providers and sport clubs were of equal ranking in 2004. 16% of the active Europeans prefer to engage in sports in clubs, while 15% exercise in commercial gyms (van Bottenburg et al., 2005: 45). At pan-European level, the development of membership in sport clubs creates a heterogeneous image. In countries, in which sport clubs are traditionally fixed (the Netherlands, Germany, Belgium, Ireland, Denmark and Great Britain), organised club sport has grown, while other countries have witnessed a decrease in club sport (France, Luxembourg, Italy and Greece). The largest section of the European population (52%)

exercises on a self-organised level, this applies predominantly to the elderly population (van Bottenburg et al., 2005: 47).

Non-organisational sport

It is not easy to define self-organised sport, meaning exercising independently of institutions and organisational Constitutions. Leisure sport is associated with non-organisational sports, which is seen as being independent from formal, temporal and institutional forces. The term non-organisational sports refers to activities performed during leisure time for which no regulations or rules are needed (cf. Dieckert & Wopp, 2002). Moreover, professional athletes' individual training schedule can contain elements of self-organised training (e.g. jogging, gymnastics). Accordingly, self-organised sport is not congruent with leisure sport, even though Dieckerts' and Wopps' definition is generally correct.

According to Dieckert and Wopp (2002), the social background to the development of self-organised sport in Germany is the appearance of a "self-help culture". People do not need the experience of sport clubs or professionals (e.g. trainers) to exercise. Based on the informal character of this sport context, the data available tends to be imprecise and inconsistent. Though in 1996 Opaschowski stated that 11.9 million Germans were exercising at non-organisational level; this corresponds to 19% of the population. It was proven in further studies that exercising and clubs and self-organised sport are not seen as an "either-or-model". Membership in a football club does not exclude additional jogging or cycling outside the organisation. A study covering several German communes conducted by Hübner (1994) showed that 50% of the population who engage actively in sports exercise on a self-organised bases (as well). For years, the most popular sports that are self-organised have consistently been cycling, swimming and running. This can even be translated to the Member States of the European Union. While there is a lack of detailed studies, they coincide, by and large, with information on the most popular leisure time activities and the data regarding organised and non-organised sport participation.

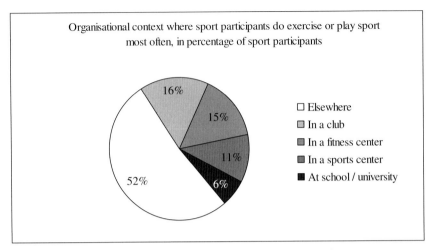

Figure 3: Organisational context of sport activity in %
(Based on European Commission 2004: Eurobarometer 62.0 (213)

Sport in clubs

The European Union designates sport clubs and federations as one of the characteristic features of the European Model of Sport (cf. European Model of Sport). Up until the 1980s, sporting activity was confined almost exclusively to sport clubs in the majority of European countries. This pattern has changed considerably over the past two to three decades. Although sport clubs continue to play an important role, they have certainly lost their organisational monopoly (cf. Steinbach et al., 2007). New commercial and non-profit-making providers have begun to emerge alongside sport clubs, creating much greater diversity in terms of sport providers.

As mentioned above, in respect of membership figures, the dominance of sport clubs in Europe has been put into perspective by a growth in the commercial fitness industry. When regarding developments at European level, commercial providers and sport clubs are almost of equal importance nowadays. Around 16% of Europeans who actively engage in sport give preference to sport clubs as providers whereas 15% use commercial gyms and fitness facilities. 11% use mainly local sport centres, 6% opt for sporting activities offered by schools or universities. Other providers are less important (Eurobarometer 62.0; van Bottenburg et al., 2005: 45). For Austria, for instance, the same study revealed slightly higher values regarding the preference for sport clubs and commercial providers (18% respectively). This places Austria in the upper medium bracket by European standards in relation to the importance of sport clubs. Sport clubs play a much more important role in Denmark, Germany and the Netherlands. In nearly all European countries, the number of men who exercise in sport clubs is much higher, whereas women tend to prefer commercial sport providers.

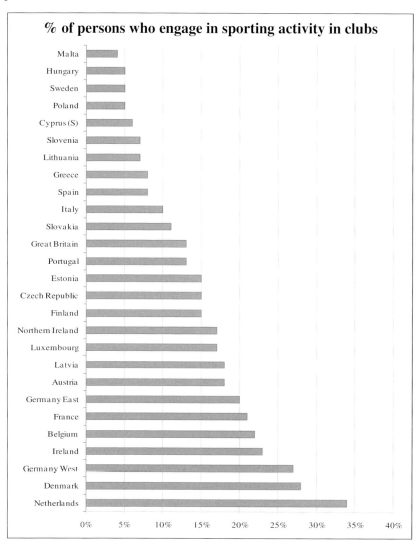

Figure 4: Sport clubs as the preferred provider for exercising.
(Based on European Commission 2004: Special Eurobarometer 62.0)

Sport with other providers

Until a couple of decades ago, most people engaged in sport in sport clubs of which they were a member. Since the early 1980s, sport clubs faced competition not only from self-organised exercise, but also from private competitors, especially in the fitness industry as well as from other providers such as adult education centres or ecclesiastical institutions. This chapter will elaborate on the different organisational forms of clubs, commercial providers and other providers. Subsequently, the meaning of sport clubs will be highlighted. This will be followed by an evaluation of organised sport.

General overview of providers:

- Commercial companies (company sports)
- Pedagogical institutions
- Social institutions
- Ecclesiastical institutions
- Adult education centres
- Health insurance companies
- Foundations
- Hybrid forms (co-operation between companies and clubs)

In the 1980s and 1990s, the welfare-based and some social campaigns were gradually replaced by a health-oriented policy in most European countries (cf. van Bottenburg et al., 2005). The "Sport for all" campaign in the 1960s, 1970s and 1980s was replaced in the 1990s by the "Europe on the move" campaign. Accordingly, fitness-oriented sport, which is offered by commercial providers, experienced enormous growth. People began to attach more importance to health, fitness and a slender and muscular body and on developing self-confidence and reaching a special social status. Even the growing focus on older age-groups enabled special sport offers to become established in the field of health-promotion, which can only be achieved under educated supervision and within a certain framework that cannot be self-organised.

At pan-European level, it can be said that exercising in an organisational framework depends on a person's gender and age. Fitness, strength and endurance are much more popular among young people, resulting in a bigger representation of this group in gyms. In all countries in which statistical data are available for the organisational aspects of sport, this data shows that men are over-represented in sport and in sport clubs. Women tend to exercise at gyms and their numbers are much higher than men's in this field of sport. Gyms and health clubs have established themselves as an addition to or as an alternative to sport clubs and other sports groups. They give people the opportunity to decide themselves when they want to exercise; social contact (in contrast to sport clubs) does not involve any commitment. Dancing, fitness and aerobics, but also some other new trends or extreme sports are mainly offered and implemented by commercial organisations. These providers are able to respond to the changing needs of their customers with new offers, independent of traditional structures. Here, specified service details take the place of honorary posts, which are much needed in clubs. The commercial sports industry promotes special effects regarding body styling, weight loss and promoting fitness and strength. They try to reach their goals by having modern studios, professional equipment, even very flexible opening hours, customer-oriented management, individual supervision, etc.

Schubert (2008: 144ff.) distinguishes commercial providers as follows:

- Gyms and fitness facilities
- Commercial sporting facilities (e.g. tennis courts and squash centres)
- (Commercial) schools for sport disciplines (e.g. sailing schools, surf schools or riding schools)
- Ballet, dance and gymnastics studios
- Commercial sport providers who provide service at specific times in different venues: sport tour operators, personal trainers and event organisers

According to Schulke (2002) besides a wide range of commercial sporting providers, a lot of non-profit organisations like ecclesiastical organisations or pedagogical and social institutions offer sports-like leisure activities. These range from games and exercise in nursery schools to leisure sports offered by social services for the elderly like functional or chair-gymnastics, walking tours and relaxation classes.

A lot of health prevention alternatives are offered especially in co-operation with health insurance companies. In particular osteoporosis-prophylaxis groups or back strengthening classes are offered to health-endangered groups. These classes are funded by employers' liability insurance associations, social insurances and health insurance companies, if the quality is secured for special prevention classes.

More and more sporting programmes are departing from traditional competition and training concepts and are moving towards individual, exercise-orientated leisure activities. In 1974, the German Sports Federation founded runners' meetings (Lauftreffs) which became a great success. This "sports-offer" is widely known in Germany and has been imitated globally. Whether organised by clubs, company sport clubs, privately or based on a spontaneous combination of people, interest groups comprising people of all ages, both male and female, of different performance levels came together to exercise (Dieckert & Wopp, 2002). In addition to runners' meetings, more offers were developed for new trend sports such as Nordic walking or skating. Many trainers initialised small training sessions or interest groups and educated individuals asked their neighbours if they would like to join them on a walk in a nearby forest.

The traditional sport offers apart from gyms and sport clubs are available in company sport clubs. Company sport is organised in comprehensive federations, just like the club system. Like the Austrian Company Sport Federation, most of the Company Sports federations are independent institutions. They are organised at federal state level and are a member of the National Sports Confederations. For example, the Austrian company sports federation is a member of the Austrian Sports Organisations and the European Company Sports Federation.

In 1962, the European Federation for Company Sport (EFCS) was founded in Switzerland, guaranteeing the promotion of company sports at international level. The international organisation combines 25 member countries, whose objective it is to exchange professional knowledge regarding health promotion at company level and to promote company sport in Europe. Fair play and a company sports-related corporate identity are promoted by the European Company Sport Games in summer and winter (cf. www.efcs.org).

The European Agency for Safety and Health Protection at the Workplace, which has its headquarters in Bilbao, is a three-tiered institution that brings together representatives from governments, employers' and employees' organisations. The Agency's task is to make workplaces more secure, healthier and more productive. To achieve this goal and to support a culture of risk-prevention, knowledge and information are pooled and passed on. The agency helps to interpret European legislation regarding safety and health protection at work. Among other things, promotion of physical activity at the workplace and company sports offers after finishing time are found.

Besides the huge sport offers provided for example by health insurance companies and other companies, a lot of small examples of alternative sport concepts and offers can be found in many European countries. For example, the biggest fitness centre chain in Sweden is breaking new ground in a very commercial fitness industry. From a welfare perspective, there are 140 branches with 400,000 members in 10 European countries today. The concept offers easy access to sport for everyone. The aim is to create a positive and active life-style and build a bridge between health-promotion and sporting activity.

8.2 Development of sport clubs and the societal role of sport

The real migration movements of athletes away from sport clubs towards commercial providers or self-organised sporting activity could be observed more soberly if it was irrelevant from the health perspective in which organisational form people engage in sport. However, it is the societal role of sport clubs and the values that set them apart from the majority of other commercial providers that make then a special object of research. Sporting activity should not just be fostered in sport clubs specifically in relation to youth work (educating people to engage in sport), but also in order to support personal development (education through sport) (Balster and Brettschneider, 2002: 16). This gives rise to the question whether and to what extent sport clubs are capable of fulfilling this requirement.

We assume that the characteristic features of a sport club creates the basis for an environment that can teach values in which the above-mentioned goal of educating people through sport can be achieved, at least in theory.

According to Jütting (2008: 133), clubs have the following characteristics:

- Orientation to members' interests
- Voluntary membership
- Democratic decision-making structures
- Voluntary involvement
- Independence from non-members

The above-mentioned proof that sport clubs have lost their organisational monopoly has, inter alia, given rise to conflicts between those who wish to abandon traditional concepts within sport clubs and those who wish sport to be oriented to the principles of modern service companies (cf. Heinemann, 1999: 29). There is also no doubt about the fact that sport clubs are undergoing a process of radical change which is aptly reflected in the terms "differentiation", "centralisation" and "professionalisation" (Heinemann, 1999: 29). This change in conjunction with the tendency to apply rules of the market economy to sport clubs too is leading to a depletion of traditional sporting values (Rugutzer, 2008: 95), with many an author urging people to call these values to mind.

Grupe (2007: 46) recalls four basic values and orientation patterns which define the self-conception of organised sport. First the effort involved in organising sport based on the idea of man, in which people can move freely and independently, without following any ideology or doctrine. Secondly, it highlights the meaning of sport for people's physical and mental health. Thirdly, it is the realisation that trust needs to be included in the educational impact of sport. Fourthly, the social importance of sport is highlighted which is based on fairness and a sense of community which has been destroyed by the use of tyranny (not referring only to Germany, contrary to what Grupe does).

Putnam and Goss (2001) talk more generally about the social capital of voluntary unions, which can be distinguished into formal/informal social capital, high/low density of social capital, intrinsic/extrinsic social capital and bridge-building/binding social capital. To sum up the social-capital-theory, it indicates that social networks evoke effects. The positive effects can be combined into three theorems, according to Jütting (2003: 13f.):

- Clubs produce reasonable goods and output (productivity theorem)
- Clubs contribute majorly to social integration (integration theorem)
- Clubs are the institutional expression of an active, democratic civil society (democracy theorem)

The dark sides which even voluntary unions can have (oligarchic or authoritarian structures), are not disregarded. However according to Jütting (2003: 219) networks and the production of goods emerges from the activities of voluntary unions which can be referred to without restriction as social wealth.

The issue of the future orientation of sport clubs has become a topic of some controversy. Whereas some authors advocate that sport clubs should perceive themselves as service providers in future, others support the view that sport clubs are important as solidarity communities. Opaschowski established that sport clubs are no longer clubs for idealists. He sees opportunities for sport clubs that will be able to offer their members consumption-oriented and service-oriented services in future (cf. Opaschowski, 2000). By contrast, the latest discussion about sport science in Germany proves the keen interest club members have in relationship patterns and patterns of action based on solidarity communities (cf. Braun & Nagel, 2005). The relevance of the social and emotional ties members have with their sport club which has been proven in empirical surveys (cf. Nagel, Conzelmann & Gabler, 2004: 148) mitigates against adopting a simple strategy of sport clubs imitating commercial sport providers.

Notwithstanding this, the data of empirical surveys and observations of trends in club practice indicate that the offers, particularly of leisure sport, sport for all and sport to enhance health and fitness, need to be expanded. A (partial) professionalisation of organisational structures, greater orientation to members' interests, upgrading honorary posts and greater orientation to quality standards are all needed. In particular the quality of care provided by trainers and coaches and the competency of club managers seem to be of paramount importance to the members of sport clubs (cf. Weiß et al., 2007: 76; Nagel, Conzelmann & Gabler, 2004).

This professionalisation and service orientation of sport clubs must not, however, be at the expense of the basic orientation of clubs as solidarity communities. In order to accomplish this, according to Steinbach et al. (2007), it is important that as many members as possible be involved in the decision-making processes and services provided by the sport clubs. This does not necessarily happen through formal voluntary activity. Rather, there are less binding forms of involvement and participation. This task of "achieving one goal as well as the other" constitutes a major challenge for organisational development. Sports federations should therefore provide comprehensive advisory services to the sport clubs that are their members.

8.3 Characteristics of structure and organisation

Describing the similarities of the diverse European sports models against the background of the definite diversity is only possible at a superficial level; a detailed comparison would not allow uniform conclusions to be drawn. According to Tokarski et al. (2004) a simplified, but for all countries applicable scheme for describing the structure of organised sport is used, which is based on the following characteristics: legislation, functionality and the role of governmental, semi-governmental and non-governmental sporting organisations.

Legislation

The huge variety within the sport systems in Europe is highlighted by the inclusion of sport in the EU Member States' Constitution and a further consideration in sport-related laws. It extends from sport being referred to in the Constitution as in Spain, through explicit sports legislation as in France, or to no specific reference being made to sport by issuing statutory regulations as in the Leisure Time Act in Denmark, to little mention being made of sport in legislation, which is characteristic of the German and Austrian sporting system (cf. Ternes, 2002). According to Tokarski and Steinbach (2001) as the lowest common denominator, it can be identified that in young democracies like Spain and Portugal, sport has been incorporated into the Constitution, using specific sports legislation. Last but not least, it depends on an increased awareness of the social role of sport, which is validated by a trend towards more sport-related regulations. For example, Italy discusses tax advantages for sport clubs (cf. Madella, 2004) and the Netherlands, which had a liberal sport system, have plans to adopt their own sport-related laws (cf. Veldhoven, 2004). Existing sport-related laws are based on interventionist models and give authority to the government to influence the self-administration of sport. The most extreme example is Spain. The Sports Council, the Consejo Superior de Desportes, which is joined directly to the Ministry of Education, Culture and Sports has the right to dismiss chairmen and members of sports federations (cf. Tarragó, 2004). The difference compared to laws such as the "Act over body-culture and sport in the Russian Federation" passed in 1999, are striking. The Russian government can influence sport in financial and organisational terms, by organising sporting events in the field of public and competitive sport (cf. Burk, 2001). The EU Member States do not have the legal background to have such a direct influence of sport, but according to Jütting (1999) a "performance mixture" based on four sporting systems, is guaranteed. Even the schools' sporting system is based on governmental institutions, while to a large extent, exercising in private, non-commercial and commercial areas takes place without governmental intervention. A further similarity within the framework of sport-related legislation in Europe are the two conventions, whose ratification can be seen as the readiness to subordinate themselves to supranational legislation. As a restriction, the voluntariness of the ratification of these conventions needs to be mentioned.

Governmental and semi-governmental sport organisations

The institutional diversity does not decrease within the field of governmental, sport-related responsibility. Direct competency for the Ministère des Sports in France or the Department of Tourism, Sport and Recreation in Ireland has been created, while in Denmark's or Italy's Ministries of Education, only subdivisions are in charge of sports. The governmental responsibility in centralistic controlled countries is at national level, e.g. in France or Greece, while in countries with a federal system the responsibility lies with the federal states, e.g. as in Germany or Austria. In Belgium, sport is part of the responsibility of the three-language community. Furthermore, the existence or non-existence of consulting institutions can be taken into consideration in relation to the responsibility for sport. The Irish Sport Council, initiated by the Irish government, plays an important role for the self-administration and development of sport in Ireland. By contrast, the National Sport Council in Finland deals only with questions regarding national sport policies. The Portuguese Secretary of State is supported by up to three public institutions in promoting sport federations, in sport education and sport infrastructure (cf. Tokarski & Steinbach, 2001). Even the extent of influence accorded in individual national legislation ranges between financial support to delegating and controlling tasks in sport-related administration. In summary it can be said that no consistent conclusion can be drawn regarding institutionalisation and liability at national level for sport in Europe (cf. Ternes, 2002). But causal structures are distinguishable, because countries with explicit sport legislation possess diverse governmental structures, some even have their own Ministry of Sport, and the political system influences the institutional integration of sport at governmental level (cf. Jütting, 1999). An extended international comparison with China and the USA shows pan-European similarities. First of all, every

European country has an institution that is in charge of sport, and secondly, the government does not have exclusive competence for sport.

Non-governmental sport organisations

The basis for the European sport system is created by the national federations with their approximately 700,000 sport clubs (Eurobarometer, 2004). In almost every EU Member State, sport is represented by umbrella associations, combining the national sports federations. A typical example is the German Olympic Sports Committee (DOSB) that emerged from the merger of the German Sport Association (DSB) and the National Olympic Committee (NOC) on 20 May 2006. The National Olympic Committees are either the representatives of Olympic sport in their respective country or, as in some EU Member States, are entrusted with the function of the National Sports Confederation. One exception is Spain which has no umbrella association and where the national sports federations represent the highest organisational level. In some countries, sport clubs and sports federations are combined in several umbrella associations, for example in Austria, where sports federations and politically-oriented associations are present at national level. Moreover, some European NOCs are financially and/or administratively dependent on governmental institutions like the CNOSF in France and the HOC in Greece, whereas these organisations in Sweden and Austria are completely independent in their actions. The jurisdiction of some umbrella associations is limited by the influence of semi-governmental institutions, like the British umbrella association Central Council of Physical Recreation (CCPR) and its relationship with sport in the UK (cf. Henry, 2004). The NOCs' umbrella organisation at European level is the EOC (European Olympic Committee). At European level, national sports federations are organised in European federations, such as the Union of European Football Associations. European Non-Governmental Sports Organisations (ENGSO) has National Sports Confederations and the National Olympic Committees as members if and when they are the national umbrella organisations for sports. The members represent sport in the widest sense and fully respect the diverse nature of sport, miscellaneous target groups and the manifold social and cultural dimensions of sport (ENGSO, 2007). The almost independent structure of the European sport system gives rise to the question why the European Union is not addressing the needs of sport. Even within the non-governmental organisations, controversy prevails regarding this issue. The huge diversity within the non-governmental sport organisations in Europe creates the opportunity to filter common characteristics extending beyond the existence of an NOC in each country. Umbrella organisations differ in form, number and competency, but act as national representatives for sport specific clubs (normally, there is only one umbrella association for each sport discipline) in each country. An extended international comparison shows different structures in the area of umbrella associations. Co-existence of several sport confederations for only one sport is charac-teristic of the USA. But even within Europe, Great Britain creates ex-clusion. According to Tokarski and Steinbach (2001) "athletes and clubs of one sport are partly organised in separate confederations for native countries, men and women, professionals and amateurs."

Financing of sport

Another basic characteristic that has rarely been the subject of re-search and is hence not mentioned in the country profiles for sport systems in the EU Member States is financing of sport. It is safe-guarded by public funds as well as through budgets of regional and local authorities. Overall it can be said that sport is financed by public funds in all EU Member States. Differences only exist regarding the particular source of finance. Even the allocation of funds is organised differently, as a result of several different institutions being responsi-ble for sport and to the diversity of legislation in the individual na-tional sporting system. The main objective of the financial support granted by the Belgian government is, for instance, to raise sport par-ticipation, while governmental funds in Great Britain mainly finance the semi-governmental Sports Council.

In some countries that have an explicit sports legislation, the manner of financial support is legally regulated; for example in Finland and Portugal. In some countries that do not have any sport laws, like in the Netherlands, the "government and semi-governmental sports federa-tions assume a responsibility for sport that is not prescribed by law" (Tokarski & Steinbach, 2001: 197). In the Netherlands, as well as in Germany, the government, federal states and communes become ac-tive regarding to the subsidiarity principle only if the subordinated sports self-administration is not able to develop and realise a responsi-ble sports policy. Communes raise the biggest part of governmental sport-related funds within this type of system. The lions' share of those funds goes into building and maintaining sporting facilities.

A form of direct governmental sports promotion in many countries is represented by the lottery system; for example the Lotto and Totto

Block in Germany or the national Bingo Lotto in Sweden. According to Miège (2000) these amounts - except for Totocalcio in Italy - account for approximately 1% of the total revenues generated by sport. Even in this field, the purpose and cash flow vary in country comparisons - in Germany, even at the level of federal states, no similarities can be identified. In Denmark, Finland and Italy private funding is important in the financing of sport. Detailed similarities regarding sport sponsoring or, for example, marketing of TV rights cannot be identified at this point. The population basically contributes to sport financing with membership fees and honorary posts.

Populations' sports participation
The sport participation, accordingly a population's active involvement in sport, is a further characteristic of the national sport structure. Justifiably so, it can be said that this is one of the most significant characteristics, because, on the one hand, exercising is the core of the organisational aspects, which were created around sport at the end of the 19th century. On the other hand, studies on sport participation provide a very exact picture of the extent to which the population engages in sport, what prompts them to exercise, which organisational forms are preferred and which sports top the popularity scale, to name but a few factors which can be examined within such a study. Within the country profiles, the general sporting behaviour will be partially addressed.

8.4 Categorisation of national sport systems

It seems to be attractive to divide the profiles of the national sport systems into clear units. Besides the Institute for European Sports Development and Leisure Studies at the German Sports University Cologne, Camy et al. (2003) spoke about these issues regarding the comparison and classification of the European sports system in their final report for the EU-project "Vocasport". While the Institute for European Sports Development and Leisure Studies takes a comparative position and highlights and describes the differences between individual countries separately (cf. Tokarski & Steinbach, 2001; Tokarski et al., 2004; Steinbach, Ternes & Petry, 2004; Tokarski, 2003), the scientists around Camy try to create a classification and systematisation of the national sport systems.

The following explanations referring to the differences and similarities of the national sports systems in terms of the governmental and non-governmental structure are based on Tokarski (2003), the issue of the differences in funding and usage of money will not be covered in the following paragraphs.

Differences and similarities at governmental level

A closer look at the integration of sport into every single European Member State's Constitution and more sport-related legislation reveals the huge variety of sports systems in Europe. It ranges from sport being mentioned in the Constitution as in Spain, to explicit sports legislation, as in France or the direct contact of sport through other legal mandates, like the Leisure Time Act in Denmark (cf. Ibsen & Jorgensen, 2002), to a very marginal legal settlement of sport which is characteristic of the German, Dutch and Austrian sports system.

Especially in young democracies like Portugal, Spain and Slovenia, sport has been incorporated into the Constitution - individual sport laws reflect this. By contrast, older Constitutions do not mention sport, because at the time the law was passed, the social meaning of sport was not widely acknowledged. It seems that a trend towards more sport-related regulations is emerging: in Italy legal actions for introducing tax advantages and other privileges for sport clubs are in the pipeline (cf. Madella, 2004), and even in the Netherlands, which were an example of a liberal sports system, plans are being discussed to shield sport from the negative impact of other legal orders by adopting a law on sports (cf. Veldhoven, 2004).

The different political structures of the Member States increase the institutional diversity, because the governmental responsibility in centralistically controlled countries is at national level, such as Greece and France. In countries with a federal structure (decentralised countries) like Germany or Austria sport falls within the remit of the federal states. In Belgium, for instance, sport is part of the responsibility of the three-language community. The degree of governmental influence on sport ranges basically between the provision of financial support for some sporting activities up to delegation and controlling tasks within the self-administration. A consistent statement assigning institutionalisation und responsibility for sport in Europe to governmental level cannot be made. But it can be ascertained that countries that have explicit legislation for sport, like France, have more sophisticated governmental structures, some having their own Ministries for Sport.

The observation of similarities and differences at non-governmental level in the EU Member States refers firstly to the responsible umbrella association and secondly to the sport clubs as the basis for exercising as well as the local, regional and national federations. At first glance, only one single institutional similarity can be identified. Yet though some big differences come to light upon closer scrutiny. At national level, self-administration exists in every country that has a National Olympic Committee. Although this is not an exclusive European phenomenon, it can be ascribed to the structures and rules of the International Olympic Committee (IOC) and can be found globally. Moreover in some countries, the NOC is directly connected to the National Sports Federation of the Confederations, like the NOC*NSF in the Netherlands, the DOSB in Germany or the CONI in Italy. In other countries, the NOC and the National Sport Federation are organised separately, as in the British sport system. Furthermore, some European NOC's are financially and/or administratively dependent on governmental institutions, such as the CNOSF in France and the HOC in Greece. By contrast, these organisations in Sweden and Austria are completely independent in their actions.

However, not all countries possess their own sport-spanning umbrella association, such as Spain, where confederations represent the highest organisational level. Conversely, in some countries sport clubs and federations are combined into several umbrella associations as in Austria, where besides National Sports Federations politically-oriented umbrella associations represent sport at national level. Furthermore, the umbrella associations' liability is limited through the influence of semi-governmental institutions in some countries, such as the Central Council of Physical Recreation (CCPR) and its links with sport in the UK (cf. Henry, 2003). Despite the existing diversity, common characteristics can be identified which extend beyond the NOCs' existence in all countries. The umbrella associations differ in terms of structure, number and competency, but in every country National Sports Confederations act as national representatives of clubs for one single sport, whereas normally only one Confederation exists per sport. One exception within the EU Member States is Great Britain where "athletes and clubs of one sport are partly organised in separate confederations for home countries, men and women, professionals and amateurs" (Tokarski & Steinbach, 2001: 216).

Camy et al. (2003: 52ff.) developed another systematisation for the different national profiles. They say that the sport systems can be characterised by four key parameters:

- Firstly, it is necessary to know which role governmental institutions play regarding the systems' regulation. "This may involve intervention in actually defining the role of sport in the country, intervention in the structuring of the national sports framework (...), deciding on the conditions for funding the activity, providing and maintaining sports facilities and the staff necessary, etc." (Camy et al., 2003: 52)
- Secondly, it is necessary to consider the way in which the parties involved in this system are co-ordinated. The spectrum ranges from complete autonomy to a rigid way of "co-operation" through laws. "We may see very loosely structured systems, where each party has complete autonomy, without any organised coordination. Conversely, some countries extensively coordinate the contributions of those involved in the sport system" (Camy et al., 2003: 52)
- As a third parameter, the arrangement of the three providers (public, voluntary, commercial; following the three social sectors state, civil society and the market) needs to be known. These three providers play the ultimate characterising role in the national systems
- The fourth parameter is the ability to change offerings to new demands. How rapidly or conversely how flexibly can offers be readjusted?

Based on these parameters, Camy et al (2003) identified four configurations for national sport in Europe:

- Bureaucratic configuration
  The state plays a very active role within this configuration, regarding the system regulation. A legal framework exists especially for sport; partners in sport are informed but not consulted. Voluntary initiatives are delegated and outsiders like customers or companies have practically no influence at all on the introduction of new ideas. Examples of bureaucratic systems are Belgium, Cyprus, the Czech Republic, France and Greece

- Missionary configuration
  The voluntary sector plays a dominant role within this configuration. Referring to decisions, the movement of honorary posts has a lot of autonomy. The state or regional authorities delegate much responsibility for orientation of sports policy, even though they may become gradually involved in a contractual logic with it. Examples of the missionary system are Germany, Denmark, Italy and Luxembourg

- Entrepreneurial configuration
  This category is defined by the system regulation using the social and economic demand for sport. The market behaviour regarding supply and demand is not regulated from the outside; governmental institutions set the framework in which the market can express itself. Examples of the entrepreneurial system are Ireland and the United Kingdom

- Social configuration
  The social configuration is a multi-faceted system in which social players dominate. This system is characterised by collaboration and co-operation between governmental, civil-social and commercial forces. Governance plays an important role in this context. The Netherlands represents the social system

In summary, Camy et al. (2003) state that at least 16 out of the 25 EU Member States possess such a sport structure, which can be assigned to the bureaucratic configuration and in which the government or a governmental dependent institution plays a key role. Due to the EU enlargement from 15 to 25 Member States, the part of the missionary sport structures has been reduced enormously, and all ten new EU Member States had bureaucratic structures (at this time). In historic terms, the missionary structure is the one which emerged under the lead of honorary posts in the sport policy arena, before bureaucratic systems, led by nationalistic movements, gained ground. The origin of entrepreneurial configurations are assumed by the authors to be in the USA, spreading only to Great Britain, where the entrepreneurial system was promoted by Margaret Thatcher's policies and where a service market sport developed. The social configuration emerged as a new system that is characterised by the presence of social players. The new partners are not dominant, but they appear next to other players, a trend which can be found in other configurations and whose change can be most aptly translated by the "principle of government" to "principle of governance".

Henry and Ko (2009) uses this typology and describes in which way the various sectors differ with regard to aspects of governance and political content. According to that, the greatest weakness of the bureaucratic system (i.e. the governmental sector) is that it focuses on the so-called "throughputs", i.e. the workflow is the focus rather than the outcome which supports distinguishing individual players and follows a "silo-mentality". The private sector (the entrepreneurial configuration) concentrates on short-term output rather than on the achievement or the impact of outcomes. In the voluntary sector (missionary configuration), the effort is aimed at having short-term and medium-term success, which may support the sport sectors' autonomy. Finally, the social configuration focuses solely on long-term success, including the stakeholders' inclusion which renders it hugely complex. Referring to the changes of configuration, Henry sees three trends: Central European Member States such as France and Italy are developing from a bureaucratic (and missionary) model towards an entrepreneurial configuration. The United Kingdom is transforming itself from the entrepreneurial to the social configuration and the once strong social model in the Netherlands is beginning to weaken.

8.5 Interim conclusions: results of a new evaluation of oganised sport

The European Union considers sport clubs and sport organisations to be one characteristic of the European Sports Model (cf. European Commission, 1998). Until the 1980s, people engaged in sport almost exclusively in sport clubs in the majority of European countries. This image has changed enormously over the past two or three decades. Although clubs play an important role, they have lost their organisational monopoly. New commercial and charitable providers have emerged next to sport clubs, creating a greater diversity of providers. Furthermore, sport is becoming more self-organised without institutional connections.

What does this mean? It shows that club organised sport has been numerically overtaken by self-organised sport and commercial and other sport providers. To put it in a nutshell, the pyramid is losing its foundations. The head and umbrella associations which represent sport organised by clubs in the European Union and their interests, are not entitled to act singly for all sports. But who can represent self-organising athletes? This is where communities and cities should step in and support sport in general, without neglecting any single form of organisation. To highlight another positive example, an illuminated running track has been built in the municipal area of Cologne, which can be used by all runners even in the dark.

Several publications covering the issue of the organisation of sport in Europe reveal that it is characterised by its own diversity (cf. Heinemann, 1999; Heinemann & Schubert, 2001; Jütting, 1999; Miège, 2000; Tokarski & Steinbach, 2001). The above-mentioned authors emphasise this variety and call its comparability more or less into question. There might be a huge difference regarding the relations between the state and sport, the role and functionality of self-administration or even the structure of sport clubs. Tokarski and Steinbach (2001: 168f) talk about an "almost unclear variety", while Heinemann and Schubert (2001: 11) exclude the development of a "One-Society-Model" in view of sport. The development of one single sport system is closely associated with the respective historical, political, cultural and societal circumstances in every single nation. Seven years ago, Heinemann und Schubert accused the European Commission of failing to acknowledge the existing diversity of sport after launching the European Sports Model in 1998. They demanded that the cultural diversity, the manifestation and relevance thereof be taken into account.

Henning Eichberg (2008) criticises the pyramidal structure of the European Sports Model as well. This criticism is directed in particular at the Independent European Sport Review, which was published by José Luis Arnaut in 2006 and which was subsequently endorsed by the Belet-Bulletin. Eichberg doubted the bulletin's independence and insinuated they had been influenced by UEFA and FIFA. He thought problems in sport were described as if superior intervention at political and legal level was required. Moreover, the bulletin focused on football which does not cover the diversity of sport. Eichberg provides a number of examples focusing on the area of football. A bigger part of football takes place beyond the pyramidal structure, such as street football, company sports, childrens' football, grassroots football, so called "bar-teams" or campaigns like "Football 4 Peace".

Eichberg does not see the diversity of the sport model "Sport for all" just as a base for a sport "controlled from above". As an independent model it has been taken into consideration by the sport-related legislation and administration; therefore creating dual or even threefold systems in sport administration. As an example, Eichberg talks about Denmark, where DIF works as a governmental sport administration in the sport structure, DGI is based on the local and regional sports movement and the DFIF is responsible for company sports. Following the Danish or even the Scottish idea, a (dual or even threefold) base-structure of sport, according to Eichberg, is more capable of adequately representing the diversity of sport in society than the original pyramidal concept created by UEFA and FIFA (this concept was already published in 2005 in the "UEFA Vision Europe" bulletin). Such a structure sees the following representatives in sport:

- Umbrella associations of several sports and the Olympic head organisations for professional competitive sport
- Popular sport associations (sport for all) for recreational sport, leisure sport, company sport, etc.
- Partners for sport, which represent cultural and social values in a sporting context (e.g. UNESCO, WHO)

According to Eichberg, such a system can integrate former "outsiders" into sport (dancing, traditional games, outdoor sports, creative movement). Eichberg positively exposes that the White Book on Sport, published by the European Commission in 2007, does not follow this very concept. The pyramidal structure is mentioned as a characteristic of sport, but not as an organisational structure. A consistent organisational model of sport in Europe has been evaluated as unrealistic by the Commission. Eichberg construes the explanations made in the White Book on Sport to the effect that the Commission has distanced itself from the aims of the interest groups in competitive sport (especially in football) and sees severe criticism being founded in this distance which UEFA and FIFA have created in relation to the White Book on Sport.

Given the development and professionalisation of sport over the past couple of years, the EU more clearly defined its position on sport, having been urged to do so by governments and sport organisations of different Member States. In the past, European sport policy focused on people exercising within the framework of organisations. Recognising the decline in participation especially in organised and competitive sport in some countries, the increasing (commercial) fitness industry and the ongoing diversification of sport, sport policy seems to be too one-sided. New sports and activities, which are organised beyond the existing international system of sport clubs and associations, are emerging all the time (cf. Eichberg 2008). Cultural and demographic developments, such as individualisation, a growing supply of information and an ageing population are being quoted as reasons for the decrease in club and competitive sports. All this suggests that the Structured Dialogue with all stakeholders of sport needs to be strengthened, not only with representatives of organised club sport. Only time will tell if the new diversity of sport has been taken into consideration or if "old wine is merely being presented in new skins".

8.6 National sports systems in the EU Member States[3]

8.6.1   Austria

The federal structure of the country is reflected in the organisation of sport, just as it is in Germany. Some sport-related matters of national interest are handled at federal level by the Federal Ministry for Public Services and Sport. The latter promotes top-level sport, in particular, by sending national teams to competitions abroad. However, the state's main responsibility for sport lies with the provinces.

Despite the government's existing responsibility for the promotion of sport, the latter is organised independently in Austria. The Austrian Federal Sports Organisation BSO is the country's supreme self-governing sports body. It was registered as an association in 1969 and has since represented sport in the entire federal territory as a non-profit-making sports association. It is responsible for promoting sport in the interest of all citizens and for acting as a service facility for its members. The BSO distributes the funds allocated from the federal budget as well as the "special federal funds for the promotion of sports" (lottery funds).

59 national sports federations and three umbrella organisations belong to the BSO as ordinary members and the Austrian Federation of Sport for the Disabled belongs to the BSO as a "member with special tasks". Furthermore, a number of federations, facilities and institutions that are of special importance for sport in Austria, in particular the Austrian Olympic Committee (ÖOC) and the nine provincial sports organisations, are extraordinary members. The work performed by the

---

[3] For further information visit www.sport-in-europe.eu

three umbrella organisations: Association for Sport and Physical Education in Austria (ASKÖ: Arbeitsgemeinschaft für Sport und Körperkultur Österreichs), SPORTUNION: Austrian Gymnastics and Sport Union (Österreichische Turn- und Sportunion), General Sport Federation of Austria (ASVÖ: Allgemeiner Sportverband Österreich) focuses on sport for all and leisure sport.

In total, a number of 14,400 sport clubs exist in Austria. The average sports club has 280 members, although more than half the clubs have less than 200 members, and it is a fact that there are a number of very large clubs with over 1,000 members that raises the average.

8.6.2   Belgium

Sport as a sub-area of culture falls within the remit of the language communities. Although Belgium does not have a homogeneous law on sport, a number of statutory provisions relating to sport are in place which may vary according to the language community. This applies, for instance, to regulations governing the recognition of sports federations or financial support for federations. The communities perceive the promotion of participation in sport and the support of private sport initiatives to be among their tasks.

The organisation of Belgian sport is characterised not just by Belgium's administrative policy structures at national level but by those in the private sector as well. This means that institutions which operate autonomously are responsible for sport within the above-mentioned language communities both at governmental and non-governmental level.

On the part of the government, the central Flemish Sport Administration (BLOSO) supports sport in the Flemish language community, the Sport and Training Administration (ADEPS) does so in the francophone community whereas this task is performed in the German-speaking community by the Ministry of the German-speaking community (Division of Cultural Affairs). In parallel, there are the regional sports federations in the Flemish language community, the French-speaking community and the German-speaking community, all of which are included in the governmental sports support.

The umbrella sport federation in the Flemish community is the Vlaamse Sport Federatie (VSF), in the francophone community the Association Interfédérale du Sport Francophone (AISF) and in the

German-speaking community the Sportrat which was just founded in 2002. Both the VSF and the AISF have around 80 member federations. Members of the Sportrat are among others representatives of the sports federations, the local Sporträte (sport boards) and of the sport clubs which are not organised in federations.

The National Olympic and Interfederal Committee of Belgium (BOIC) plays a very special role against the backdrop of this regional fragmentation. It performs both the tasks of the Belgian representative of the Olympic movement and of the non-governmental sport representative of the whole of Belgium. The BOIC incorporates 34 Olympic and 42 non-Olympic sports, which are administrated in Flemish, Welsh and German federations.

Belgium has a total of approximately 20,000 sport clubs comprising around 1.5 million members. This shows that around 15% of Belgians are involved in some form of organised sport.

8.6.3   Bulgaria

The main sports authority responsible for sports in Bulgaria is the State Agency for Youth and Sport (SAYS). The Agency has the status of Ministry and subsidises all sports federations. The SAYS is the state body that develops national strategies, national and annual programmes for the development of physical education, sport, youth policy and social tourism in the Republic of Bulgaria.

Youth organisations in the country for the implementation of state youth policy are supported by drafts and annual proposal programmes for youth activities to be approved by the Council of Ministers. A team of skilled experts makes proposals and opinions in relation to the harmonisation of the legislation of the Republic of Bulgaria in the field of youth, sport and social tourism with the international legal regulations.

The State Agency for Youth and Sports supervises the activities of sport organisations complying with the Law on Physical Education and Sports. Together with the sports federations and with the Bulgarian Olympic Committee, the Agency funds a programme for training and participation of Bulgarian athletes in Olympic Games. Bulgaria hosts many prestigious tournaments, European and World Championships in different types of sport. On behalf of the state, the State Agency for Youth and Sports promotes athletes, sport specialists and officials, as well as young talents in different fields of public life with different awards on a regular basis. Special attention is paid to the development of sport at schools and to the implementation of extracurricular sports facilities for children an young people, as one of the best alternatives to crime and drug addiction. The Agency supports coordination and organisation of school and university games and competitions, as well as other youth sport activities.

Another priority in the Agency's activities is the prevention and control of doping in sport, as well as the fight against violence and hooliganism in sport. The State Agency of Youth and Sports manages the state-owned sport infrastructure and develops a strategy for the development of physical education, sport and social tourism sites and facilities. Pursuant to the requirements of the Law on Physical Education and Sports, the State Agency for Youth and Sports ensures the rules of use are observed and ensures the national youth and sport sites and facilities in state- or municipal ownership are managed well and meet the needs of youth, physical education, sport and social tourism in Bulgaria. As the primary distributor of budget credits, the Agency allocates the state budget and other state sourced subsidies for youth activities, physical education, sport and social tourism, finances different programmes, youth projects and sport organisations, as well as projects relating to the development of persons with disabilities and people in unequal positions.

8.6.4   Cyprus

The Cyprus Sport Organisation is a semi-governmental organisation enacted by the 1969-1996 law upon the Cyprus Sport Organisation, acting as the supreme authority in the Republic of Cyprus.

The main objectives of the organisation involve the development of sports outside schools, the coordinating of the sport life in Cyprus, the cultivation of the Olympic ideal and the promotion of Cyprus in the international sports arena. A nine-member Board of Administration runs the Cyprus Sport Organisation. It comprises a president, a vice-president and seven members. The services of the organisation are divided into four sectors including the sport sector, sport grounds sector, financial management branch, and human resources branch.

Owing to the support the Cyprus Sport Organisation and the Cyprus National Olympic Committee give to the national sports federations, they are heavily involved in international events. Cyprus is also represented in a range of international sports competitions.

Apart from competitive sport, the Cyprus Sport Organisation promotes the Sport For All programme in its attempt to upgrade the quality of life of all Cypriot citizens.

The Cyprus Sport Organisation at government level is in charge of sports policy. At non-governmental level, the National Olympic Committee is entrusted with the task of international participation (Olympic Games, Mediterranean Games, Games of the Small States of Europe etc.) as well as with the dissemination of the Olympic ideals through the educational system.

8.6.5   Czech Republic

At governmental level, the Ministry of Education, Youth and Sports is a leading umbrella for governmental focus on physical activities for all and competitive sports (including international cooperation - in general as well as within the framework of European programmes).

At non-governmental level, there are different sports federations, including the Czech Sports Federation, which is an organisation of sport clubs and institutions for competitive sports for all. The Czech Sports For All Association is an organisation of sport clubs, institutions and civic associations which is, only at recreational level, responsible for physical activities of people of all ages, including the commercial area (limited by special rules and legislation).

The Czech Sports Association (CSA) represents sports federations, sport clubs and their civic unions established in compliance with the Act of Citizen Associations NR. 83/1990 CL.

The goal of the CSA is to advance sports, physical education, tourism and sports representation. Other goals of the organisation are to represent and protect the rights and interests of associated organisations, to offer them useful services and to create an optimum platform for cooperation. The organisations associated with CSA maintain their full independence, property and individual activities.

The CSA was founded in 1990. It comprises 43 sports federations and 5,521 sport clubs. At present the CSA includes 93 sports federations and 9,222 sport clubs. The CSA has more than 1.5 million members. The goals and organising structure of the CSA conforms to European standards of European Non-Governmental Sports Organisation

(ENGSO). CSA is a democratic organisation, being autonomous, fully independent and politically non-partisan.

The CSA General Assembly is the supreme organ of the CSA. The CSA General Assembly consists of a board of federations and its clubs' representatives. It meets regularly once a year. In between meetings of the CSA Executive Committees are held, meeting all the requirements of the CSA.

Similarly, the Regional CSA (RCSA) sports associations develop their activities in each region of the Czech Republic. The CSA Statutes are the basic document for CSA activities.

8.6.6   Denmark

In Denmark, the Ministry of Culture is responsible for sport, because in Denmark both elite sport and sport for all are considered to be an important feature of Danish culture. However the most significant law regarding sport - the Leisure Time Act - falls under the jurisdiction of the Ministry of Education. The Danish government, though, interferes very little in sport-related matters. Danish sport is based on the freedom of association and it is a very independent and autonomous sector.

Denmark has never had a unified organisation in the field of sports. The sport clubs are organised in three main national organisations: "Denmark's Sports Federation", "Danish Gymnastics and Sports Associations" and "Danish Companies' Sports Federation". There is also a semi-public body that concentrates on elite sport, TEAM DENMARK. The federations have three main purposes: they organise tournaments, competitions and festivals, they devote considerable resources to holding courses for members and they provide support, advice and inspiration to sport clubs.

Denmark's Sports Federation (DIF), founded in 1896 and merged with the Danish National Olympic Committee in 1993, has approx. 1.6 million members. DIF is an umbrella organisation of 56 specialised federations such as the "Danish Football Union". The specialised federations in Denmark organise "sports for all" as well as elite-sport and are generally divided into smaller regional federations.

The other main organisation, Danish Gymnastics and Sports Associations (DGI), also has approx. 1.3 million members. Most of the sport clubs under the DGI, however, are also members of the specialised federations under the DIF. The organisation of the DGI differs from the DIF, since it does not consist of specialised federations, but includes 24 regional associations. Competitions and tournaments are primarily held at county level, but in addition to these, there are displays and sports meetings. The DGI has no elite sport.

The third federation, Danish Companies' Sports Federation (DFIF), founded in 1946, has about 340,000 members, and consists of about 75 local associations of corporate sport clubs. Unlike traditional sport clubs, where sport is the primary camaraderie, a company sports club consists of members whose main bond is that they work in the same company. Most of the corporate sport clubs do not organise training and exercise, and members primarily take part in local football, bowling and badminton tournaments.

The club system is particularly widespread in the voluntary sport sector. A quarter of the adults and around two-thirds of the children in Denmark are active members of a sports club. The total number of sport clubs is about 16,300, this boils down to one club per 400 citizens. Furthermore, there are about 8,000 company sport clubs. On average, sport clubs have approx. 340 members, but this tends to fluctuate, with 1/4 of the clubs having fewer than 50 members.

8.6.7   Estonia

The Sport Law was passed in the Estonian Parliament, Riigikogu, in April 2005 and entered into force in January 2006. The previous Sport Law was adopted in 1998. The Sport Law regulates the following issues: the organisational and legal basics of sport, the rights and obligations of athletes and coaches, the application for government-financed support for Olympic champions, the financing of sports, and the requirements for organising sporting competitions and other events and the corresponding responsibilities. According to the Sport Law, sport is organised and promoted at different levels by the state, local government units and sports organisations. The aim of the respective activities is to promote the physical and mental health of the nation as well as a sportive lifestyle and to enable young people to reach their full sporting potential.

Within the government, sport is administered by the Ministry of Culture where there is the Department of Sport. Its main task is to coordinate the creation of conditions for sports development and governmental sports policy. Furthermore the Ministry divides governmental support into sports organisations, projects and facilities. The tasks of the Ministry in the public organisation of sports are outlined in detail in the Sports Act and in the Statute of the Ministry.

The Estonian Olympic Committee (EOC) is the umbrella organisation, bringing together sports associations, sports unions, regional sports unions in counties and, on conditions stipulated in the Olympic Charter, also individuals. The task of the Estonian Olympic Committee is to organise joint activities, develop and promote sports and the Olympic movement in Estonia. The Estonian Paralympic Committee joins five sports organisations for persons with disabilities.

The 67 sports associations join the 2,048 sport clubs all over the country. The 12 sports unions operate in specific areas, e.g. recreational sports, school sports, student sports, sports for persons with special needs, company sports, veteran sports, etc. In the country, there are 19 regional sports unions. The most popular sports regarding the number of people practising it and registered in the relevant clubs and associations are football, hunting sport, and basketball.

8.6.8   Finland

The law most relevant to public sport financing and administration is the Sports Act (1054/1998), which entered into force in January 1999. Under Section 1, the purpose of the Act is to promote "Sport-for-All, competitive and top-level sports and related civic activities, to enhance the population's well-being and health and to support children's and young people's growth and development through sports".

Within the Government, sport is administered by the Ministry of Education, which has a Sport Division at its Department for Cultural, Sport and Youth Policy, the National Sport Council, which is a consultative expert body attached to the Ministry; and the sport authorities of the five regional state offices. At regional level, the responsibility for sport development rests with the provincial sport authorities and at local level with the local authorities.

The Finnish Sports Federation FSF is the umbrella organisation. In 2006, the FSF adopted the FSF Strategy 2006-2010 in the FSF´s General Assembly. The strategy defines the roles of the different member organisations in accomplishing the following goals of the strategy:

- To increase the number of people who actively engage in sports and to develop the quality and effectiveness of sports
- To ensure the working environment of non-profit-making, volunteer sport clubs and organisations and thus to promote possibilities of sport as citizens' activity in Finland
- To add cooperation between the different partners to the programme

Most of the sports activities are organised by sport clubs and federations. There are 7,800 sport clubs, 130 sports federations and other national sports organisations in Finland. 97% of the sport clubs are non-profit-making. Over 20% of the population (1.1 million Finns) are members of sport clubs.

However the basis of the Finnish sports culture is formed by voluntary activities. There are 500,000 volunteers, meaning that 10% of the population takes part in voluntary work in sports in their leisure time. The value of voluntary work is estimated to be   1.5 billion per year.

8.6.9   France

Ordinance 2006-596 of 23 May 2006 ratifies the legislative part of the Code of Sport. The Code of Sport comprises all laws and regulations applicable to the field of sports in one single coherent and comprehensive document. The code is the reference document for sports law in France.

The organisation of sport in France is based on cooperation between the state, which plays a supervisory role, local authorities, and the sporting movement, entrusted with a public service mission. The state is mainly responsible for implementing sports policies in France. It empowers sports federations to organise and promote the practice of their disciplines and supports them via target agreements and by providing technical frameworks.

The Ministry of Health, Youth, Sports and its State Secretary devoted exclusively to sport-related matters draw up and implement government policy partly with regard to initiatives aimed at young people concerning physical and sports activities as well as participation in sports and community development. The Ministry coordinates initiatives undertaken in these areas whenever a number of ministerial departments are involved. In order to carry out these responsibilities, the

Ministry of Health, Youth, Sports has authority over directorates and departments of the central administration.

The principle of coexistence and cooperation between the state and the sporting movement implies permanent discourse which is assumed by the Ministry for Youth, Sports, on behalf of the state, and the Comité National Olympique et Sportif Français (CNOSF - French Olympic Committee), on behalf of the sporting movement.

The CNOSF, a state-approved association created in 1972, comprises all sports federations (Olympic single sports federations, non-Olympic single sports federations, multi-sports federations). It represents the IOC in France and is therefore subject to the requirements of the Olympic Charter. The Mission of the CNOSF is:

- To represent French sport with regard to the authorities and official organisations
- To cooperate in the training and selection of French athletes and to ensure their participation in the Olympic Games
- To encourage the promotion of athletes at social level
- To provide effective assistance to member federations: it has the task of reconciling disputes involving registered members, sports associations and clubs, and registered sports federations, with the exception of disputes involving drug abuse

The sporting federations are responsible for organising and promoting the practice of their disciplines. Articles of the Code of Sport distinguish between state-approved federations and those that have been delegated powers.

The national sports development centre (CNDS) is managed in close cooperation with the sports movement and plays a major role in the development of sport in France.

8.6.10   Germany

Parliamentary democracy and federalism characterise the basic political structure of the Federal Republic of Germany. Sport in Germany is autonomous; any action the state takes in the field of sport is based on the principle of subsidiarity.

Even though the state has no legal obligation at federal level to support sport, the Federal Ministry of the Interior has taken on some subsidiary tasks in the field of sport, such as representing the Federal Republic in international sports bodies, providing financial support for supra-regional sporting facilities and proving financial support for top-level sport and sport for the disabled.

In terms of state involvement, sport in Germany, just like culture and education, is a matter that is dealt with by the Federal States. The Federal Government's competencies in the field of sport fall within the remit of the Federal Ministry of the Interior. It coordinates all measures that are of significance for the Federal Government. The Federal States are responsible for the subsidisation of sport in the fields of leisure, sport for all, school sport, the building and administration of sporting facilities.

Rising criticism on German sports policy caused by a lack of success in German top-level sports in recent Olympic Games led to the merger of the National Olympic Committee and the German Sports Confederations to The German Olympic Sports Confederation (DOSB).

The DOSB unites 96 member organisations: 16 federal state sports confederations, 60 national sports federations (33 Olympic and 27 non-Olympic) and 20 with special tasks. With about 90.000 sport clubs comprising over 27 million members the DOSB is the largest member organisation in Germany.

It is responsible for coordinating general issues and for the common representation of the interests of its member organisations vis-à-vis the state and the public. Furthermore comparable to the National Olympic Committee of a state, the DOSB represents its interests at the International Olympic Committee.

8.6.11   Greece

Sport in Greece is influenced more by the government than in any other country of the EU. This government competency for sport-related matters has been enshrined expressly in the country's relatively young Constitution (dating back to 1975). Furthermore, laws regulate the organisation of sport in many specific areas in this Member State of the EU which has a weaker economy.

Responsibility for the planning and mapping out of the government policy on sport lies with the Deputy Ministry for Culture with responsibility for sports. The latter is also responsible for the General Sports Secretariat GSS. The main responsibility of the General Sports Secretariat (O.J./28A/1.3.1985) is planning at national level; it also has the general responsibility for all matters relating to progress, better organisation and functioning of sports in the country. More specifically, the General Sports Secretariat is responsible for monitoring sporting events of all kinds, for drawing up short and long-term sports development programmes, as well as for providing all the facilities necessary for the implementation of these programmes, which include all other programmes relating to the field of sports.

The Hellenic Olympic Committee HOC takes action to ensure the preparation, publication and distribution of special editions aiming at developing and promoting the Olympic idea, the history of Olympism, out-of-school physical education and sport in general, as well as all sorts of material in print, which may help to fulfil the mission of the International Olympic Academy. Finally, the HOC recommends to the Minister responsible for sport affairs having supervisory authority over the HOC any measures that might help the Committee fulfil its mission.

The International Olympic Academy IOA acts as a multidisciplinary cultural centre with the aim of studying, analysing and promoting Olympism. The source of inspiration for the foundation of such an institution was the ancient Greek Gymnasium that formed the Olympic Ideal, the harmonious development of the body, the will, the spirit and mind of man.

Non-governmental organised sport in Greece is characterised by the following features: the sport clubs and the 34 special sports federations are in principle self-organised and autonomous. Officially speaking, the government does not influence the actual content of decisions relating to the policies of sports federations. However, the government is responsible for monitoring sports federations. Most of the sports federations' financial resources emanate from state subsidies.

8.6.12   Hungary

The Hungarian Sport Office is the central governmental organisation of sport today. This is an independent institution linked to the Prime Minister's Office. The National Sports Office has a background institution: the Institution of Talent Development which coordinates the youth and talent development programmes of sport in Hungary. Furthermore, they develop physical education programmes and carry out research studies.

The regional and local governments in towns and other settlements usually organise sport for all, students' sport tasks and school sport programmes, even though it is not their mandatory task by law. They maintain about 71% of the sporting facilities, and they also grant subsidies to local top sport teams. The regional and local governments - especially the latter ones - play a major role in Hungarian sport today.

The Hungarian Olympic Committee plays a leading role in the sport structure in Hungary. Since 2001, there have been three prominent public utility umbrella organisations representing the interests of the different areas of sport:

- The Hungarian Sports Confederation is the umbrella organisation for the Hungarian Sports Federations involved in developing the professional, amateur and open competition system and conducting Hungarian championships
- The National Leisure Sports Confederation is the umbrella organisation for Hungarian Sports Federations involved in leisure sports, school sports, students sports
- The National Association of Disabled Athletes is the umbrella organisation for Hungarian Sports Federations engaged in sports for people with special needs

In 2004, the fourth public utility umbrella organisation, the Hungarian Paralympic Committee was founded by the Act on Sport.

The national sports federations for the individual disciplines are autonomous organisations which are based on democratic principles. Their legal status is usually that of a non-profit-making federation. The number of sports federations is steadily increasing. At present, there are 66 national sports federations, which are members of the Hungarian Sports Confederation, and several others, that are not yet officially recognised by the government as official and exclusive Hungarian sports federations. The estimated total membership of the sport clubs is around 700,000. According to a recent survey, 16% of the Hungarian population engages in sport at least once a week, yet only 9% do so regularly, at least twice a week for at least 30 minutes. About half of them engage in sport in a sport club, the rest do so informally or at a for-profit organisation.

8.6.13   Ireland

The Government Department with responsibility for Sport is the Department of Arts, Sport and Tourism which was set up in June of 1997. The Department defines its goal as 'formulating and overseeing the implementation of policies for the promotion and development of sport, and to encourage increased participation in Sport and Recreation, particularly by disadvantaged communities.'

A significant function of the Department of Arts, Sport and Tourism is to provide information, guidance, and clarification on policy in the sport and recreational sectors. The Department is also responsible for providing information and advice on schemes such as the Sports and Recreational Facilities Programme.

In May 1999, the President of Ireland signed the Irish Sports Council Act. The Act provided for the establishment of the Irish Sports Council (ISC) in July 1999 as the State Sports Development Agency. This statutory body's mission is to plan, lead and coordinate the sustainable development of sport in Ireland. Ultimately the Council reports to the Minister for Arts, Sport and Tourism. The Council is also responsible for local sports and is charged with developing strategies for increasing participation in recreational sport and coordinating their implementation to all bodies involved in promoting recreational sport.

Additionally the Council operates the International Carding Scheme for High Performance Players and Athletes which is the mechanism for supporting Ireland's elite athletes. The players and athletes qualify for support under the scheme by meeting standards and criteria set in consultation with the National Governing Bodies of Sport.

The Council also channels investment directly to those sports and individuals likely to be competing at the Olympic and Paralympic Games. As part of the high performance, the NGBs complete Performance Plans under a number of headings, for example, competition, training camps, management, sport science and equipment. The planning process involves detailed discussions between the Performance Directors and the Irish Sports Council.

The ISC is also responsible for strengthening and developing the National Governing Bodies (NGBs) of Irish Sport through designing programmes to develop and co-ordinate sport. The ISC administers funding of these bodies annually, and also to a host of athletes who have reached specific standards.

NGBs organise and administer the majority of organised sport in Ireland: they train and deploy coaches, they organise representative level sport and they provide sporting opportunities and pathways leading from local sport to national and international level competition. To date there are 72 NGBs recognised by the Irish Sports Council. These NGBs operate and coordinate both recreational and competitive sport at international, national, regional and local level.

8.6.14   Italy

As part of institutional innovation in the cultural sector, introduced by the Budget Law for 2007, responsibility for sport was transferred from the Ministry for Heritage and Cultural Activities to a newly-established Ministry for Youth Policies and Sport Activities. The Ministry was entrusted with a) performing central government tasks in relation to sport, and b) policy-making and coordination tasks regarding youth policies (Decree-Law No 181 of May 2006).

With regard to sport, the remit of the Ministry for Youth and Policies and Sport Activities comprises "a) proposing, coordinating and implementing legislative, regulatory, administrative and cultural initiatives relating to sport; b) managing relations with intergovernmental agencies and institutions responsible for sport, particularly with the European Union, the Council of Europe, UNESCO and WADA (World Anti-Doping Agency); c) managing relations with sports entities and other parties working in the sports sphere; d) preventing doping and violence in sport that comes under the ministerial remit; e) exercising oversight over the Italian National Olympics Committee (CONI) and, jointly with the Minister for Culture in relation to areas within their respective jurisdiction, overseeing and policy-making for the Institute for Sports Credit."

The National Italian Olympic Committee (CONI) is a public but non-governmental body. It was created in 1942 as the National Governing Body for Sport and by the early 1960s had a strong central and territorial structure.

At the same time, the CONI is a body that represents the sport movement and is the public body responsible for the regulation of the sport movement at national and (partly) at local level. It is assisted by a special company (CONI Servizi Spa) owned by the state that carries out operational tasks and activities.

CONI is represented by 45 national sports federations (with many sub-disciplines) and another 19 non-Olympic federations called "associate disciplines" with a lower status and limited funding. The national sports federations are now private bodies with public relevance. All of them have a central and territorial structure. The personnel of the federation is mostly provided and paid by the CONI. For the federations recognised by CONI, the total number of clubs in Italy is currently around 65,000.

8.6.15   Latvia

Sports are among the major tools for creating a physically and mentally healthy nation and asserting a national identity. The goal of the Latvian national sports policy is to promote healthy, physically and mentally highly-developed citizens.

100 approved non-governmental sports federations were registered in Latvia in 2008. An approved sports federation has the right to lead and coordinate work in certain sport disciplines and in the field of sport, to represent the state in international sport organisations as well as to obtain financing from the national budget. Sport clubs are societies in which associated physical and legal persons engage in certain kinds of sports and promote its development in fulfilling their own interests. Sport clubs can be affiliated with sport federations. There are around 600 sports organisations in Latvia.

The Sport Administration Ministry of Education and Science implements the unified government sports policy. The governmental sports organisation, the Latvian Sports Department of the Ministry of Education and Science is responsible for promoting the project of governmental budget programme "sport" implementing, and approving sport federations and monitoring their activities, coordinating activities of sport educational institutions and sports centres in area of sport.

The Latvian Sports Federation's Council is the umbrella non-governmental sport organisation that represents Latvia in European Non-Government Sport Organisation - ENGSO.

The Latvian Olympic Committee together with the government institutions participates in the development and implementation of the national sport and education policies, introduction of the youth sport competition system and improvement of the sport infrastructure.

In 1994, the Latvian Olympic Team was founded to help athletes to achieve good results in international competitions, especially in the Olympic Games. The IOC Olympic Solidarity Programme also supports the training of Latvian athletes who are to participate in the Beijing Olympic Games.

The Latvian Olympic Committee pursues the regional development programme. Nine regional Olympic centres were founded in Latvia to promote the Olympic ideas and to facilitate sport development in major administrative areas.

8.6.16   Lithuania

The Law on Physical Education and Sports, which was adopted in 1995, has been replaced with a new law. In the spring of 2008, the Parliament of the Republic of Lithuania adopted the Law amending the Law on Physical Education and Sports. The new law sets out the main principles for physical education and sports: it allocates competencies between governmental and municipal institutions; monitors physical education and sports planning and implementation in educational and academic institutions; it defines competencies of non-governmental physical education and sports institutions participating in the training of sportsmen and women and organises sporting events; it regulates activities of physical education and sports specialists; it establishes a basis for the development of professional sports; it defines the main principles for organising sports events, and determines the requirements to be met by sports buildings.

All issues connected with physical education and state sports administration are managed by the Physical Education and Sports Department, a governmental institution set up in 1990. Furthermore organisers of physical education and sport activities for children and young people in Lithuania are the Ministry of Education and Science, the Ministry of National Defence, the Ministry of Internal Affairs, the Ministry of Health and the Teachers Professional Development Centre. Municipalities throughout the country run 103 specialised sports centres that are attended by nearly 52,000 schoolchildren, and all 56 municipalities in the country have PE and sports departments.

In 1991, the National Olympic Committee of Lithuania re-established its membership of the International Olympic Committee and various sports federations in the country also re-established their membership of other international organisations. Lithuanian athletes have been granted the right to participate in the Olympic Games, European and World Championships, the Universal Games and the Paralympic Games. Lithuania has been granted the opportunity to organise the European and World Championships of various disciplines of sport. The Lithuanian Olympic Sports Centre is involved in training skilled sportsmen and sportswomen.

There are 78 Olympic and non-Olympic sports federations in Lithuania, which practise 96 disciplines of sport. In 1993 the Lithuanian Union of Sports Federation was founded to unite the sports federations.

The "Sports for All" association was founded to promote a healthy way of life and physical education for all the people of Lithuania.

8.6.17   Luxembourg

The country's Constitution does not contain any reference to sport. The Sport and School Sport Act adopted in 1976 stipulates the shared responsibility of the state and the independent sport movement for sport. A new Law on Sport replaced this older version in 2005 and highlights new opportunities for the development of sports in Luxembourg in all respects (leisure, school, competition and elite sports).

The Ministry of Sport and School Sport was dissolved in 1999. Until 2004, the Ministry for National Education, Vocational Training and Sport has been in charge of sport at government level. Since 2004, a Ministerial Sport Department, directed by the Sport Minister, has been responsible for Sport.

The state also runs the National Sport Institute, sport classes, a National Sport School and a National Sport Centre. At local level, there are local sport commissions in larger municipalities. The state is not heavily involved in the organisation of sport; the principle of subsidiarity also applies to the Luxembourg sport system.

At non-governmental level, the National Olympic Committee COSL is the umbrella organisation of sports in Luxembourg. 61 governing bodies of sports which have around 1,550 club members are represented in the General Assembly of the COSL. With sport clubs accounting for around 120,000 members, the level of organisation is around 28%.

8.6.18   Malta

The Sports Act (Act XXVI of 2002) entered into force on 27 January 2003 and defines the roles of the Malta Sports Council (MSC- KMS), a governmental organisation, and the Malta Olympic Committee (MOC), a non-governmental organisation.

The MSC is the supreme authority of sport whose mission includes increasing participation in sports especially amongst children and young people, promoting a culture of excellence in sport, and monitoring and evaluating all practices, operations and activities relating to sports. Physical education and sport in schools falls within the Education Division, a remit of the Ministry of Education, Culture and Youth.

The main objective of the MOC is to ensure that preparations by prospective participants are of a standard for the major competitions in which Malta takes part, such as the Olympic Games, Commonwealth Games, Mediterranean Games, Games of Small States of Europe, and other International games. National Sports Federations (also known as Associations and Unions) have representatives on the KMS and the MOC.

The Physical Education Association Malta (PEAM) is an independent body that aims to facilitate the improvement of professional performance of physical educators and to promote good practices in schools.

Sports federations and clubs are mainly run by volunteers at administrative level. Most athletes lack the financial support to turn their sport into a profession. This often puts Maltese athletes at the bottom of league tables in Europe.

8.6.19   Netherlands

The Netherlands has no special 'Law on Sport'. There were plans to develop one in 2006, but these were stopped. Since January 2007, the general framework for the sports policies of the different authorities has been provided by the Social Support Act and the Law on VWS-subsidies. The Social Support Act defines the framework within which each municipality can adopt its own welfare policy, based on the composition and demands of its inhabitants. The Law on VWS subsidies provides the framework for the application of subsidies to non-governmental organisations for the benefit of sport.

When the Ministry of Welfare, Health and Culture was changed to the Ministry of Health, Welfare & Sport in 1996, the term 'sport' appeared in the name of a Dutch ministry for the very first time. Since this change, the budget for sport has been multiplied almost five-fold, from 21 million in 1996 to 99 million in 2007. This budget has been used in particular to provide impetus to sport for all programmes at local level, to implement a national action plan for sport and exercise, to support social inclusion via sport, and to support the aim of the sports sector to ensure the Netherlands ranks among the top ten countries in the international sports world.

Although the central government has gained momentum in sports policy, its role is primarily one of coordination and encouragement. The 458 local authorities are responsible for implementing governmental sports policy in practice.

Of all sports participants, more than the half are members of a sports club. Of all sport clubs, 27,000 are affiliated to one of the 72 national sport associations, which are in turn members of Netherlands Olympic Committee * Netherlands Sports Confederation (NOC*NSF). Since a merger established this sports umbrella organisation in 1993, NOC*NSF has performed both the (elite sport and sport for all) tasks of an NOC and an NSF.

The sport clubs have a total of 4,686,000 club members. More than 1,000,000 people are actively involved in volunteering for one of these sport clubs. The clubs are autonomous bodies, founded and run by their own members. Nevertheless, they depend to some extent on local governments.

The same goes for their umbrella organisations. As in the sport clubs, the General Assembly is the highest decision-making body of the national sport associations; in this case consisting of the chairmen or other representatives of the sport clubs. Apart from the sport clubs, there are over 6,700 commercially run sports centres in the Netherlands, such as health and fitness clubs, sailing schools, and riding-schools.

8.6.20   Poland

Activity in the area of physical culture is regulated in Poland by the Physical Culture Act of 18 January 1996, - and ordinances issued by the Minister of the National Education and Sport (15 acts). In addition, matters associated with physical culture are regulated by general law, pertaining to all areas of public life. The most frequently invoked acts are the Mass Events Safety Act, Association Law, Commercial Companies Code, the Civil Code and legal regulations concerning financial activity in sports.

The central body of government administration concerned with matters of physical culture in Poland is the Ministry of National Education and Sport.

On 1 July 2002 at central level, Poland set up the Polish Sports Confederation (Polska Konfederacja Sportu) which is a state agency having the status of a legal person included in the sector of public finances. The purpose of the Confederation is to create suitable conditions for activity in the area of high level sports, including professional sports, their development and promotion.

The leading organisation of the non-governmental sector having a nationwide character and operating at central level is the Polish Olympic Committee (Polski Komitet Olimpijski), a federation of associations and other legal persons acting to ensure participation of Poland in Olympic games, fostering Olympic principles, representing Polish sports in the international Olympic movement and communicating with the national Olympic committees of other countries.

Poland also has two types of sports federations functioning at central level that deal with top level (competitive) sport:

- Multidisciplinary federations (multi-sport)
- Polish sports federations (mono-disciplinary federations)

It is no easy task to determine how many Poles participate in sports. One of the reasons is that in Polish the term "sports" is associated unequivocally with competitive sports. At present just over 300,000 individuals, i.e. 0.8% of the entire population of Poland, are registered in 57 Polish sports federations.

8.6.21 Portugal

Sport is mentioned in the Portuguese Constitution. It grants citizens both a social and a cultural right to engage sporting activity and a specific legal entitlement to partake in sport. Since 1990, the sports policy goals and role distribution between the government and sports organisations have also been regulated by a Law on Sport. Honorary functions and private initiatives are acknowledged as the hallmarks of sport. As such, clubs and federations constitute the basis for organising sport. Nonetheless, the basic responsibility for accomplishing objectives in sport lies with the government.

At government level, a State Secretary for Youth and Sport (Secretaria de Estado do Desporto) has been set up within the Prime Minister's Office, which discharges the sport-related duties of the government. As such, the Secretariat is assisted in its day-to-day operations by three public institutions:

The IND (Instituto Nacional do Desporto), which is responsible for directly supporting sport associations, the CEFD (Centro des Estudos e Formacao Desportiva), which deals with the field of non-academic training in sport, and the CAAD (Complexo de Apoio às Actividades Desportiva), which is responsible for maintaining the sport infrastructure. On 1 June 2003, those three structures were merged in a single Institute: the Portuguese Sports Institute (Instituto do Desporto de Portugal).

The Portuguese sports system has a National Sports Council (CSD - Conselho Superior do Desporto) which acts as a consultative body.

Around half a million people are organised privately in around 10,000 sports clubs, most of which are multi-sport clubs. The clubs constitute the regional sports federations and the 69 national sports federations. A national umbrella organisation has only been in place since the Portuguese Sport Federation was set up in 1993, although not all federations belong to it. The federations, including those representing non-Olympic sports disciplines are, however, also organised within the General Assembly of Federations (AGF - Assembleia Geral das Federaçoes) that is linked to the National Olympic Committee (COP).

8.6.22   Romania

In the Romanian system of physical education and sport, the structures of sport are private or public entities. Multiple sporting disciplines are promoted and practiced by its members, who, for instance, participate in competitions.

The organisation and functioning of the national sports structure and physical education is regulated under the provisions set forth in Section 69 of the Law on Physical Education and Sport which came into effect on 28 April 2000, as subsequently amended (the latest amendments pursuant to the provisions of Law 472 of 4 November 2004) (the "Law").

According to the Law, the definition of "physical education and sport" incorporates all forms of physical activity of an independent nature or organised participation with the purpose of expressing, improving and developing the physical and intellectual well-being of the individual and of establishing and developing civilized social norms, conducive to competitive results at all levels.

The National Agency for Sport is the central public administrative entity in charge of coordinating the activities of physical education and sport. It organises the registration of sporting structures by maintaining a sporting registry, allocating each structure an identity number and issuing a certificate of sporting identity. Physical education and sport activities in educational institutions are organised by the Ministry of Education and Research; they are governed by school/university associations under the provisions of Law 69/2000 and supervised by the Federation of School Sports or the Federation of University Sports. Regional directorates for sport, including the Bucharest municipal offices are decentralised agencies of the National Agency for Sport collaborating with local government administrations to organise and promote sporting activities.

The Romanian Olympic and Sport Committee (legal entity, of public interest, autonomous, non-profit-making, non-governmental, non-political, non-lucrative entity) (the "COSR") is an association of national interest that acts and operates according to its own statutes, issued in conformity with the provisions of the Olympic Charter and Law 69/2000, as subsequently amended.

The various National Sports Federations are organised under the auspices of the COSR. They can be constituted only pursuant to the approval of the National Agency for Sport.

8.6.23   Slovakia

Sport is not mentioned in the Slovak Constitution. In 1997, the new National Council Law on Physical Culture No. 288 was approved, which also included articles on educational and commercial activity in sport. The law on state funding of physical culture no. 264 of the 1993

National Council approved the financing of sport through lottery funds. In 1992, the National Council approved the Law on Public Sport and Tourist Events no. 315, addressing the necessary precautions to prevent violence at sporting events. In 1993 Slovakia ratified the European Convention of violence and misbehaviour of spectators at sporting events especially on football grounds (no. 255/93). The European Sport Charter was accepted by 254/93, and the Council of Europe Anti-Doping Convention no. 256/93. In 1994, the National Council approved the use and protection of all Olympic symbols and the Slovak Olympic Committee Law No. 226. Many other legislative acts in the Slovak Republic as well as regulations and decrees by the government, Ministry of Education, and others are related to the field of sport.

The central authority of state administration responsible for sport is the Directorate General for Sport of the Slovak Ministry of Education. The main responsibilities of the sports department include fostering international co-operation, issuing sports legislation, dealing with nationwide issues on sport for all and providing grants to non-governmental sport organisations from the state budget. An organisation directly supported by the Ministry of Education is the National Sport Centre, which creates favourable conditions for the best Slovak athletes in the area of sport science and healthcare, providing coaches, referees and sport officials with all the latest up-to-date information and managing the sports information system. Other organisations for supporting the training of top-level athletes are training centres directly supported by the Ministry of Interior and the Ministry of Defence. Since 2002, competencies in accordance with the Slovak decentralisation policy have consistently been transferred to regional and local self-administration in the fields of sport for all, sporting facilities, school sports, and partly in the training of talented youth. Governmental sports institutions at all levels transfer a large number of competencies to non-governmental organisations at all levels.

The most important nationwide non-governmental sport organisations are national sports federations which are responsible for developing their appropriate sport and selected national teams. There is no unique umbrella organisation for all national federations. Among the most important of them are the Confederation of Slovak Sports federations and the Association of Technical and Sporting Activities of the Slovak Republic. In addition to nationwide sports federations, there are a large number of organisations which provide services to sports federations or other associations with nationwide competencies. The specific task of the Slovak Olympic Committee is to arrange the participation of the national team at the Olympics, as well as to spread the ideals of the Olympic movement. At regional and local level there are some 7,000 sport clubs which provide appropriate services for practicing organised and non-organised sports.

8.6.24   Slovenia

Since April 1998, Slovenia has had its own Law on Sport. The fact that this law was adopted is intended to reflect the important role sport plays in society and in citizens' lives. In this law, the state accepts responsibility for safeguarding the public interest in sport, which encompasses sports education, leisure sport, competitive sport, top-level sport and sport for the disabled. The Law on Sport regulates the competencies of the individual sport-related institutions in Slovenia and the way in which they cooperate with each other and it also contains provisions governing the important general framework for sporting activity.

The concrete principles governing the safeguarding of the public interest in sport that is defined in the Law on Sport are set forth in the Slovenian National Sport Programme that was adopted by the Slovenian Parliament on 3 March 2000. With the aid of this fundamental document on Slovenian sports policy, the state is to create the necessary prerequisites for the further development of areas relating to the public interest in sport. The goals defined in this programme are to be accomplished via the annual sports programmes to be implemented at national and local level.

The main player in sport at national level is the Ministry of Education, Science and Sport which was set up in 1991 as soon as Slovenia gained independence.

The Council of Sports Experts constitutes a consultative body for action by the institutions responsible at governmental and non-governmental level. The compilation, tasks and activities of the institutions set up by the Government and financed from the state budget are specified in Slovenia's Law on Sport. Another semi-state body is the Slovenian Sports Office, which was set up jointly by the Ministry of Education and Sport and the OCS-ASF in May 1995. The Sports Office is responsible for gathering all information on sport from the various areas, above all sport for children and young people, and for making this information accessible to interested parties.

The Olympic Committee of Slovenia (OCS) and the Association of Sports Federations (ASF) are Slovenia's top sports self-administration bodies. The OCS was set up on 19 October 1991, a few months after the country gained independence, and was recognised officially by the International Olympic Committee in 1992. These two organisations, which have worked separately, joined forces in December 1994 to become the OCS-ASF and since then they have represented the bulk of organised sport in Slovenia. In accordance with the umbrella organisation's tasks, the OCS-ASF represents the interests of its members, comprising National Sports Federations and Communal Sports Federations at national and international level, promoting the Olympic idea. The organisation of sport in Slovenia is based on the 7,200 sport clubs with their approximately 370,000 members.

8.6.25   Spain

In Spain there is no umbrella organisation which compiles the demands of the different organisations and discusses them with the public authorities. In fact the communication channels between the different organisations involved in the sport system are confusing and have not been sufficiently defined (Burriel & Puig, 1999).

The Sports Act 10/1990, of 15 October 1990 is the basic legislation of sport in Spain. It defines the National Sports Agency (Consejo Superior de Deportes - CSD) as an Autonomous Administrative Body, attached to the Ministry of Education and Science, through which the State Administration operates in the field of sport.

The powers of the National Sports Agency are to authorise or revoke the Constitution with justification and to approve the statutes and regulations of Spanish Sports Federations; to establish, in conjunction with the Spanish Sports Federations, their objectives, sports programmes (especially in high-level sport), their budgets and organic/functional structures, subscribing to the corresponding agreements; to grant economic subsidies for sports federations and other sporting bodies and associations, carrying out inspections and verifying that they comply with the aims set out in the current legislation; to classify official, professional, state competitions; to act in coordination with the Autonomous Regions regarding general sporting activity and to cooperate with these regional governments in the development of the powers vested in them by their respective statutes. (Sports Act/10/90, of 15 October, Art. 8) Furthermore there is the Spanish

Disciplinary Committee for Sports, a state-controlled body, organically attached to the National Sports Agency, which, acting independently of the Agency, decides as a last resort, in an administrative capacity, on matters of discipline in sport within its jurisdiction. Its resolutions can be appealed in contentious-administrative jurisdiction.

The Spanish Olympic Committee and the Spanish Paralympic Committee are devoted exclusively to the development of the Olympic movement in the terms established by the Sports Act 10/90. Moreover there are private non-profit-making sports federations, privately-run international organisations and public limited sports companies to which all professional clubs or teams participating in professional sports competitions at national level must conform. The private entities regulate top level and professional sport, control and authorise international selections, regulate sport titles, promote scientific investigations and, for example, are involved in the fight against doping. There are 59 national sports federations, 5 sports federations for sports disciplines for persons with disabilities and 2 club associations. In total, Spain has 91,268 sport clubs with approximately 3,325,984 registered sport members.

8.6.26 Sweden

Sport and the organisation of sport are autonomous in Sweden. Sport is not enshrined in the Constitution, nor is there any special sport legislation.

The role the government plays is limited to providing financial support for sport. The Ministry of the Interior is responsible for distributing and monitoring the targeted use of government funds at government level. Despite this great reluctance on the part of the government to become involved in the field of sports policy, the Swedish Government issued a declaration on sport known as "Sports Policy for the 21st Century" in 1999. It mentions three pillars of national sports policy: specifically, the active promotion of public health and the independent sports movement as well as commercial top-level sport as part of the entertainment industry, for which promotion from public funds is, however, expressly rejected. However, from the late 1990s onwards, the Swedish government has, together with trade and industry, given substantial economic support to top-level sport, especially to Olympic sports.

The Swedish Sport Confederation plays a key role in respect of sports self-administration (Riksidrottsforbundet-RF). The roughly 3 to 3.5 million Swedes who take part in some kind or organised sport are members of approximately 20,500 sport clubs. 7,000 of these clubs are company sport clubs. The sport clubs are organised into around 1,000 regional sports federations which, in turn, constitute the 68 currently existing national sports federations.

Apart from the Swedish Sport Confederation (RF), there is the Swedish Olympic Committee (SOC) and the Federation for Adult Education in Sport, SISU (Svenska Idrottsrörelsens Studieförbund), which organises the multi-sports training for persons involved in sport.

The SOC is a support organisation. The Committee is made up of 35 permanent member federations and twelve recognised federations acknowledged by the IOC. The federations for each respective sport have the main responsibility for development within their sport. The SOC can help to reinforce developments initiated by these federations.

8.6.27   United Kingdom

The UK has no written Constitution and does not have a comprehensive law on sport. Its Constitution is to be found partly in conventions and customs and partly in statutes. Most legislation pertaining to sport is permissive in that it allows (but does not require) different levels of government to be active in the field of sports and in sports funding.

The government department responsible for sport differs according to the particular home country. Responsibility for sport at UK level and for England lies with the Department of Culture, Media and Sport (DCMS). DCMS policies help to deliver Government's 'sport for all' policy and realise its ambitions for sporting success at elite level. The Department oversees the work of Sport England and UK Sport (the Non-Departmental Public Bodies set up in 1997 to replace the Sports Council for Great Britain) and helps set the Government strategy for a whole range of sporting issues, from sport in schools, and community sport to international sports policy, and the distribution of National Lottery funding.

In Scotland, sport is under the responsibility of the Minister for Culture and Sport. Sportscotland (formerly the Scottish Sports Council) provides advice on sport-related matters to the Scottish Executive (in effect the Scottish Government), and to local authorities, governing bodies and others involved in sport in Scotland.

In Wales, sport is the responsibility of the Ministry of Culture, Sport and the Welsh Language, which is advised by the Welsh Sports Council. In Northern Ireland sport is the responsibility of the Minister of Culture, Arts and Leisure, advised by the Sports Council for Northern Ireland.

There are two principal umbrella bodies operating at national level in addition to the National Governing Bodies or National Federations for individual sports (NGBs). These are the Central Council for Physical Recreation (CCPR) and the British Olympic Association (BOA).

The British Olympic Association is described as a unique blend of elected officials and professional staff. The National Olympic Committee (NOC) is made up of the elected officials, one from each of the Olympic sports. The Committee is the Association's decision and policy-making body.

9 Bibliography

Alemann, U. von (1987). Organisierte Interessen in der Bundesrepublik. Grundwissen Politik 1. Opladen: Leske + Budrich.

Balster, K. and Brettschneider, W.-D. (2002). Jugendarbeit im Sportverein. Duisburg: Sportjugend NRW.

Becker, F. and Lehmkuhl, D. (2003). Multiple Strukturen der Regulierung: Ursachen, Konflikte und Lösungen am Fall des Leichtathleten Baumann. Bonn: Max-Planck-Institut zur Erforschung von Gemeinschaftsgütern.

Benner, T. and Reinicke, W. H. (1999). Politik im globalen Netz: Globale Politiknetzwerke und die Herausforderung offener Systeme. *Internationale Politik* 8, 25-32.

Benz, A. (2004). Governance - Regieren in komplexen Regelsystemen. Wiesbaden: Verlag für Sozialwissenschaften.

Bieling, H.-J. and Lerch, M. (2005). Theorien der europäischen Integration. Wiesbaden: Verlag für Sozialwissenschaften.

Bitsch, M.-T. (1999). Histoire de la construction européenne de 1945 à nos jours. Paris: Edition Coplexe.

Blockmans, S. & Prechal, S. (Eds.) (2008). Reconciling the Deepening and Widening of the European Union. Cambridge: TMC Asser Press.

Boldt, H. (1995). Die Europäische Union. Geschichte, Struktur, Politik. Mannheim: B. I. Taschenbuchverlag.

Bollmann, P., March, U. and Petersen, T. (1987). Kleine Geschichte Europas. Gütersloh: Prisma Verlag.

Borchardt, K-D. (1995). European Integration: The Origins and Growth of the European Union 4th ed., Office for the Official Publication of the European Communities, Luxembourg.

Borneman, J. and Fowler, N. (1997). Europeanization. In Annual Review of Anthropology 26, 487-514.

Börzel, T. A. (2000). Why There Is No Southern Problem. On Environmental Leaders and Laggards in the European Union. *Journal of European Public Policy* 7, 141-162.

Börzel, T. A. (2001). Non-Compliance in the European Union. Pathology or Statistical Artifact? *Journal of European Public Policy* 8(5), 803-824.

Bottenburg, M.van., Rijnen, B. and Sterkenburg, J. van (2005). Sports participation in the European Union. Trends and differences. Nieuwegein: Arko Sports Media.

Brand, A. and Niemann, A. (2007). Europeanisation in the societal/transnational realm: What European Integration Studies can get out of analysing football. *Journal of Contemporary European Research* 3, 182-201.

Brand, A. and Niemann, A. (eds.) (2007). Interessen und Handlungsspielräume in der deutschen und europäischen Außenpolitik. Dresden: TUDpress.

Braun, S. and Nagel, M. (2005). Zwischen Solidargemeinschaft und Dienstleistungsorganisation. Mitgliedschaft, Engagement und Partizipation im Sportverein. In Alkemeyer, T.,Rigauer, B. and Sobiech, G. (eds.), Organisationsentwicklungen und De-Institutionalisierungsprozesse im Sport. Schorndorf: Hofmann, 123-150.

Brunn, G. (2002). Die europäische Einigung von 1945 bis heute. Stuttgart: Reclam.

Burk, V. (2001). Russland. In Bohr, J. (ed.). Handbuch internationale Sportstrukturen. Frankfurt am Main: Deutscher Sportbund.

Centre D'action pour la Federation Européenne (ed.) (1945). L'Europe de Demain. Neuchatel: Editions de la Baconnière.

Chabod, F. (1963). Der Europagedanke. Von Alexander dem Großen bis Zar Alexander. Stuttgart: Kohlhammer.

Croci, O. and Forster, J.J. (2004). Webs of Authority: Hierarchies, Networks, Legitimacy, and Economic Power in Global Sport Organizations. In Papanikos, G.T. (ed.) (2004). The Economics and Management of Mega Athletic Events: Olympic Games, Professional Sports, and Other Essays. Athens: ATINER, 3-10.

Crosier, D., Purser, L. and Smidt, H. (2007). Trends V: Universities shaping the European Higher Education Area. Brussels: European University Association.

Davies, N. (1996). Europe - A History. Oxford: Harper Perennial.

Delanty, G. (1995). Inventing Europe. Idea, Identity, Reality. Houndmills: Palgrave.

Dieckert, J., Wopp, C. and Ahlert, G. (eds.) (2002). Handbuch Freizeitsport. Beiträge zur Lehre und Forschung im Sport 134. Schorndorf: Hofmann.

Digel, H. (2001). Leistungssportsysteme im internationalen Vergleich. In Digel, H. (ed.). Spitzensport. Chancen und Probleme. Schorndorf: Hofmann, 212-230.

Digel, H. (2001). Spitzensport. Chancen und Probleme. Schorndorf: Hofmann.

Dinan, D. (2004). Europe recast. A history of European Union. Basingstoke: Palgrave Macmillan.

D'Sa, R. (1998). European Community Law on State Aid. London: Sweet & Maxwell.

Elias, N. (1983). Über den Rückzug der Soziologen in die Gegenwart. *Kölner Zeitschrift für Soziologie und Sozialpsychologie* 39,(1), 29-40.

Elvert, J. (2006). Die europäische Integration. Darmstadt: Wissenschaftliche Buchgesellschaft.

Feiden, K. and Blasius, H. (2002). Doping im Sport. Wer-womit-warum. Stuttgart: Wissenschaftliche Verlags Gesellschaft.

Foerster, R. H. (1967). Europa. Geschichte einer politischen Idee. Mit einer Bibliographie von 182 Einigungsplänen aus den Jahren 1306 bis 1945. München: Nymphenburger.

Frei, D. (1985). Integrationsprozesse. Theoretische Erkenntnisse und praktische Folgerungen. In Weidenfeld, W. (ed.). Die Identität Europas. Studien zur Geschichte und Politik. Bonn: Bundeszentrale für Politische Bildung, 113-131.

Frensch, R. (1996). Geschlechterverhältnisse in Europa oder: Wie geht es Europa? In Münch, D. and Thelen, E. (eds.). Forum Frauenforschung. Vorträge aus fünf Jahren. Darmstadt: FiT Verlag, 77-92.

Fritzweiler, J. (1998). Praxishandbuch Sportrecht. München: Beck.

Gehler, M. (2005). Europa: Ideen, Institutionen, Vereinigung. München: Olzog.

Giering, C. (1997). Europa zwischen Zweckverband und Superstaat. Die Entwicklung der politikwissenschaftlichen Integrationstheorie im Prozeß der europäischen Integration. Bonn: Europa Union Verlag.

González, J. and Wagenaar, R. (2003). Tuning Educational Structures in Europe. Final Report Phase One. Bilbao: Socrates, Education and Culture.

González, J. and Wagenaar, R. (2005). Tuning Educational Structures in Europe II. Universities´ contribution to the Bologna Process. Bilbao: Socrates, Education and Culture.

González, J. and Wagenaar, R. (2007). Tuning Educational Structures in Europe. Final Report Phase 3. Bilbao: Socrates, Education and Culture.

Greenwood, J. (2007). Interest Representation in the European Union. Basingstoke: Palgrave.

Grodde, M. (2007). Der Einfluss des Europarechts auf die Vertragsfreiheit autonomer Sportverbände in Deutschland. Ausgleich zwischen nationalem Verfassungsrecht und europäischem Freizügigkeitsrecht. Rechtswissenschaft und Praxis 11. Berlin: Lit.

Groll, M. (2005). Transnationale Sportpolitik. Analyse und Steuerungsansatz sportpolitischer Interaktionen. Sportforum 14. Aachen: Meyer & Meyer.

Groll, M., Gütt, M. and Mittag, J. (2008). Political Aspects of Sport in the European Union. Status Report within the framework of the project "Sport in Europe - Social, Political, Organisational, Legal Transparency in Europe", available at www.sport-in-europe.eu. German Sport Universitiy Cologne.

Grupe, O. (2007). Ist die Einheit des Sports gefährdet? *Olympisches Feuer* 6, 46-49.

Güldenpfennig, S. (2003). Politikwissenschaft und Sport - Sportpolitik. In: Friedrich, G. and Haag, H. (eds.). Theoriefelder der Sportwissenschaft (2nd edition). Schorndorf: Hofmann, 165-199.

Gugutzer, R. (2008). Sport im Prozess gesellschaftlicher Individualisierung. In Weis, K. and Gugutzer, R. (eds.). Handbuch Sportsoziologie. Schorndorf: Hofmann, 88-99.

Haas, E.B. (1975). The obsolescence of regional integration theory. Research Series 25. Berkeley/CA: University of California/Institute of International Studies.

Hauchler, I. (1995). Globale Trends 1996. Fakten, Analysen, Prognosen. Frankfurt: Fischer Taschenbuch Verlag.

Haug, G. and Tauch, C. (2001). Towards the European higher education area: Trends in learning structures in higher education II. Follow-up Report prepared for the Salamanca and Prague Conferences of March/May 2001.

Hay, D. (1968). Europe. The Emergence of an Idea. Edinburgh: University Press.

Head, D. (2004). Europeanization through football. The cross-cultural impact of Jürgen Klinsmann and Sven-Göran Eriksson in England. *European journal for sport and society* 1, 23-33.

Heinemann, K. (1996). Staatliche Sportpolitik und Autonomie des Sports. In Lüschen, G. (ed.). Sportpolitik. Sozialwissenschaftliche Analysen. Sozialwissenschaften des Sports 3. Stuttgart: Naglschmid, 177-198.

Heinemann, K. (ed.) (1999). Sport clubs in various European countries. Schorndorf: Hofmann.

Heinemann, K. and Schubert, M. (2001). Sport und Gesellschaften. Schorndorf: Hofmann.

Henry, I. and Ko, L.-M. (2009). European Models of Sport: Governance, Organisational Change and Sports Policy in the EU. In Tokarski, W. and Petry, K. (eds.). Handbuch Sportpolitik. Schorndorf: Hofmann (in preparation).

Henry, I. (2004). United Kingdom. In Tokarski, W., Steinbach, D., Petry, K. and Jesse, B. (eds.). Two players-one goal? Sport in the European Union. Aachen: Meyer & Meyer, 263-270.

Herz, D. (2007). Die Europäische Union. (2nd edition). München: C.H. Beck.

Hübner, H. (ed.) (1994). Von lokalen Sportverhaltensstudien zur kommunalen Sportstättenentwicklungsplanung. Beiträge zu einer zeitgemäßen kommunalen Sportentwicklung. Münster: Lit.

Ibsen, B. and Jørgensen, P. (2002). Denmark. In daCosta, L. P. and Miragaya, A. (eds.). Worldwide experiences and trends in sport for all. Aachen: Meyer & Meyer, 293-322.

Jesse, B. (1995). Die Sportpolitik der Europäischen Union. Entwicklung eines Kommunikations- und Marketingkonzeptes zur Nutzung des Sports als Integrationsinstrument in Europa. Diploma Thesis. Cologne: German Sport University.

Joas, H. and Wiegandt, K, (eds.) (2005). Die kulturellen Werte Europas. Frankfurt am Main: Fischer.

Judt, T. (2006). Die Geschichte Europas seit dem Zweiten Weltkrieg. München/Wien: Hanser.

Jütting, D. H. (ed.) (1999). Sportvereine in Europa zwischen Staat und Markt. Münster: Waxmann.

Jütting, D. H., van Bentem, N. and Oshege, V. (2003). Vereine als sozialer Reichtum. Empirische Studien zu lokalen freiwilligen Vereinigungen. Münster: Waxmann.

Jütting, D.H. (2008). Sport im Verein. In Weis, K. and Gugutzer, R. (eds.). Handbuch Sportsoziologie. Schorndorf: Hofmann, 133-142.

Kaiser, K. (1969). Transnationale Politik. Zu einer Theorie der multinationalen Politik. In Czempiel, E.O. (ed.). Die anachronistische Souveränität. *PVS-Sonderheft* 1, 80-109.

Kevenhörster, P. (2008). Entscheidungen und Strukturen der Politik. Politikwissenschaft 1 (3). Wiesbaden: Verlag für Sozialwissenschaften.

Klein, G. (2005). L'échelle Européenne - Europe, formation universitaire et sciences du sport - quelques repéres. *Revue* 313, 7-8.

Knipping, F. (2004). Rom, 25. März 1957. Die Einigung Europas. München: Deutscher Taschenbuchverlag.

Koenig, Ch. (2000). Fremd- und Eigenkapitalzufuhr an Unternehmen durch die öffentliche Hand auf dem Prüfstand des EG- Beihilfenrechts. *ZIP* 2000, 53-59.

Koenig, Ch. and Kühling, J. (2000). Grundfragen des EG-Beihilfenrechts. *NJW-Neue Juristische Wochenschrift*, 1065.

Koenig, Ch., Kühling, J. and Ritter, N. (2001). EG-Beihilfenrecht. Heidelberg: Verlag Recht und Wirtschaft.

König, W. (1997). Sportpolitik in Europa-Eine Einführung. *DVS-Informationen* 12, 25-34.

Koopmann, O. (2008). Sportwetten in Deutschland. Eine Analyse des deutschen Sportwettenmarktes. Hamburg: Diplomica.

Kornbeck, J. (2006). Governance als Softlaw: Innovation oder Notwendigkeit im sportpolitischen Handeln der EU? In Tokarski, W., Petry, K. and Jesse, B. (eds.) (2006). Sportpolitik. Theorie- und Praxisfelder von Governance im Sport. Veröffentlichungen der Deutschen Sporthochschule Köln 15. Cologne: Strauß, 31-52.

Lehner, F. (1983). Interesse als Paradigma der sozialwissenschaftlichen Analyse. In von Alemann, U. and Forndran, E. (eds.). Interessenvermittlung und Politik. Interesse als Grundbegriff sozialwissenschaftlicher Lehre und Analyse. Opladen: Westdeutscher Verlag, 102-115.

Lipgens, W. (ed.) (1986). Documents on the History of European Integration, Vol. 2: Plans for European Union in Great Britain and in Exile 1939-1945. Berlin/New York: W. de Gruyter.

Loth, W. (1996). Der Weg nach Europa. Geschichte der europäischen Integration 1939-1957. Göttingen: Vandenhoeck & Ruprecht.

Madella, A. (2004). Italy. In Tokarski, W., Steinbach, D., Petry, K. and Jesse, B. (eds.). Two players - one goal? Sport in the European Union. Aachen: Meyer & Meyer, 191-198.

Meier, Ch. (1993). Athen. Ein Neubeginn der Weltgeschichte. Berlin: Siedler.

Meier, R. (1995). Neokorporatistische Strukturen im Verhältnis von Sport und Staat. In Winkler, J. & Weis, K. (eds.). Soziologie des Sports: Theorieansätze, Forschungsergebnisse und Forschungsperspektiven. Opladen: Westdeutscher Verlag, 91-106.

Meyers, R. (1997). Grundbegriffe und theoretische Perspektiven der Internationalen Beziehungen. Grundwissen Politik. Schriftenreihe der Bundeszentrale für Politische Bildung (3). Bonn: Bundeszentrale für Politische Bildung, 313-434.

Michalowitz, I. (2007). Lobbying in der EU. Wien: Facultas.

Miège, C. (2000). Les organisations sportives et l'Europe. Paris: Institut National du Sport et de l'Education Physique.

Mittag, J. and Nieland, J.-U. (2007). Das Spiel mit dem Fußball. Interessen, Projektionen und Vereinnahmungen. Essen: Klartext.

Mittag, J. (2008). Kleine Geschichte der Europäischen Union. Von der Europaidee bis zur Gegenwart. Münster: Aschendorff.

Mittag, J. (2009). Die konstitutionelle Erfassung des Sports in der Europäischen Union. In Tokarski, W. and Petry, K. (eds.). Handbuch Sportpolitik. Schorndorf: Hofmann (in preparation).

Moravcsik, A. (1998). The Choice for Europe. Social purpose and state power from Messina to Maastricht. Ithaca/NY: Cornell University Press.

Nagel, S., Conzelmann, A. and Gabler, H. (2004). Sportvereine - Auslaufmodell oder Hoffnungsträger? Tübingen: Attempto-Verlag.

Nonon, J. and Clamen, M. (1991). L´Europe et ses Couloirs. Paris: La Découverte.

Opaschowski, H.-W. (2004). Deutschland 2020. Wie wir morgen leben - Prognosen der Wissenschaft (1). Wiesbaden: Verlag für Sozialwissenschaften.

Parrish, R. (2003). Sports law and policy in the European Union. European Policy Research Unit Series. Manchester: University Press.

Patzelt, W. J. (2001). Einführung in die Politikwissenschaft. Grundriß des Faches und studiumbegleitende Orientierung (4). Passau: Wissenschaftlicher Verlag Rothe.

Pegg, C. H. (1983). Evolution of the European Idea, 1914-1932. Chapel Hill: University of North Carolina Press.

Petry, K., Froberg, K., Madella, A., Tokarski, W. (Eds.) (2008). Higher Education in Sport in Europe. From Labour Market Demand to Training Supply. Aachen: Meyer & Meyer.

Petry, K., Gütt, M. and Fischer, Ch. (2008). European Education Policy and the implementation oft he Bologna Process in Sport. In Petry, K., Froberg, K., Madella, A., Tokarski, W. (Eds.) Higher Education in Sport in Europe. From Labour Market Demand to Training Supply. Aachen: Meyer & Meyer, 10 - 43.

Petry, K., Froberg, K. and Madella, A. (2006). Thematic Network Project AE-HESIS - Report of the Third Year. Cologne: German Sport University.

Petry, K., Jesse, B. and Kukowka, D. (2006) Move your body - stretch your mind. Das Europäische Jahr 2004 als sportpolitischer Steuerungsprozess der Europäischen Kommission. In Tokarski, W., Petry, K. and Jesse, B. (2006). Sportpolitik - Theorie- und Praxisfelder von Governance im Sport. Veröffentlichungen der deutschen Sporthochschule Köln 15. Cologne: Strauß, 91-104.

Petry, K., Steinbach, D. and Tokarski, W. (2004). Sport systems in the countries of the European Union. *European Journal for Sport and Society* 1(1), 15-21.

Pfeiffer, G. (1995). Eurolobbyismus. Organisierte Interessen in der Europäischen Union. Frankfurt: Peter Lang.

Pfister, B. (1998). Das Bosman-Urteil des EuGH und das Kinass-Urteil des BAG. In Tokarski, W. (ed.). EU-Recht und Sport. Aachen: Meyer & Meyer, 151-171.

Putnam, R. D. and Goss, K.A. (2001). Einleitung. In Putnam, R. D. (ed.). Gesellschaft und Gemeinsinn. Sozialkapital im internationalen Vergleich. Gütersloh: Bertelsmann-Stiftung, 15-43.

Reding, V. (2003). Bildungspolitik - Europa: Wirkungsvoll in die allgemeine und berufliche Bildung investieren - die europäische Perspektive. *Der Landkreis* 73. Stuttgart: Kohlhammer, 548-549.

Risse, T., Caporasoj J. and Green Cowles, M. (2001). Transforming Europe: Europeanization and Domestic Change. Ithaca/NY: Cornell University Press, 1-20.

Rittberger, V. and Boekle, H. (1997). Das Internationale Olympische Komitee - eine Weltregierung des Sports? In Grupe, O. (ed.) (2002). Olympischer Sport. Rückblick und Perspektiven. Schorndorf: Verlag Karl Hofmann, 127-155.

Ronge, V. (2006). Governance: Begriff, Konzept und Anwendungsmöglichkeiten im Sport. In Tokarski, W., Petry, K. and Jesse, B. (eds.) (2006). Sportpolitik. Theorie- und Praxisfelder von Governance im Sport. Veröffentlichungen der Deutschen Sporthochschule Köln 15. Cologne: Strauß, 9-20.

Rosamond, B. (2000). Theories of European integration. The European Union Series. Basingstoke, Hampshire: Palgrave (Reprint).

Rosenau, J. N. and Czempiel, E.O. (1992). Governance without government: order and change in world politics. Cambridge: Cambridge University Press.

Röthel, A. (2000). Kompetenzen der Europäischen Union zur Dopingbekämpfung. In Röhricht, V. and Röhricht-Vieweg (eds.). Doping-Forum. Aktuelle rechtliche und medizinische Aspekte. Sondertagung des Konstanzer Arbeitskreises für Sportrecht. Stuttgart: Boorberg, 109-123.

Sattler, R.-J. (1971). Europa. Geschichte und Aktualität des Begriffes. Braunschweig: Albert Limbach Verlag.

Savola, J. (2002). Finland. In DaCosta, da Lamartine P. and Miragaya, A. (eds.). Worldwide experiences and trends in sport for all. Aachen: Meyer & Meyer, 333-351.

Schädler, T. (2008). Die Europäische Union und der Sport: Eine Analyse des Weißbuches „Sport" der Europäischen Kommission. Diploma Thesis. Cologne: German Sport Universitiy.

Schmale, W. (2000). Geschichte Europas. Wien/Köln/Weimar: Böhlau.

Schmeilzl, B. (2004). Sport und Recht - Was dürfen Spielervermittler und Sportmanager? *Leistungssport* (34). Münster, 32-40.

Schneider, H. (1977). Leitbilder der Europapolitik 1. Der Weg zur Integration. Bonn: Europa Union Verlag.

Schneider, P. (1998). Traumfrau Europa. *Der Spiegel* 14 (30/03/1998), 226-231.

Schubert, M. (2008). Kommerzielle Sportanbieter. In Weis, K. and Gugutzer, R. (eds.). Handbuch Sportsoziologie. Schorndorf: Hofmann, 143-151.

Schulke, H.-J. (2002). Gemeinnützige Institutionen. In Dieckert, J., Wopp, C.and Ahlert, G. (eds.). Handbuch Freizeitsport. Beiträge zur Lehre und Forschung im Sport 134. Schorndorf: Hofmann, 150-158.

Schulze, H. (1995). Europäische Identität aus historischer Sicht. In Henrichsmeyer, W., Hildebrand, K. and May, B. (eds.). Auf der Suche nach europäischer Identität. Bonn: Europa Union Verlag, 17-43.

Siegert, E. (2008). Anti-Doping-Maßnahmen der Europäischen Union. Ein Vergleich der Anti-Dopingpolitik von Deutschland und Frankreich. Dissertation. Cologne: German Sport University.

Siekmann, R. and Soek, J. (2005). The European Union and sport. Legal and policy documents. The Hague: Asser Press.

Sommer, R. (1997). Europa in Märchen und Mythen. In Weitz, N. (ed.). Europa. Vision und Wirklichkeit. Probleme, Fakten, Perspektiven. Aachen: Meyer & Meyer, 147-150.

Steinbach, D. and Popp, R. (eds.) (2007). Zukunft - Freizeit - Sport. Situation und Perspektiven des Freizeit- und Breitensports in Salzburg. Salzburg: FHS Forschungsgesellschaft mbH.

Stirk, P. (2001). A History of European Integration since 1914. London/New York: Pinter Publishers Ltd.

Tarragó, A. (2004). Spain. In Tokarski, W., Steinbach, D., Petry, K. and Jesse, B. (eds.). Two players-one goal? Sport in the European Union. Aachen: Meyer & Meyer, 245-257.

Tauch, C. and Rauhvargers, A. (2002). Übersicht über Master-Abschlüsse und gemeinsame Abschlüsse (joint degrees) in Europa. Genf: European University Association.

Ternes, E. (2002). Sportstrukturen in Mittel- und Osteuropa. Eine Analyse der Entwicklungen vor dem Hintergrund der Europäischen Integration. Diploma Thesis. Cologne: German Sport University.

Tokarski, W. (2003). Sportstrukturen in den Europäischen Nachbarländern. "Europa hautnah". Cologne: Unpublished paper.

Tokarski, W. and Schmitz-Scherzer, R. (1985). Freizeit. Studienskripten zur Soziologie 125. Stuttgart: Teubner.

Tokarski, W. and Steinbach, D. (eds.) (2001). Spuren. Sportpolitik und Sportstrukturen in der Europäischen Union. Edition Sport und Freizeit 6. Aachen: Meyer & Meyer.

Tokarski, W. and Petry, K. (eds.) (2009). Handbuch Sportpolitik. Schorndorf: Hofmann (in preparation).

Tokarski, W., Petry, K. and Jesse, B. (eds.) (2006). Sportpolitik. Theorie- und Praxisfelder von Governance im Sport. Veröffentlichungen der Deutschen Sporthochschule Köln 15. Cologne: Strauß.

Tokarski, W., Steinbach, D., Petry, K., Jesse, B. (eds.) (2004). Two players-one goal? Sport in the European Union. Aachen: Meyer & Meyer.

Unger, M. (2006). Sportpolitik in der Europäischen Union. Dissertation. Cologne: German Sport University.

Veldhoven, N.van (2004). The Netherlands. In Tokarski, W., Steinbach, D., Petry, K. and Jesse, B. (eds.). Two players - one goal? Sport in the European Union. Aachen: Meyer & Meyer, 201-208.

Vieweg, K. (2007). Legal comparison and the harmonisation of doping rules. Pilot study for the European Commission. *Beiträge zum Sportrecht* 27. Berlin: Duncker & Humblot.

Vitanyi, I. (1985). The European Paradigm. European Culture - World Culture. Budapest: ELRA Press.

Voelzkow, H. (2003). Neokorporatismus. In Andersen, U. and Woyke, W. (ed.). Handwörterbuch des politischen Systems der Bundesrepublik Deutschland (5th edition). Opladen: Leske + Budrich.

Weber, M. (1973). Die protestantische Ethik. In Winckelmann, J. (ed.). Eine Aufsatzsammlung. Hamburg: Mohr.

Weidenfeld, W. and Wessels, W. (eds.) (2007). Europa von A bis Z. Taschenbuch der europäischen Integration (10th edition). Baden-Baden: Nomos.

Weidenfeld, W. (2007). Europäische Einigung im historischen Überblick In Weidenfeld, W. and Wessels, W. (eds.). Europa A-Z. Taschenbuch der europäischen Integration. Baden-Baden: Nomos, 13-48.

Weidenfeld, W. and Wessels, W. (eds.) (1997). Europe from A to Z: Guide to European Integration. Luxembourg: European Commission.

Weiler, S. (2006). Mehrfachbeteiligungen an Sportkapitalgesellschaften. Berlin: Duncker & Humblot.

Weiß, O. et al. (2007). Sport 2000. Entwicklungen und Trends im österreichischen Sport. In Weiß, O. (ed.). Entwicklungstendenzen im Sport. Vienna: Lit Verlag, 61-77.

Weitz, N. (1997). Europa - Vision und Wirklichkeit. In Weitz, N. (ed.). Europa. Vision und Wirklichkeit. Probleme, Fakten, Perspektiven. Aachen: Meyer & Meyer.

Welz, C. and Engel, C. (1993). Traditionsbestände politikwissenschaftlicher Integrationstheorien: Die Europäische Gemeinschaft im Spannungsfeld von Integration und Kooperation. In Bogdandy, A. von (ed.). Die europäische Option. Eine interdisziplinäre Analyse über Herkunft, Stand und Perspektiven der europäischen Integration. Baden-Baden: Nomos, 129-169.

Wessels, W. (1992). Staat und (west-europäische) Integration, Die Fusionsthese. In Kreile, M. (ed.). Die Integration Europas. PSV Sonderheft 23, 36-61.

Wessels, W. (2006). Theoretischer Pluralismus und Integrationsdynamik: Herausforderungen für den „acquis académique". In Bieling, H.-J. and Lerch, M. (ed.) (2006). Theorien europäischer Integration (2nd edition). Wiesbaden: VS Verlag, 427-459.

Wessels, W. (2007). Das politische System der Europäischen Union. Wiesbaden: Verlag für Sozialwissenschaften.

Wessels, W., Maurer, A. and Mittag, J. (2002). Fifteen into One? The European Union and its Member States. Manchester: Manchester University Press.

Wiener, A. and Diez, T. (2004). European integration theory. Reprinted. Oxford: University Press.

Wilkens, A. (ed.) (2004). Le Plan Schuman dans l'Histoire. Intérêts nationaux et projet européen. Brüssel: Bruylant.

Wilson, K. and van der Dussen, J. (eds.) (1995). What is Europe? The History of the Idea of Europe. London/New York: Routledge.

Witte, J. K. (2006). Change of degrees and degrees of change. Comparing adaptations of European higher education systems in the context of the Bologna Process. Enschede: CHEPS/Universiteit Twente.

Woll. C. (2006). Lobbying in the European Union: From Sui Generis to a Comparative Perspective. Journal of European Public Policy, 13(3), 456-469.

Wopp, Ch. (2008). Soziologie des Freizeitsports. In Weis, K. and Gugutzer, R. (eds.). Handbuch Sportsoziologie. Schorndorf: Hofmann, 321-330.

Documents and other sources

Arnaut, J. L. (2006). Independent European Sport Review. http://www.independentsportreview.com, 18/01/2009.

Eichberg, H. (2008). Pyramid or Democracy in Sports? Alternative ways in European Sports Policies. http//www.idrottsforum.org/articles/eichberg/eichberg080206.html, 05/06/2008.

Euractiv (2006). Report: European football needs major reform. http://www.euractiv.com/en/sports/report-european-football-needs-major-reform/article-155587, 05/06/2008.

Euractiv (2007). First EU step on sports policy receives cool welcome. http://www.euractiv.com/en/sports/eu-step-sports-policy-receives-cool-welcome/article-165445, 05/06/2008.

European Commission (1998). Entwicklung und Perspektiven der Gemein-schaftsaktion im Bereich Sport.

European Commission (1999). Mitteilung von Frau Reding an die Kommission: Bekämpfung des Doping im Sport: Entwurf für eine vom Internationalen Olympischen Komitee vorgeschlagene Weltagentur zur Bekämpfung des Do-pings im Sport. Brussels.

European Commission (2000). Gemeinsam gegen Doping. http://europa.eu.int/comm/dg10/sport/doping/legalaspects/a_legal_de.html, 31/05/ 2000.

European Commission (2004). Special Eurobarometer 62.0 (213): The citizens of the European Union and Sport. Brussels.

European Commission (2005). Reports from the Consultation Conference with the European Sport Movement. http://ec.europa.eu/sport/whatsup/index05_en.html, 05/06/2008.

European Commission (2006). What's up? Year 2006. http://ec.europa.eu/sport/whatsup/index06_en.html, 05/06/2008.

European Commission (2007). Whitepaper on sport. http://ec.europa.eu/sport/whitepaper/wp_on_sport_de.pdf, 12/07/2007.

European Parliament (2006). The future of professional football in Europe. Reporter: Ivo Belet. Strasbourg.

Eurostat (2008). Population in Europe 2007. First results - No. 81/2008. Brussels.

Fígel, J. (2007). EU-Kommission nimmt Weißbuch „Sport" an. http://europa.eu/rapid/pressReleasesAction.do?reference=IP/07/1066&format =HTML&a-ged=0&language=DE&guiLanguage=en, 15/09/2007.

International Olympic Committee (1998). Rules govering Doping and Drug Trafficking in the various countries. www.nodoping.org/contributions_pdf/rules_doping_e.html, 18/02/2000.

Kreuzer, H.P. (2008). Mehr als nur ein Wirtschaftsfaktor. Die Europäische Kommission veröffentlicht ihr Weißbuch des Sports. http://www.dradio.de/dlf/sendungen/hintergrundpolitik/645696/, 05/06/2008.

Matuschek, G. (1998). Neokorporatismus als Form politischer Steuerung. Unpublished paper. Berlin: Institut für Sozialwissenschaften/Institut für Sozialwissenschaften.

Netopilek, F. (2003). Role and future of the European Sports Conference. Proceedings. http://public.mzos.hr/fgs.axd?id=11415, 05/06/2008.

Olsen, J.P. (2002). The many faces of Europeanization. Arena working paper 2.

Schimank, U. (2002). Der Vereinssport in der Organisationsgesellschaft. Organisationssoziologische Perspektiven auf ein spannungsreiches Verhältnis. Unpublished paper. Oldenburg: Deutsche Vereinigung für Sportwissenschaften.

Spindler, B. (2005). Die Organisation des Sports in Österreich und Europa. Struktur, Projekte und Internationale Aktivitäten. Sektion Sport des Bundeskanzleramtes, Abteilung VI/1. www.austria.gv.at/Docs/2005/11/9/Sportstruktur.pdf, 05/06/2008.

Sports Division, Council of Europe (1998). The Council of Europe and Sport, 1966-1998. Volume I-IV.

Tokarski, W. (2003). Sportstrukturen in den Europäischen Nachbarländern. "Europa hautnah". Cologne: Unpublished paper.

Tuning Educational Structures in Europe (Tuning) (2007). http://tuning.unideusto.org/tuningeu, 21/11/ 2007.

Tuning Educational Structures in Latin America (Tuning Latin America) (2007). http://tuning.unideusto.org/tuningal, 21/11/2007.

10 Index of figures

THE BUSINESS
OF SPORTS

This Sport Management Book Series aims to incorporate cutting edge work which is designed to transcend the boundaries between business and sport.

The series will be used as a forum for research and scholarly insight surrounding the major issues of importance for those concerned with sport management and sport marketing. The series will provide an opportunity to illustrate and highlight the ways in which the business of sport has expanded to become a global industry.

Editors of the Series:
Dr. James Skinner, Griffith University, Queensland, Australia
Prof. Paul De Knop,
Free University Brussels, Belgium

The Business of Sports, Volume 1
James Skinner/Allan Edwards
The Sport Empire

192 pages, 3 charts
Paperback, $6^1/2''$ x $9^1/4''$
ISBN: 978-1-84126-168-3
$ 19.95 US / $ 32.95 AUS
£ 14.95 UK/€ 18.95

The Business of Sports, Volume 2
Annelies Knoppers/
Anton Anthonissen (Eds.)
Making Sense of Diversity in Organizing Sport

120 pages, 2 charts
Paperback, $6^1/2''$ x $9^1/4''$
ISBN: 978-1-84126-203-1
$ 19.95 US / $ 32.95 AUS
£ 14.95 UK/€ 18.95

Maastricht School of Management
Remmé, Jones, van der Heijden
& De Bono
Leadership, Change and Responsibility

240 pages,
30 Illustrations
Paperback, $6^1/2''$ x $9^1/4''$
ISBN: 978-1-84126-238-3
$ 34.00 US / $ 49.95 AUS
£ 16.95 UK/€ 24.95

MSM-SERIES

This series makes excellent, affordable textbooks for students worldwide. By emphasizing the international, multicultural sustainability, and social responsibility dimensions of management, and by giving special attention to change issues in transitional economies, these volumes aim to define the way management subjects should be taught to multicultural audiences. It provides students all over the world with essential advice for successful studies.

Maastricht School of Management
De Bono, van der Heijden & Jones
Managing Cultural Diversity

288 pages,
9 Illustrations, 9 charts
Paperback, $6^1/2''$ x $9^1/4''$
ISBN: 978-1-84126-239-0
$ 34.00 US / $ 49.95 AUS
£ 16.95 UK/€ 24.95

Each book is a concise but complete treatment of the topics covered in a core course, based on the philosophy of the Maastricht School of management's MBA program. Targeted readers are students enrolled in other universities, and practicing managers in countries worldwide, as well as MBA students in MSM's overseas outreach programs.

Competence in Sports Science

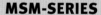

MEYER
& MEYER
SPORT